PERSPECTIVES ON
AMERICAN COMPOSERS

The *Perspectives of New Music* Series

Perspectives on American Composers
Perspectives on Contemporary Music Theory

PERSPECTIVES ON AMERICAN COMPOSERS

Edited by

Benjamin Boretz and Edward T. Cone

W · W · NORTON & COMPANY · INC ·

NEW YORK

The following essays are reprinted from issues of *Perspectives of New Music,* a journal published twice yearly by Princeton University Press for the Fromm Music Foundation, and copyrighted in the years indicated by Princeton University Press:

Roger Sessions: In Honor of His Sixty-fifth Birthday: © 1962

Stefan Wolpe: For His Sixtieth Birthday: © 1963

A Composer's Influences; Copland on the Serial Road: An Analysis of *Connotations;* Walter Piston: For His Seventieth Birthday; Conversation with Steuermann; Elliott Carter and the Postwar Composers: © 1964

Ives' Quarter-Tone Impressions: Conversation with Varèse; Expressionism and American Music: © 1965

The Liberation of Sound; Edgard Varèse: A Few Observations of His Music; "Open Rather Than Bounded"; A Varèse Chronology; Conversation with Roger Sessions; Arthur Berger: The Composer as Mannerist: © 1966; To the Editor: © 1967

Charles Ives' Quotations: Manner or Substance?; Conversation with Aaron Copland; Conversation with Walter Piston; Aspects of Tonality in the Music of Ross Lee Finney: © 1968

The emblem on the cover is a reproduction of a drawing made by Igor Stravinsky as a visual representation of his "recent music." Used by permission.

ACKNOWLEDGMENTS

—————————■■■■■■■■—————————

Music examples are reprinted by kind permission of the copyright owners as follows:

Associated Music Publishers, Inc., New York. Piston: Partita for Violin, Viola, and Organ, Copyright 1951; Symphony No. 2, Copyright 1945, both by Arrow Music Press, New York; Quintet for Wind Instruments, Copyright 1957; Symphony No. 4, Copyright 1953; Symphony No. 7, Copyright 1961. Ives: "Fourth of July" from the *Holiday Symphony,* Copyright 1932.

Boosey and Hawkes, Inc., New York. Copland: *Connotations,* Copyright 1962. Piston: Violin Concerto, Copyright 1948.

Franco Colombo, Inc., New York. Varèse: *Déserts,* Copyright 1954; *Ionisation,* Copyright 1933.

Edward B. Marks, Inc., New York. Sessions: Quintet, Copyright 1960; Violin Concerto, Copyright 1959.

McGinnis and Marx, Inc., New York. Wolpe: Form for Piano, Copyright by Edition Tonos, Darmstadt; Sonata for Violin and Piano, Copyright 1955.

C.F. Peters Corporation, New York. Finney: String Quartet No. 6, Copyright 1950; Symphony No. 3, Copyright 1960, both by Henmar Press, Inc., New York.

Theodore Presser Co., Bryn Mawr. Wolpe: Passacaglia, Copyright 1947 by New Music Edition.

PREFACE

In more than a purely formal sense, this compilation can be regarded as a sequel to *Perspectives on Schoenberg and Stravinsky* (Princeton University Press, 1968) ; perhaps that book should have been called *Perspectives on American Composers,* Volume I. For the two masters to whom the earlier collection was devoted—like some of those who appear in the present volume—became Americans not only by long residence and citizenship, but also through productiveness and influence in their adopted country.

In the preface to the first collection we wrote that "the views . . . here presented perhaps reveal important aspects of contemporary American composition as much as they generate insight into the works actually under discussion"; and further, that "the essays themselves were not originally written at the prompting of an 'Aspects' survey, but only out of their authors' immediate and particular interests." Those statements are equally true in the present case. It cannot be emphasized too strongly that the roster of composers presented here is by no means a deliberately contrived list of the "ten best," nor an attempt to cover "recent tendencies"; it is merely a representative selection from *Perspectives of New Music.* If one wonders, for example, why so much attention is expended on composers of the older generations, or why certain obvious names are missing altogether, the answer is simply: these are the musicians that other musicians have wished to write about. (Some of the interviews, it is true, were in a certain sense "commissioned" by the magazine; but in each case the interviewer chose a subject particularly close to his personal and professional interests.)

Certain kinds of articles were considered out of place in a compilation of this nature: for example, memorial notices (of which there have, alas, been many in recent years) , and essays on individual compositions, which we are saving for a projected book of "analyses." (On this ground some objection might be raised to the inclusion of Peter Evans's article on Copland; but in this case we felt that the discussion of Copland's development as a composer, and of the place of *Connotations* in his oeuvre, balanced the strictly analytic aspects of the essay.)

In a word, this is a book by and about *composers,* but composers as musicians, not as "personalities." Personality, it is true, emerges in these pages, but through the composer's relation to his craft. This is, after all, the only approach that gives a real meaning to the phrase "the personality of the composer"—as opposed to "the composer as a personality." The latter we are content to leave to the world of entertainment and public relations; it is to the definition and interpretation of the former that this book is dedicated.

B.A.B.
E.T.C.

Princeton, N.J.
February 1971

CONTENTS

PERSPECTIVES ON
AMERICAN COMPOSERS

IVES' QUARTER-TONE IMPRESSIONS

HOWARD BOATWRIGHT

I

In the post-World War II period, it has become common for composers with experimental tendencies to write about their work. Charles Ives wrote a great deal of prose, but only in one case did he write specifically about a musical experiment. This one case was the article, "Some 'Quarter-tone' Impressions," written in 1924–25, at approximately the end of his composing years, to explicate his Three Quarter-tone Pieces for Two Pianos.[1]

During the period when Ives was turning out music which found its way into nearly every new niche that was eventually opened to the twentieth-century composer (*c.* 1900–20), he wrote not technical prose but semi-philosophical essays concerned with the broadest aspects of artistic creation, and other writings which expanded his philosophical viewpoints (derived mainly from Emerson and Thoreau) into the areas of economics and politics. All the while, he was solving in his music the problems of chord-building other than by the traditional pyramiding of thirds, utilizing the full chromatic tone-supply, escaping overmetrical rhythmic practices, and building fluid, prose-like forms rather than rigidly organized phrase-structures relying extensively on repetition. Had he attempted to describe, even briefly, all that he had accomplished along these lines by, let us say, 1915, he would have had to write a very large treatise, or several treatises. But no one could have written so much music in so short a time, or could have written it the *way* Ives did (rapidly, and without over-self-conscious cerebration about the technical side) and at the same time have formulated verbal accounts of the theory and technic —especially not Ives, whose time was already divided between music and a major business career.

By 1923–24 (the date proposed by John Kirkpatrick[2] for the Three Quarter-tone Pieces), Ives was beginning to taper off both in composing

[1]The article is included in Charles Ives, *Essays Before a Sonata and Other Writings,* ed. Howard Boatwright, New York: W. W. Norton & Co., Inc., 1962, pp. 107–119. This edition collates material from three manuscript versions in the Ives Collection at Yale University and the first printed version of the article, in the *Franco-American Music Society Bulletin,* March 1925. All references here are to the 1962 edition.

[2]In *A Temporary Mimeographed Catalogue of the Music Manuscripts of Charles Edward Ives (1874–1954)* given by Mrs. Ives to the Library of the Yale School of Music, September 1955, New Haven, 1960.

and in business. He had managed to get his major works into print by then—the Concord Sonata with its accompanying *Essays Before a Sonata* (1920), and his collection of 114 Songs (1922)—and it may even have been with a bit of backward-looking nostalgia that he readily accepted a suggestion from the French pianist, E. Robert Schmitz, to meet Hans Barth (b. 1897), a Swiss composer then experimenting with a quarter-tone piano in New York. The subject of quarter-tones undoubtedly took Ives back to memories of his father, the remarkable George Ives, who was the real experimenter of the family, although never a composer of consequence. In his article, Ives tells how his father got interested in quarter-tones:

> One afternoon, in a pouring thunderstorm, we saw him standing without hat or coat in the back garden; the church bell next door was ringing. He would rush into the house to the piano, and then back again. "I've heard a chord I've never heard before—it comes over and over but I can't seem to catch it." He stayed up most of the night trying to find it on the piano. It was soon after this that he started his quarter-tone machine.

George Ives' "quarter-tone machine" was a device made with twenty-four or more violin strings that could be tuned in various ways. He used to pick out quarter-tone melodies on this device and try to get his family to sing them. But, as Charles relates, "he gave that up except as a means of punishment—though we got to like some of the tunes which kept close to the usual scale and had quarter-tone notes [MS. 2: quarter-tone runs] thrown in. After deciding that quarter-tone chords were needed to train the ear for quarter-tone melodies, the elder Ives found a way of sustaining chords with violin bows set in motion by means of weights "but in this process he was suppressed by the family and a few of the neighbors."

It can be seen from these autobiographical reminiscences that Ives was aware of quarter-tone possibilities long before he wrote the Three Pieces in 1923–24. It is not certain when he first attempted to write a quarter-tone piece, but Kirkpatrick lists a "Chorale for strings in 1/4 tones" of 1913–14 or earlier,[3] which became the third piece (Chorale) in the 1923–24 set. The "Epilogue" of *Essays Before a Sonata* contains a reference to quarter-tones written not later than 1920, and perhaps several years earlier, which places quarter-tones in an evolutionary context similar to that of Joseph Yasser in his *A Theory of Evolving Tonality* (1932). The Ives passage reads: "In some century to come, when school children will whistle popular tunes in quarter-tones—when the diatonic scale will be as obsolete as the pentatonic is now—then . . . borderland experiences may be both easily expressed and readily recognized."[4]

[3]Perhaps 1903–1904. One of Ives' lists gives 1903–1914 (see Kirkpatrick, p. 104).
[4]Page 71. This and other references are to the 1962 edition of *Essays Before a Sonata*.

In any case, Ives' meeting with Barth in 1923–24, while it by no means provided his first experience with quarter-tones, was the direct stimulus which led to the composition of the Three Quarter-tone Pieces.

Barth and Ives were working on quarter-tone problems at the same time as the man who was later to become the most renowned exponent of this medium—the Czech composer, Alois Hába. Hába wrote for a quarter-tone piano brought out by A. Förster in Prague in 1923; it had two keyboards, one tuned a quarter-tone higher than the other. Ives seems to have been familiar with a similar instrument in New York, as he mentions in his article a quarter-tone piano of this type by "Dr. Stoehr, Mehlin & Sons."[5]

In February of the year Hába published his *Von neuer Musik* (1925), the Franco-American Music Society (founded by Schmitz) sponsored a concert of quarter-tone music arranged by Barth at Town Hall in New York. Ives' Three Pieces were performed, and a month later the bulletin of the Society (later called *Pro Musica Quarterly*) carried his explicatory article.

Ives' manuscript[6] contained a paragraph about Barth which was somehow deleted from the printed article. It reads as follows:

Another way of treating the general subject is as Mr. Barth has done. He uses practically the same number of notes as in the diatonic system dividing them between two pianos—each using six or seven notes a whole-tone apart—a plan of substitution rather than of extension but the more I hear his music the more I like it—it has many beautiful periods and effects, it produces a composite result that is fascinating. It is a practical way of accustoming the ear to 1/4 tone combinations and intervals. It attempts no pure 1/4 [tone] harmonic basis and the usual rules of the diatonic system may apply. It has the advantage that any piano music may be readily transcribed. But the plan obviously can include no perfect fifths & a good part of the twenty-four quarters are not used—or if so only as passing notes.

Ives' pieces in final form were for two pianos, as were Barth's. But two of them, according to Ives, were intended originally for a double-keyboard instrument (Stoehr's?).

Ives' reaction to a number of curious effects that he observed in the pieces is expressed near the end of the article with characteristic humor: "I'm getting ready to say with the man who went to the horse race: 'What I expected didn't happen and I didn't expect it would.'" But the fact is, he worked out his system carefully, and he records in a more serious vein

---

[5]Possibly Richard Stoehr (b. 1874), an Austrian theorist and composer. Mehlin & Sons was a New York firm.

[6]That is, MSS. 2 and 3 of the Yale Collection, as designated in the 1962 edition. For a complete description of the manuscript material relative to this Ives article, see the Introductory Note to that edition, pp. 105–106. The excerpt given here is the version of MS. 2, which is the longer one.

a number of acute observations which show at once the flexibility of his approach to new material and the keenness of his aural perception.

II

Whether it came from his Emersonian belief in man's capacity, and need to master new material,[7] or from the example set by his iconoclastic father, or both of these sources, Ives never shared—even as a boy—that stifling belief in the rightness and inevitability of traditional practice which stultified the ears of even so intelligent a man as his teacher at Yale, Horatio Parker. Ives was prepared by his father from the start to "stretch his ears," and his early attempts to do so were tolerated by Parker only because—again through George Ives' teaching—he had an unquestionable command of harmony and counterpoint, those solid skills which Parker required of all his students.

George Ives apparently found stimulation and support for his unorthodox experiments in Helmholtz's *On the Sensations of Tone.* Cowell says (p. 19) that "one of Helmholtz's books was in the family library" during Ives' youth. Such a passage as the following one could have served George Ives as a basis for challenging the status quo during the 1880's:

> Hence it follows,—and the proposition cannot be too vividly present in the minds of our musical theoreticians and historians—*that the system of Scales, Modes, and Harmonic tissues does not rest solely upon inalterable natural laws, but is at least partly also the result of esthetical principles, which have already changed, and will still further change, with the progressive development of humanity.*[8]

Such a viewpoint, passed on to a remarkably gifted youngster like Charles, was enough in itself to have served as a springboard for progress into a then unknown world of new sounds. Ives does, in fact—near the beginning of his article—quote this very passage to support his plea for an "extension of medium." But curiously enough, he derives the passage not directly from Helmholtz but from a book by one William Pole called *Philosophy of Music* (Boston, 1879), the text of which is also quoted by Ives in this article.[9] Pole writes in the same vein:

> No doubt, in the simplest elements of music, the ear has been the guide; and we shall see that there are physical and physiological rea-

[7]In the "Emerson" chapter of *Essays Before a Sonata,* Ives quotes the following passage from Emerson's essay, "Culture" in *The Conduct of Life:* "Man's culture can spare nothing, wants all the material. He is to convert all impediments into instruments, all enemies into power."

[8]Page 358 in the edition, London, 1875. This is the edition Ives' father would have had, and it is the one quoted by the source from which Ives quotes (see below).

[9]William Pole (1814–1900) was an engineer, composer, and examiner in music to the University of London. He wrote with quite remarkable freedom and insight for his time, though relying heavily on Helmholtz and Moritz Hauptmann. There are variants in the Helmholtz text as given by Ives which coincide exactly with variants in Pole's quotation of Helmholtz, indicating that Ives drew the passage from Pole's book.

sons why certain preferences should have existed. But this appeal to the ear must not be carried too far; and when the ear is appealed to to sanction complicated effects of harmony, it amounts simply to begging the question. We approve certain things, not because there is any natural *propriety* in them, but because we have been accustomed to them, and have been taught to consider them right; we disapprove certain others, not because there is any natural *impropriety* in them, but because they are strange to us, and we have been taught to consider them wrong.

Ives then continues:

It will probably be centuries, at least generations, before man will discover all or even most of the value in a quarter-tone extension. And when he does, nature has plenty of other things up her sleeve. And it may be longer than we think before the ear will freely translate what it hears and instinctively arouse and amplify the spiritual consciousness.

But that needn't keep anyone from trying to find out how to use a few more of the myriads of sound waves nature has put around in the air (immune from the radio) for man to catch if he can and "perchance make himself a part with nature," as Thoreau used to say.

Even in the limited and awkward way of working with quarter-tones at present, transcendent things may be felt ahead—glimpses into further fields of thought and beauty.

III

Ives believed that the best way to approach quarter-tone music (his father had thought so too) was through harmony "with the melodic coming as a kind of collateral, simultaneously perhaps, and just as important, but very closely bound up [MS. 2: and dependent on] with the former—in a sense opposite to the way our present system has developed." It seemed to him that "a pure quarter-tone melody needs a pure quarter-tone harmony not only to back it up but to help generate it."

In setting up a quarter-tone harmony, Ives takes an interesting initial leap when he says "chords of four or more notes, as I hear it, seem to be a more natural basis than triads." In this supposition he is again in agreement with Yasser, whose nineteen-tone "supradiatonic" system also rejects the triad as the simplest complete verticality, and treats a hexad as the basic chord.

Ives invokes the psychology of expectation when he explains why the triad using a quarter-tone pitch for its third sounds badly, while a four-note chord using two such pitches sounds well (I rearrange the sequence of statements somewhat in quoting):

[On a quarter-tone piano with the upper keyboard tuned a quarter-tone sharp] strike C and G on the lower keyboard and D sharp on the upper. . . . This chord to most ears, I imagine, sounds like a C major or C minor chord [triad], out of tune . . . the third note [D♯] enters as a kind of weak compromise to the sound expected. . . . While if another note [A♯] is added which will make a quarter-tone interval with either of the two notes [C-G] which make the diatonic [i.e., lower keyboard] interval, we have a balanced chord which, if listened to without prejudice leans neither way, and which seems to establish an identity of its own . . . if listened to several times in succession, it gathers a kind of character of its own—neither major, minor, nor even diminished.

Here is a diagram showing the chord described above:

Two other possibilities for a fundamental chord are examined:

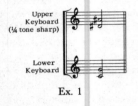

Ex. 1

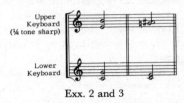

Exx. 2 and 3

The first of these (Ex. 2) is rejected because the narrow interval between B plus and the octave makes it impractical when inverted. The second (Ex. 3) is rejected because its fifth is out-of-tune (a quarter-tone flat).

The interval of the fifth receives an unexpected citation from Ives at this point:

[The fifth]—that inexorable thing—[is] a part of the natural laws which apparently no aesthetic principle has yet beaten out. The fifth seems to say, "You can't get away from the fact that I am boss of the overtones—the first *real* partial. I have the octaves to walk on. If I'm not land, I'm sea, and you can't travel around the world without me." He forgot the airplane.

However, some day, perhaps, an Edison, a Dempsey, or an Einstein will or will not suppress him with a blow from a new natural law.

Ives sought a "secondary chord corollary to the fundamental." He describes it necessary character:

The chord in itself, I think, should give a feeling of less finality than the first. It should be absorbed readily by the fundamental, it should have lesser [MS. 1: shorter] intervals, and, in general, a contrasting character, and a note in common [with the primary chord], though I don't know that this is so important; it depends on the direction of the general motion or melody.

Without explaining any of the stages by which he arrives at such a chord, he presents his choice: it is a chord built of intervals each of which is measured by five quarter-tones (i.e., minor thirds a quarter-tone flat, or major seconds a quarter-tone sharp), except for the last interval completing the octave (Ex. 4).

Ives, again entirely on the basis of his aural impression, suggests that "if the second note . . . is thrown up an octave, the chord has a more malleable sound and is in a more useful form—that is, considering it as above in the first position, and not an inversion."

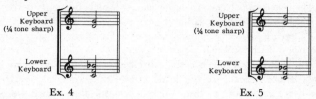

Ex. 4   Ex. 5

When he first describes them, Ives' fundamental and secondary chords seem to suggest an analogy with the tonic and dominant of conventional usage. But further along in the text, he writes:

> These two chords outlined above might be termed major and minor —more because their intervals are larger and smaller than because they carry the usual feeling between our diatonic major and minor chords, and partly because the five-quarter-tone intervals offer possibilities for a minor or lesser scale which I won't try to go into now.

Ives does not conceive of the two fundamental chords as belonging exclusively to any one scale degree (in the manner of tonic and dominant) but as verticalities that may be erected over any one of the twenty-four steps of the quarter-tone scale (as major or minor triads may be erected over any step of the twelve-tone scale).

Ives uses Helmholtz' method in measuring the roughness of quarter-tone harmonies: calculating the difference tones or beats formed between the partials.[10] The results indicate that "these chords [MS. 2: especially the first] stand up only fairly well." But Ives is critical of this method of evaluation:

> It has seemed to me that the value of measuring "roughness" is relative. I can't see why a great deal doesn't depend on how hard the notes are struck (their amplitude) or on the instruments playing them. The average ear feels the fundamental primarily and thinks in its terms. But as the effect of the vibration numbers of the fundamental is so closely bound up with those of the overtones—that is, the vibrations of all the partials as a sounding unit—on the whole the "general difference" is the safest thing to measure by. Still I don't see how one can always measure by vibrations he doesn't always hear.[11]

[10]Here again, the form of the diagram used in Ives' illustration indicates that he learned the method from Pole rather than directly from Helmholtz.

[11]Ives does not take into account the effect of aural harmonics which supply the overtones even when the fundamentals are overtoneless.

One of Ives' most interesting observations, made after actually experiencing quarter-tone harmonies in the composition of his Three Pieces, has to do with the problem of redundance. He feels that these new sounds "offer permutations and combinations that won't do our music any harm . . . they may be played quite continuously without holding you up, as a repetition of diatonic chords seems to do." He thinks this may be because the "ear" has to make certain adjustments which prevent it from lazily accepting the sounds through habit. An instinctive awareness of the usefulness of serial procedures in reducing redundance to a minimum is touched upon in the following paragraph:

In a movement of music, a structure built primarily on a progression of chords not necessarily the same but of the same relative intervals seems more and more to hold up that organic flow which we feel the need of—it halts us so severely that a resort to other material is almost forced on us. As an instance, we may go perhaps to a series of chords, each different, occurring in cyclic repetition [MS. 2: a series of chords each different which do not repeat except as the cycle repeats and then not literally]. The process of finding whatever one feels is wanted in each case is mostly instinctive, but that there are underlying laws is evidenced by the fact that they may be traced in a general way after the notes are written down.

In their ability to relieve monotonous repetitions, Ives believes that the new quarter-tone harmonies may also have useful effects on both rhythm and form. They have a "sense of humor," too, but, he says, "that's a dangerous thing to refer to: it depends as much on where the catcher's mitt is as on the pitcher's curves."

IV

At the end of his article, Ives describes several curious impressions or "aural illusions" he had observed in the context of quarter-tone harmony which reveal well his sensitivity to pitch relationships. They show that Ives' way of listening was of the type which can imaginatively project finer pitch distinctions upon the artificial regularities of equal-tempered tunings—a gift not always common to composers whose main musical experience has involved keyboard instruments.[12]

[12]In an incomplete and rather confused rough draft (perhaps dating from the '40's), Ives attempts to explain the rationale of the spellings in the Concord Sonata, probably after one of his encounters with engravers, who always had great difficulty understanding his notation. The gist of the manuscript is that a note *must* be written as a sharp if it is felt that way or a flat if it is to be understood as such, even though there is really no difference between them on a tempered instrument. The implication is that one actually imagines slightly higher or lower pitches under the influence of a feeling for functional relationships, and that the spelling should be coordinated with these feelings.

John Kirkpatrick relates an incident in which he attempted to suggest a change of spelling to Ives, and was literally blown off his feet by a storm of temperament which the suggestion released. The note *had* to be just as Ives had written it.

One of Ives' "aural illusions" concerns the effect of diatonic harmony on quarter-tone melodic progressions. In one instance cited, the descending quarter-step, C-B plus, is sounded against a G-major triad played on the lower (diatonic) keyboard, and the ascending form, B plus-C, is played against a C-major triad. Ives finds that the descending interval sounds shorter than the ascending one. "I've tried it several times on different days," he writes, "some time apart, and I get the same impression."

What he is observing, of course, is that the ascending quarter-tone step, B plus-C, sounds more "normal" when it is used melodically as a leading tone over a C-major triad than the descending step against a G-major triad, which leaves the ear with an unresolved and poorly blended third in a terminal harmony. The B plus would sound sharp, in any case, against the twelve-tone tempered B on the lower keyboard. One would wish the B plus to be lower, and the melodic progression, C-B plus, to be wider. Therefore, it seems in retrospect that the progression *was* shorter than the other ascending one, which, though just as short, left one with a feeling of satisfactory resolution, in that no contrasting intonations were unresolved in the terminal harmony.

These impressions, Ives says, are opposite to those he gets from the same progressions with tempered half-steps in the diatonic system: there the ascending progression, B-C, against a C-major triad sounds *shorter* than the descending one, C-B, against a G-major triad.

A possible explanation here is that Ives projects imaginatively (in the way referred to in note 12) the cadential leading-tone function on the ascending progression, but does not do so with the descending one, which is less final in its cadential implications. The feeling of attraction and desire for closeness to the tonic, which compels singers and players of untempered instruments to sharpen leading tones as much as (or more than) the harmonic context will tolerate, leads Ives in this case to hear the interval as shorter, though it is not, because he *wishes* it to be so.

It is clear from Ives' response to these "aural illusions" that he was thoroughly aware of the curious problems created by the introduction of small melodic steps into the orderly world of twelve-tone equal temperament, in which harmonic and melodic functions are normally neutralized and at peace with each other.

In further observations, Ives suggests that parallel motion in this system is "just as agreeable as opposite motion," and that "the need of passing notes is felt less." [MS. 1: Does this mean that contrapuntal feeling will be lessened by a quarter-tone system. I hope not.] Also, he finds that "inversions of quarter-tone chords do not seem as different in character

as those [of] purely diatonic [chords]." But, he proposes, "in this as in
the other reactions, it is quite probably my ear and not the system that
is at fault."

V

Ives' quarter-tone pieces (although they are a small and relatively
unimportant part of his total output) and his theoretical probing into the
effects of the new medium (although more intuitive than thorough) supply
us with yet one more illustration of how much was probably lost by Ives'
arrival on the musical scene at a time when there was so little opportunity
for a composer with experimental tendencies to develop fully. If he were
living now, and were, say, thirty years old, what fascinating new media
there would be for him to try his hand at! And perhaps now he could
have managed to live in music without having to sell insurance.

Or would he have liked things as well without Rollo[13] to complain
about?

Would he have lashed out against foundations as he did against the
proposals to establish an American Academy at Rome?[14]

What would he have said about new media in 1965 if he could write
before 1920 that "the intensity today with which techniques and media
are organized tends to throw the mind away from a "common sense" and
towards manner, and thus to resultant weakened mental states?"

Ives would probably have reacted to contemporary problems as he
reacted to those of his day. In his own words (advice to "a poet or
a whistler"),[16] he would have stood "unprotected from all the showers
of the absolute which may beat upon him," and he would have learned
"to use . . . whatever he can of all lessons of the infinite that humanity has
received and thrown to man, that nature has exposed and sacrificed, that
life and death have translated, . . . growing and approaching nearer and
nearer to perfect truths—whatever they are and wherever they may be."

---

[13]Ives' personification of the Victorian conservative. A frequent marginal note in Ives
manuscripts is: "Rollo won't like it."

[14]"We hear that Mr. Smith [David Stanley Smith, Dean of the Yale School of Music and
classmate of Ives with Horatio Parker] or Mr. Morgan [J. Pierpont Morgan, whose name
appears with Smith's in the list of Members of the Council of the American Academy in Rome
for 1921–22], etc., *et al.,* design to establish a 'course at Rome,' to raise the standard of American
music, (or the standard of American composers—which is it?); but possibly the more our composer accepts from his patrons '*et al.,*' the less he will accept *from himself.* It may be possible that
a day in a 'Kansas wheat field' will do more for him than three years in Rome" (*Essays Before
a Sonata,* pp. 92–93).

[15]*Ibid.,* p. 91.

[16]*Ibid.,* pp. 91–92.

CHARLES IVES' QUOTATIONS: MANNER OR SUBSTANCE?

DENNIS MARSHALL

ONE OF IVES' most frequently mentioned compositional practices is his extensive use of borrowed material; he draws upon the vast body of contemporary social music—hymn tunes, patriotic songs, ragtime, college songs—as "raw material" for his works. Little has been said, however, about the relationship of these borrowed elements to the overall musical structure. It has been generally assumed that this previously composed material is used principally for its programmatic significance and that these borrowed tunes bear little or no *musical* relationship to each other or to the composition as a whole.

However, in his *Essays Before a Sonata* (first published by Ives in 1920 as a preface to his *Second Pianoforte Sonata: "Concord, Mass., 1840–1860"*) the composer seems to hint at the possibility that this borrowed material might take on a much more fundamental musical role. In the Epilogue, Ives elaborates on the dualism present in any art work between its fundamental "substance" and its more superficial, external "manner."[1] He points out that an "overinsistence upon the national in art" may cause some composers to borrow from local musical sources merely for surface effect.[2] On the other hand, he then gives examples of how such materials may become part of the real substance of an artist's work:

> The man "born down to Babbit's Corners" may find a deep appeal in the simple but acute Gospel hymns of the New England "camp meetin'" of a generation or so ago. He finds in them—some of them—a vigor, a depth of feeling, a natural-soil rhythm, a sincerity—emphatic but inartistic—which, in spite of a vociferous sentimentality, carries him nearer the "Christ of the people" than does the *Te Deum* of the greatest cathedral. . . . If the Yankee can reflect the fervency with which "his gospels" were sung—the fervency of "Aunt Sarah," who scrubbed her life away for her brother's ten orphans, the fervency with which this woman, after a fourteen-hour work day on the farm, would hitch up and drive five miles through the mud and rain to "prayer

[1] Charles Ives, *Essays Before a Sonata and Other Writings*, ed. Howard Boatwright (New York, 1962), p. 75.
[2] *Ibid.*, pp. 78–79.

meetin'," her one articulate outlet for the fullness of her unselfish soul
—if he can reflect the fervency of such a spirit, he may find there a local
color that will do all the world good. If his music can but catch that
spirit by being a part with itself, it will come somewhere near his ideal
—and it will be American, too. . . . In other words, if local color,
national color, any color, is a true pigment of the universal color, it is a
divine quality, it is a part of substance in art—not of manner.[3]

A closer examination of Ives's compositions reveals that his use of borrowed material is indeed at the very core of his compositional thought.
The two scherzo movements of his First Piano Sonata, completed in 1909,
illustrate this fundamental role which borrowed elements play in the over-
all design. The many motivic and structural interrelationships which unite
this pair of symmetrically placed second and fourth movements in the
five-movement sonata justify considering them as a single scherzo, interrupted by the central third movement (a rhapsodic series of variations on
"What a Friend We Have in Jesus"). Each half of the scherzo is further
divided into two sections, labeled by the composer IIA, IIB, IVA, and
IVB. Three of these are arrangements from a *Set of Four Ragtime Pieces* for
small orchestra which Ives completed in 1904.[4] He originally intended to
use all four early ragtime pieces in the sonata, but around 1909 he replaced the third piece with a newly composed section IVA.[5] This section,
probably one of the last parts of the sonata to be composed, is also harmonically and rhythmically the most advanced. The ragtime piece dis-
carded from the sonata was later used in the *Second Orchestral Set* (finished
in 1915).[6]

As a young man starting his career in the insurance business in New
York City, Charles Ives had enjoyed spending an occasional Saturday
night playing ragtime piano in some local beer garden,[7] and this exuberance is reflected in the interrupted scherzo. But this scherzo also reflects
another kind of exuberance: that of the New England "prayer meetin',"
and the composer utilizes three Gospel hymn tunes in the scherzo: "I
Hear Thy Welcome Voice," "Bringing in the Sheaves," and "Happy
Day" (Exx. 1a, 1b, and 1c).

This combination of ragtime and hymn tunes may seem incongruous—
perhaps even a bit sacrilegious—to some, but Ives is expressing not ridi-
cule, but intense admiration. He feels, with the New England Trans-

---

[3] *Ibid.*, pp. 80–81.
[4] John Kirkpatrick, *A Temporary Mimeographed Catalogue of the Music Manuscripts of Charles Edward Ives (1874–1954) given by Mrs. Ives to the Library of the Yale School of Music, September 1955*, Yale University, 1960, p. 40.
[5] *Ibid.*, p. 85.
[6] *Ibid.*, p. 18.
[7] Henry Cowell and Sidney Cowell, *Charles Ives and His Music* (New York, 1955), p. 40.

I Hear Thy Welcome Voice

Lewis Hartsough

Ex. 1a

cendentalists, "that all occupations of man's body and soul in their diversity come from but one mind and soul!"[8] Thus Ives is not merely unafraid to draw upon the whole of his varied musical experiences for use in his compositions; he actually feels obligated to do so. He writes in the *Essays*:

If he (this poet, composer, and laborer) . . . is willing to use or learn to use (or at least if he is not afraid of trying to use) whatever he can of any and all lessons of the infinite that humanity has received and thrown to man, that nature has exposed and sacrificed, that life and death have translated—if he accepts all and sympathizes with all, is influenced by all (whether consciously or subconsciously, drastically or humbly,

[8] Ives, *Essays Before a Sonata and Other Writings*, p. 96.

audibly or inaudibly) whether it be all the virtue of Satan or the only evil of Heaven—and all, even at one time, even in one chord—*then* it may be that the value of his substance, and its value to himself, to his art, to all art, even to the Common Soul, is growing and approaching nearer and nearer to perfect truths—whatever they are and wherever they may be.[9]

Bringing in the Sheaves

George A. Minor

Chorus

Ex. 1b

Ives's choosing to ignore the traditional boundaries of "sacred" and "secular" reminds the present writer of the medieval musicians who found nothing improper about singing a motet with a sacred Latin text in one voice part and a secular French text in another.

[9] *Ibid.*, p. 92.

The most obvious characteristic shared by the three hymn tunes used in this scherzo is their formal structure, a series of verses, each followed by the repeated chorus (or refrain). Ives uses this as a model for the four ragtime pieces, each of which also exhibits the verse-chorus structure. (The formal similarity is more than likely not a coincidence: of the over fifty hymn tunes which John Kirkpatrick has traced in the music of Ives,[10]

Happy Day

from Edward F. Rimbault

Ex. 1c

only fifteen utilize the verse-chorus structure, and the hymn tunes used in the other movements of the sonata are not based on this formal plan.)

Each of the four chorus sections of the scherzo is based on the refrain of the same hymn tune, "I Hear Thy Welcome Voice" (see Ex. 1a). The

---

[10] Kirkpatrick, *A Temporary Mimeographed Catalogue*, pp. 264–65.

chorus of movement IIA presents all but the final note of the hymn
tune's chorus, accompanied by a ragtime-inspired rhythmic figure (Ex. 2).
The chorus of movement IIB (Ex. 3) makes use of only the first half of the
melody; in the published score (page 19) Ives describes the section as "an
impromptu affair" and has included suggestions for several alternate ways
of playing the second and fourth measures.

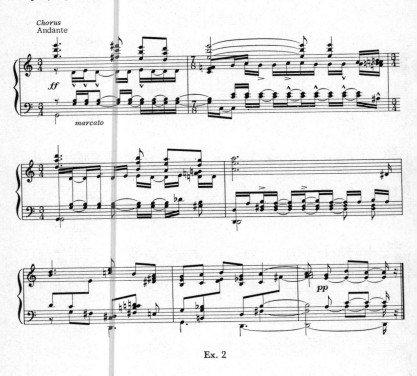

Ex. 2

The chorus of the ragtime piece originally intended as movement IVA is
similar to that of the first piece, but the chorus of the substituted section
merely suggests the hymn tune using parallel fifths (Ex. 4). The last ragtime
piece has a chorus, vacillating between B major and B♭ major, which
returns to a more nearly complete (though distorted) statement of the
original hymn tune chorus (Ex. 5).

The four verse sections in the scherzo introduce motivic elements from
two additional hymn tunes, "Bringing in the Sheaves" and "Happy
Day" (see Exx. 1b and 1c). The latter melody is also associated with a
secular text: "How Dry I am." The dual significance renders the tune

Ex. 3

singularly appropriate for this scherzo, which is consciously ignoring the usual sacred-secular dichotomy. A fragment of the tune is first heard at the very beginning of movement IIA (Ex. 6). The verse of "Bringing in the Sheaves" also makes an early appearance (Ex. 7).

Movement IIB was the first part of the sonata to be published (by *New Music*) with the title *In the Inn*. Ives relishes this verbal pun, and later we will see the "musical pun" which he uses to add motivic cohesion to the scherzo.

A marginal note by Ives describes the new movement IVA as "a study

Ex. 4

Ex. 5

in 'Rag' for 5's 3's and 2's together, changing accents, etc."[11] Its verse
and chorus lead directly to the final ragtime piece, which recapitulates

Ex. 6

some of the material of IIB and then breaks into a "ragged" verse and
jubilant refrain of "Bringing in the Sheaves" before the final chorus sec-

Ex. 7

[11] *Ibid.*, p. 86.

tion described above. This last ragtime piece differs from the first three in that there is a passage following the chorus which serves as a coda to the entire scherzo (Ex. 8).

Ex. 8

Ives's choice of the particular three hymn tunes which he uses in this scherzo—rather than another set of three with the same verse-chorus structure—is influenced by an important melodic similarity: each verse and chorus in all three hymn tunes ends with a rhythmic variant of the same re-do-mi-re-do cadential formula (see Exx. 1a, 1b, and 1c). This "musical pun" has been hinted at several times during the ragtime pieces, but Ives has carefully avoided presenting the complete five-note figure in any of the four chorus sections. Finally, in the coda, two of the hymn tune refrains (those of "I Hear Thy Welcome Voice" and "Bringing in the Sheaves") are stated simultaneously, and at the point where each has the five-note motive, Ives combines them into a single melodic line (at the 2/4 measure in Ex. 8).

It now seems clear that Ives has chosen his borrowed material very carefully, and the term "quotation" seems hardly adequate to describe the fundamental importance of these hymn tunes as formal models and as unifying factors in the sonata. Even in the first and last movements of the work, which make comparatively less use of borrowed elements, Ives introduces a single hymn tune, "Lebanon," at certain strategic points in both movements to strengthen the symmetrical structure of the entire composition.

This use of previously composed elements which are carefully selected for their motivic relationships can be found in much of the composer's

work. One of the best-known examples of this is his choice of the hymn
tune "Missionary Chant" in the "Concord" Sonata because of the tune's
melodic similarities to the "Beethoven Fifth" motive, which also plays an
important role in the composition (Ex. 9).

Missionary Chant

Heinrich C. Zeuner

Ex. 9

In addition, the technique of basing the formal plan of an extended
movement upon the structure of a much simpler borrowed melody can be
found in other Ives works. For example, the first movement of the Third
Violin Sonata, like the scherzo previously described, consists of four verse
sections, each followed by a chorus. This movement is modeled on the
hymn tune "Beulah Land," which also serves as an important motivic
element.[12]

Even in a complex orchestral movement such as "The Fourth of July"
from the *Holidays Symphony*, Ives makes use of a single borrowed tune at
the very core of the structure of the composition: "The Red, White and
Blue" ("O Columbia the gem of the ocean . . .") serves as a structural
framework for the entire movement in much the same way that a Lutheran
chorale melody would serve as the formal model and motivic source for a
cantata movement or an organ chorale prelude of J. S. Bach. "The Red,
White and Blue" can also be heard as the principal motivic material of the
orchestral movement from the very first measure; Ex. 10 illustrates the use
of the tune as both a melodic and harmonic source.

The chords in fourths, fifths, and seconds (derived from the intervals in

[12] *Ibid.*, p. 78.

Ex. 10

the opening phrase of the patriotic tune) also appear in the strings at the climax of the movement, beginning at rehearsal letter X.

As Ives introduces other popular melodies into "The Fourth of July," he is always concerned with their relationship to the principal source, "The Red, White and Blue." An excerpt from one of the composer's preliminary sketches for the passage beginning at rehearsal letter S reveals the composer experimenting with the contrapuntal combination of "The Red, White and Blue" and "The Battle Hymn of the Republic" (Ex. 11).[13] The melodic similarities in the second and third full measures undoubtedly influenced his decision to combine these particular tunes.

A great deal of Ives's music is "program music," because he feels, as he writes in a letter to Henry Bellamann:

[13] Photostats have been made of virtually all the Ives music manuscripts at Yale, and the use of the photostat negative numbers as given in the Kirkpatrick *Catalogue* is a convenient method for identifying any particular manuscript page. This example can be found on the page with negative number 0891.

You cannot set an art off in the corner and hope for it to have vitality,
reality and substance. There can be nothing *exclusive* about a substantial
art. It comes directly out of the heart of experience of life and thinking
about life and living life.[14]

Ex. 11

The previously composed materials which Ives uses are selected, of course,
partly for their programmatic connotations, but the composer is conscious
of their musical characteristics and interrelationships from the very beginning of the creative process, and these borrowed elements form a part of
the real *substance* of his musical art.

[14] Cowell, *Charles Ives and His Music*, p. 97.

THE LIBERATION OF SOUND

EDGARD VARESE

Our musical alphabet is poor and illogical.

Music, which should pulsate with life, needs new means of expression, and science alone can infuse it with youthful vigor.

Why Italian Futurists, have you slavishly reproduced only what is commonplace and boring in the bustle of our daily lives.

I dream of instruments obedient to my thought and which with their contribution of a whole new world of unsuspected sounds, will lend themselves to the exigencies of my inner rhythm.[1]

(Excerpts from lectures by Varèse, compiled and edited with footnotes by Chou Wen-chung)

━━━━━━━━━━━━━━━━━━━━■■■■■■■■━━━━━━━━━━━━━━━━━━━━

NEW INSTRUMENTS AND NEW MUSIC*

WHEN new instruments will allow me to write music as I conceive it, taking the place of the linear counterpoint, the movement of sound-masses, of shifting planes, will be clearly perceived. When these sound-masses collide the phenomena of penetration or repulsion will seem to occur. Certain transmutations taking place on certain planes will seem to be projected onto other planes, moving at different speeds and at different angles. There will no longer be the old conception of melody or interplay of melodies. The entire work will be a melodic totality. The entire work will flow as a river flows.

Today with the technical means that exist and are easily adaptable, the differentiation of the various masses and different planes as well as these beams of sound, could be made discernible to the listener by means of certain acoustical arrangements. Moreover, such an acoustical arrangement would permit the delimitation of what I call Zones of Intensities. These zones would be differentiated by various timbres or colors and different loudnesses. Through such a physical process these zones would appear of different colors and of different magnitude in

[1] "*391*," Number 5, June 1917, New York; translated from the French by Louise Varèse.

* From a lecture given at Mary Austin House, Santa Fe, 1936.

different perspectives for our perception. The role of color or timbre would be completely changed from being incidental, anecdotal, sensual or picturesque; it would become an agent of delineation like the different colors on a map separating different areas, and an integral part of form. These zones would be felt as isolated, and the hitherto unobtainable non-blending (or at least the sensation of non-blending) would become possible.

In the moving masses you would be conscious of their transmutations when they pass over different layers, when they penetrate certain opacities, or are dilated in certain rarefactions. Moreover, the new musical apparatus I envisage, able to emit sounds of any number of frequencies, will extend the limits of the lowest and highest registers, hence new organizations of the vertical resultants: chords, their arrangements, their spacings, that is, their oxygenation. Not only will the harmonic possibilities of the overtones be revealed in all their splendor but the use of certain interferences created by the partials will represent an appreciable contribution. The never before thought of use of the inferior resultants and of the differential and additional sounds may also be expected. An entirely new magic of sound!

I am sure that the time will come when the composer, after he has graphically realized his score, will see this score automatically put on a machine which will faithfully transmit the musical content to the listener. As frequencies and new rhythms will have to be indicated on the score, our actual notation will be inadequate. The new notation will probably be seismographic. And here it is curious to note that at the beginning of two eras, the Mediaeval primitive and our own primitive era (for we are at a new primitive stage in music today) we are faced with an identical problem: the problem of finding graphic symbols for the transposition of the composer's thought into sound. At a distance of more than a thousand years we have this analogy: our still primitive electrical instruments find it necessary to abandon staff notation and to use a kind of seismographic writing much like the early ideographic writing originally used for the voice before the development of staff notation. Formerly the curves of the musical line indicated the melodic fluctuations of the voice, today the machine-instrument requires precise design indications.

MUSIC AS AN ART-SCIENCE*

And here are the advantages I anticipate from such a machine: liberation from the arbitrary, paralyzing tempered system; the possibility

* From a lecture given at the University of Southern California, 1939.

Aeolian Hall

Sunday Evening, March 4, 1925, at 8.30 o'clock.

International Composers' Guild, Inc.

founded 1921

Fourth Season

Third Concert

NEW MUSIC

presented by
an Ensemble composed of

JOHN BARCLAY

and

The Leading Players of the Philadelphia Orchestra
conducted by

LEOPOLD STOKOWSKI

(*by special permission of the Board of Directors of the
Philadelphia Orchestra*)

PROGRAM

I. Serenade .... *Arnold Schönberg*
(first time in America)   (1924)
1. March
2. Minuet
3. Variations
4. Sonnet by Petrarca
5. Dance Scene
6. Song without words
7. Finale

Program continued on next page

Program of the first American performance of Schoenberg's *Serenade*
by the International Composers' Guild

of obtaining any number of cycles or if still desired, subdivisions of
the octave, consequently the formation of any desired scale; unsuspected range in low and high registers; new harmonic splendors
obtainable from the use of sub-harmonic combinations now impossible; the possibility of obtaining any differentiation of timbre, of
sound-combinations; new dynamics far beyond the present human-
powered orchestra; a sense of sound-projection in space by means of
the emission of sound in any part or in many parts of the hall as may
be required by the score; cross rhythms unrelated to each other,

Aeolian Hall

Sunday Evening, February 14, 1926, at 8.30 o'clock

International Composers' Guild, Inc.

founded by Edgar Varèse, 1921

FIFTH SEASON OF NEW MUSIC

Third Concert

PROGRAM
1

Les Noces . . . . *Igor Stravinsky*
(first time in America)   (1917)

FOR FOUR SOLO VOICES, FOUR PIANOS,
MIXED CHORUS AND PERCUSSION
conducted by
LEOPOLD STOKOWSKI
(*by courtesy of the Board of Directors of the
Philadelphia Orchestra*)

SOLO VOICES

MADAME CAHIER   MARGUERITE RINGO
RICHARD HALE   COLIN O'MORE

PIANOS

GERMAINE TAILLEFERRE   ALFREDO CASELLA
GEORGES ENESCO   CARLOS SALZEDO

MIXED CHORUS OF TWENTY-FOUR SOLO VOICES
SELECTED BY THE FRANCIS BROWN MARSH MGT.
PERCUSSION PLAYERS FROM THE PHILADELPHIA ORCHESTRA

Voices (Soli and Chorus) prepared by
CARLOS SALZEDO

Program continued on next page

Program of the first American performance of Stravinsky's *Les Noces*
by the International Composers' Guild

treated simultaneously, or to use the old word, "contrapuntally" (since the machine would be able to beat any number of desired notes, any subdivision of them, omission or fraction of them)—all these in a given unit of measure or time which is humanly impossible to attain.

RHYTHM, FORM AND CONTENT*

My fight for the liberation of sound and for my right to make music with any sound and all sounds has sometimes been construed as a

* From a lecture given at Princeton University, 1959.

desire to disparage and even to discard the great music of the past. But that is where my roots are. No matter how original, how different a composer may seem, he has only grafted a little bit of himself on the old plant. But this he should be allowed to do without being accused of wanting to kill the plant. He only wants to produce a new flower. It does not matter if at first it seems to some people more like a cactus than a rose. Many of the old masters are my intimate friends—all are respected colleagues. None of them are dead saints—in fact none of them are dead—and the rules they made for themselves are not sacrosanct and are not everlasting laws. Listening to music by Perotin, Machaut, Monteverdi, Bach, or Beethoven we are conscious of living substances; they are "alive in the present." But music written in the manner of another century is the result of culture and, desirable and comfortable as culture may be, an artist should not lie down in it. The best bit of criticism André Gide ever wrote was this confession, which must have been wrung from him by self-torture: "When I read Rimbaud or the Sixth Song of Maldorer, I am ashamed of my own works and everything that is only the result of culture."

Because for so many years I crusaded for new instruments with what may have seemed fanatical zeal, I have been accused of desiring nothing less than the destruction of all musical instruments and even of all performers. This is, to say the least, an exaggeration. Our new liberating medium—the electronic—is not meant to replace the old musical instruments which composers, including myself, will continue to use. Electronics is an additive, not a destructive factor in the art and science of music. It is because new instruments have been constantly added to the old ones that Western music has such a rich and varied patrimony.

Grateful as we must be for the new medium, we should not expect miracles from machines. The machine can give out only what we put into it. The musical principles remain the same whether a composer writes for orchestra or tape. Rhythm and Form are still his most important problems and the two elements in music most generally misunderstood.

Rhythm is too often confused with metrics. Cadence or the regular succession of beats and accents has little to do with the rhythm of a composition. Rhythm is the element in music that gives life to the work and holds it together. It is the element of stability, the generator of form. In my own works, for instance, rhythm derives from the simultaneous interplay of unrelated elements that intervene at calculated, but not regular time lapses. This corresponds more nearly to

the definition of rhythm in physics and philosophy as "a succession of
alternate and opposite or correlative states."

As for form, Busoni once wrote: "Is it not singular to demand of a
composer originality in all things and to forbid it as regards form?
No wonder that if he is original he is accused of formlessness."[2]

The misunderstanding has come from thinking of form as a point
of departure, a pattern to be followed, a mold to be filled. Form is a
result—the result of a process. Each of my works discovers its own
form. I could never have fitted them into any of the historical containers. If you want to fill a rigid box of a definite shape, you must
have something to put into it that is the same shape and size or that is
elastic or soft enough to be made to fit in. But if you try to force into
it something of a different shape and harder substance, even if its
volume and size are the same, it will break the box. My music cannot
be made to fit into any of the traditional music boxes.

Conceiving musical form as a *resultant*—the result of a process, I
was struck by what seemed to me an analogy between the formation of
my compositions and the phenomenon of crystallization. Let me quote
the crystallographic description given me by Nathaniel Arbiter, pro-
fessor of mineralogy at Columbia University:

"The crystal is characterized by both a definite external form and
a definite internal structure. The internal structure is based on the
unit of crystal which is the smallest grouping of the atoms that has the
order and composition of the substance. The extension of the unit into
space forms the whole crystal. But in spite of the relatively limited
variety of internal structures, the external forms of crystals are
limitless."

Then Mr. Arbiter added in his own words: "Crystal form itself is
a *resultant* [the very word I have always used in reference to musical
form] rather than a primary attribute. Crystal form is the consequence
of the interaction of attractive and repulsive forces and the ordered
packing of the atom."

This, I believe, suggests better than any explanation I could give
about the way my works are formed. There is an idea, the basis of an
internal structure, expanded and split into different shapes or groups
of sound constantly changing in shape, direction, and speed, attracted
and repulsed by various forces. The form of the work is the consequence of this interaction. Possible musical forms are as limitless as
the exterior forms of crystals.

[2] See note 4.

Connected with this contentious subject of form in music is the really futile question of the difference between form and content. There is no difference. Form and content are one. Take away form, and there is no content, and if there is no content there is only a re-arrangement of musical patterns, but no form. Some people go so far as to suppose that the content of what is called program music is the subject described. This subject is only the ostensible motive I have spoken of, which in program music the composer chooses to reveal. The content is still only music. The same senseless bickering goes on over style and content in poetry. We could very well transfer to the question of music what Samuel Beckett has said of Proust: "For Proust the quality of language is more important than any system of ethics or esthetics. Indeed he makes no attempt to dissociate form from content. The one is the concretion of the other—the revelation of a world."[3] To reveal a new world is the function of creation in all the arts, but the act of creation defies analysis. A composer knows about as little as anyone else about where the substance of his work comes from.

As an epigraph to his book,[4] Busoni uses this verse from a poem by the Danish poet, Oelenschläger:

"What seek you? Say! And what do you expect?
I know not what; the Unknown I would have!
What's known to me is endless; I would go
Beyond the known: The last word still is wanting."

(Der mächtige Zauberer)

And so it is for any artist.

THE ELECTRONIC MEDIUM*

First of all I should like you to consider what I believe is the best definition of music, because it is all-inclusive: "the corporealization of the intelligence that is in sound," as proposed by Hoëne Wronsky.[5] If you think about it you will realize that, unlike most dictionary definitions which make use of such subjective terms as beauty, feel-

[3] Samuel Beckett, *Proust* (1957).

[4] Ferruccio Busoni (1866-1924), *Entwurf einer neuen Ästhetik der Tonkunst* (1907); published in English as *Sketch of a New Esthetic of Music* (T. Baker, tr.; 1911).

* From a lecture given at Yale University, 1962.

[5] Hoëne Wronsky (1778-1853), also known as Joseph Marie Wronsky, was a Polish philosopher and mathematician, known for his system of Messianism. Camille Durutte (1803-81), in his *Technie Harmonique* (1876), a treatise on "musical mathe-matics," quoted extensively from the writings of Wronsky.

ings, etc., it covers all music, Eastern or Western, past or present, including the music of our new electronic medium. Although this new music is being gradually accepted, there are still people who, while admitting that it is "interesting," say, "but is it music?" It is a question I am only too familiar with. Until quite recently I used to hear it so often in regard to my own works, that, as far back as the twenties, I decided to call my music "organized sound" and myself, not a musician, but "a worker in rhythms, frequencies, and intensities." Indeed, to stubbornly conditioned ears, anything new in music has always been called noise. But after all what is music but organized noises? And a composer, like all artists, is an organizer of disparate elements. Subjectively, *noise* is any sound one doesn't like.

Our new medium has brought to composers almost endless possibilities of expression, and opened up for them the whole mysterious world of sound. For instance, I have always felt the need of a kind of continuous flowing curve that instruments could not give me. That is why I used sirens in several of my works. Today such effects are easily obtainable by electronic means. In this connection it is curious to note that it is this lack of flow that seems to disturb Eastern musicians in our Western music. To their ears it does not glide, sounds jerky, composed of edges of intervals and holes and, as an Indian pupil of mine expressed it, "jumping like a bird from branch to branch." To them apparently our Western music seems to sound much as it sounds to us when a record is played backward. But playing a Hindu record of a melodic vocalization backward, I found that it had the same smooth flow as when played normally, scarcely altered at all.

The electronic medium is also adding an unbelievable variety of new timbres to our musical store, but most important of all, it has freed music from the tempered system, which has prevented music from keeping pace with the other arts and with science. Composers are now able, as never before, to satisfy the dictates of that inner ear of the imagination. They are also lucky so far in not being hampered by esthetic codification—at least not yet! But I am afraid it will not be long before some musical mortician begins embalming electronic music in rules.

We should also remember that no machine is a wizard, as we are beginning to think, and we must not expect our electronic devices to compose for us. Good music and bad music will be composed by electronic means, just as good and bad music have been composed for instruments. The computing machine is a marvelous invention and seems almost superhuman. But, in reality, it is as limited as the mind of the individual who feeds it material. Like the computer, the machines we use for making music can only give back what we put into them. But, considering the fact that our electronic devices were never meant for making music, but for the sole purpose of measuring and analyzing sound, it is remarkable that what has already been achieved is musically valid. They are still somewhat unwieldy and time-consuming and not entirely satisfactory as an art-medium. But this new art is still in its infancy, and I hope and firmly believe, now that composers and physicists are at last working together, and music is again linked with science, as it was in the Middle Ages, that new and more musically efficient devices will be invented.

—Edited and Annotated by Chou Wen-chung

CONVERSATION WITH VARESE

GUNTHER SCHULLER

—————————————— ▪▪▪▪▪▪▪ ——————————————

GS: What were your most important early musical experiences?

EV: When I was eleven I wrote an opera on Jules Verne's *Martin Paz,* in which I was already involved with sonority and unusual sounds. I detested the piano and all conventional instruments, and when I first learned the scales, my only reaction was, "Well, they all sound alike."

Up to then, I had studied entirely by myself; my father was against my studying music and wanted me to go into mathematics and physics at the Polytechnic in Zürich. He even locked the piano at our house so that I couldn't touch it. But when I was seventeen, Bolzoni, the head of the Turin Conservatory, became interested in me and encouraged me to go back to Paris (my birthplace). There I went first to the Schola Cantorum, where I studied with Roussel and D'Indy. D'Indy was typical petty nobility, calling himself "Le Vicomte D'Indy," an anti-Semite who had been against Dreyfus, and a terribly pedantic musician. One day when he was analyzing *Parsifal,* he said "Il n'a pas modulé à temps." He was capable of such stupidities.

So I left the Schola after a year and went to Widor, a magnificent, open-minded musician and a marvelous organist. I still have the fugue, by the way, that admitted me to his class at the Conservatoire. By that time I was already disenchanted with the tempered system, though, and could never understand why we should be limited to it when our instruments can give us anything we want, and why it should be imposed as a prescriptive, as if it were the final stage of musical development. In other fields, like chemistry or physics, the basic assumption is that there is always something new to be discovered. So I left the Conservatoire as well after a couple of years (although the immediate cause for leaving was a rather nasty exchange of unpleasantries with Fauré who, as administrator of the Conservatoire, kicked me out).

By the time I was twenty, I had an enormous amount of music written, pieces like *Rhapsodie Romaine, Bourgogne, Gargantua* (written at the encouragement of Romain Rolland), *Mehr Licht,* on a Goethe poem, and many others. At that time Goethe was very important to my thinking, as was Hoéné Wronsky, an officer in Napoleon's army, who was also a physicist and philosopher, who created a phrase I never forgot: "Music is the corporealization of the intelligence that is in sound."

The composers I admired in those early days were Debussy, especially for his *Pelleas,* and then Strauss and Busoni, both of whom were very influential in my career after I went to Berlin in 1905. But I also respected composers like Satie and Scriabin. Satie was not only important as an influence on Debussy by pulling him away from the Conservatoire and Prix de Rome atmosphere, thus really broadening Debussy's horizons, but Satie also wrote some rather remarkable music, such as the Kyrie from his *Messe des Pauvres,* a music which always reminds me of Dante's *Inferno* and strikes me as a kind of pre-electronic music.

I found Scriabin's orchestral pieces simply overwhelming. His music has such a powerful seductive atmosphere, that it goes beyond questions of technique. I know that Scriabin's music is often criticized for its lack of polyphony, for example. But my answer to that is: why must it have polyphony?

But above all I admired Debussy, primarily for his economy of means and clarity, and the intensity he achieved through them, balancing with almost mathematical equilibrium timbres against rhythms and textures —like a fantastic chemist. Sometimes Strauss also had that kind of clarity; the final scene of *Salome,* for example, or the Recognition Scene in *Elektra* have that same combination of transparency and intensity. Debussy and Strauss both had a wonderful sense of using silence and the suspense and intensity latent in the musical pause.

The essential touchstone for me was Busoni's prophetic book, *Entwurf einer Neuen Aesthetik der Tonkunst.* This predicts precisely what is happening today in music—that is, if you pass over the whole dodecaphonic development, which in my view represents a sort of hardening of the arteries. I find the whole 12-tone approach so limiting, especially in its use of the tempered scale and its rigid pitch organization. I respect the 12-tone discipline, and those that feel they need such a discipline. But it reminds me of Beckmesser's *Tablatur,* and it seems much more fruitful to use the total sonic resources available to us. Although there are certain works of Schoenberg that I find magnificent—the Five Orchestra Pieces especially —his orchestration often seems quite thick and fat. Compare this to the transparency and lyricism of Webern!

GS: Eduard Steuermann was the only person I ever met who heard any of your early music, all of which I understand was lost or destroyed. He remembered your *Bourgogne* from its 1912 Berlin performance, especially a section with a lot of multiple divided string parts.

EV: I was trying to approximate the kind of inner, microcosmic life you find in certain chemical solutions, or through the filtering of light. I used these strings unthematically as a background behind a great deal of brass and percussion.

GS: How did your music of this period compare with later works like *Octandre* or *Intégrales,* for example?

EV: The earlier works were what I would call more architectonic. I was working with blocks of sound, calculated and balanced against each other. I was preoccupied with volume in an architectural sense, and with projection.

GS: How did your ideas of architectonic form and structure arise? Certainly other composers were thinking along totally different lines at that time—Debussy and Stravinsky appear to have arrived at similar concepts considerably later than you did.

EV: I was not influenced by composers as much as by natural objects and physical phenomena. As a child, I was tremendously impressed by the qualities and character of the granite I found in Burgundy, where I often visited my grandfather. There were two kinds of granite there, one grey, the other streaked with pink and yellow. Then there was the old Romanesque architecture in that part of France: I used to play in one of the oldest French churches—in Tournus—one that was started in the sixth century and built in purest Romanesque style. And I used to watch the old stone cutters, marveling at the precision with which they worked. They didn't use cement, and every stone had to fit and balance with every other. So I was always in touch with things of stone and with this kind of pure structural architecture—without frills or unnecessary decoration. All of this became an integral part of my thinking at a very early stage.

GS: Did the special kind of static continuity in your music, and its use of repetition and near-repetition of the same elements in constantly new juxtapositions and successions, arise mainly as a result of such fundamental structural preoccupations?

EV: Yes. In 1905, when I composed *Rhapsodie Romaine,* I was thinking of Romanesque architecture, not Rome! I wanted to find a way to project in music the concept of calculated or controlled gravitation, how one element pushing on the other stabilizes the total structure, thus using the material elements at the same time in opposition to and in support of one another. I think I would characterize my early music as granitic!

GS: What made you come to America in 1916, and how did you find the musical climate here?

EV: After I was discharged from the French Army, I came to America because the war conditions had really interrupted all normal musical activity. When I came here, the climate for modern music was really quite terrible. Musical organizations were run entirely by society ladies, who certainly did not want to hear any modern music. As a conductor, my programs were constantly interfered with. It was as a result of this situation, that Salzedo and I formed the International Composer's Guild, where we could perform whatever we wanted. We were very fortunate in having the disinterested collaboration of such conductors as Stokowski, Klemperer, and Goosens. It was for these concerts that I composed *Octandre, Hyperprism,* and so on.

GS: How do these compositions of the twenties compare with your earlier works?

EV: I believe they reflect a greater refinement of my earlier conceptions. I also became increasingly interested in internal rhythmic and metric relationships, as in *Ionization.* I was also interested in the sonorous aspects of percussion as structural, architectonic elements. But this was not my first percussion piece. I had already done some in Berlin and Paris, especially in connection with the choruses I conducted in Berlin. These works used special percussion instruments that I had collected myself, which the singers often played themselves.

GS: Why did you compose so little in the period after *Ionization?*

EV: In those days the situation really seemed hopeless. I'm afraid I developed a very negative attitude toward the entire musical situation. After all, great men like Mahler, Strauss, Muck, and Busoni had given me my professional start with their encouragement and esteen for my scores. By the thirties, these men had all been replaced by—in most cases —much lesser musicians. Mahler, for example, was kicked out by the New York Philharmonic and replaced by a nonentity, Stransky, and still later by that enemy of modern music, Toscanini, and the only conductor who had shown an interest in my music, Stokowski, stopped playing it. But the frustration of having my music ignored was only a part of it. I had an obsession: a new instrument that would free music from the tempered system. Having been closely associated with scientists of the Bell Laboratories, with Bertrand, inventor of one of the first electronic instruments, the Dynaphone, and with Theremin, who made two elec-

tronic instruments for my *Ecuatorial,* I knew what the possibilities were.
I wanted to work with an electrical engineer in a well-equipped labora-
tory. Individual scientists became interested in my idea but their companies did not. I tried here and in Hollywood but no doors opened. It is,
however, not exact to say that I deliberately stopped composing. I kept
working on a score that I called *Espace,* but I would tear up at night what
I had written during the day or vice versa.

GS: Did the new possibilities in electronic music bring you back to
composition?

EV: Yes, first with *Déserts* in 1954, and then with the *Poème Electronique* in
which the resources offered by Le Corbusier and Philips—11 channels,
425 speakers, all related to the acoustics and architecture of the building
—were irresistible. I am not, however, impressed by most of today's
electronic music. It does not seem to make full use of the unique possibilities of the medium, especially in regard to those questions of space and
projection that have always concerned me. I am fascinated by the fact
that through electronic means one can generate a sound instantaneously.
On an instrument played by a human being you have to impose a musical
thought through notation, then, usually much later, the player has to
prepare himself in various ways to produce what will—one hopes—
emerge as that sound. This is all so indirect compared with electronics,
where you generate something "live" that can appear or disappear in-
stantly and unpredictably. Consequently, you aren't programming something musical, something to be done, but using it directly, which gives
an entirely different dimension to musical space and projection. For instance, in the use of an oscillator, it is not a question of working against it
or taming it, but using it directly, without, of course, letting it use you.
The same pertains to mixing and filtering. To me, working with electronic
music is composing with living sounds, paradoxical though that may
appear.

GS: Your position then would seem to be directly contrary to that of
Milton Babbitt?

EV: I respect and admire Babbitt, but he certainly represents a completely
different view of electronic music from mine. It seems to me that he wants
to exercise maximum control over certain materials, as if he were *above*
them. But I want to be *in* the material, part of the acoustical vibration,
so to speak. Babbitt composes his material first and then gives it to the
synthesizer, while I want to generate something directly by electronic
means. In other words, I think of musical space as open rather than

bounded, which is why I speak about projection in the sense that I want simply to project a sound, a musical thought, to initiate it, and then to let it take its own course. I do not want an a priori control of all its aspects.

GS: Are you interested, then, in the other direction—improvisation and so-called aleatory music?

EV: For me, these means are simply *too* accidental! Cage, whom I first met in California during the thirties (he had been a painter, and was just beginning to study music), is very intelligent, talented, and certainly imaginative. But his way of making music isn't for me—it is so accidental that I can't see the *necessity* for a composer! Actually, Cage also thinks of sound as living matter, raw material, but he wants to create a spectacle with music in order to reach the public. I don't care about reaching the public as much as I care about reaching certain musical-acoustical phenomena, in other words, to disturb the atmosphere—because, after all, sound *is* only an atmospheric disturbance!

EDGARD VARESE
A FEW OBSERVATIONS OF HIS MUSIC*

MILTON BABBITT

THIS IS, to the best of my knowledge, only the second occasion on which I have been granted the somewhat unnerving privilege of speaking publicly of a composer's music in that composer's presence. On the first such occasion, the composer was Igor Stravinsky, being done homage in his 80th birthyear; now, on this second occasion, the composer is Edgard Varèse, in his 80th birthyear;[1] and it was of Varèse that Stravinsky has predicted: "His music will survive; we know that now, for it has dated in the right way." Although I have no direct knowledge of Stravinsky's survival theory of music, I infer from this statement that it derives from Darwin rather than from Gresham, and, having been obliged to have the temerity to speak of Stravinsky's music in his presence, it requires relatively little courage to conjecture as to the meaning of his prose in his absence, particularly since, for those of us who regard it as far less remarkable when Varèse's music was composed than that it was composed at all, it is not difficult to interpret Stravinsky's observation to our satisfaction. Surely, the most critical factor of the "aging" process has been the transformation of much of this body of music from works little heard in the first quarter-century of their existence to works widely heard in the past decade and a half. And just as we, who pressed our mind's ear almost beyond its capacities in attempting to re-create, or—more accurately—create, mentally the unprecedented sonorous world of this music from those scarce scores to which we had access thirty years ago, understandably measured its originality primarily, if not solely, by the extent of the difficulty of this inference from experienced and recalled sound to the sound of Varèse, so the first hearing and first rehearing of the music directed attention to the striking singularities of the single events, and induced the ultimately unjust appraisal, in the name of finally redressing injustice, that this music was most remarkable in its insular originality, its absence of

* This article consists mainly of selected and slightly altered portions of a talk given at Peterborough, New Hampshire on August 21, 1965, on the occasion of the presentation of the Edward MacDowell Society Medal of Achievement to Varèse.
[1] Varèse's birthyear is usually reported as 1885, but 1883 appears to be correct.

significant ancestry or possible progeny. Yet, it appears now to be acceptably deferential and appreciative to say that, now that those coruscating sonorities and dazzling rhythmic webs have become more familiar, we can penetrate beneath and beyond them, and—if they have lost a little of their breathtaking impact with time and repetition—we can now value the music for other, more durable properties, not excluding those of historical precedence and chronological originality. But I prefer to assert that the sonorities have lost nothing of their luster, the rhythms nothing of their fascination precisely because we have penetrated from the local to the global, from the event as separable and independent to its temporal and spatial dependencies, relationships, and influences. If we have identified possible ancestral sources, this seems of far less consequence than that we have recognized the extent to which Varèse's music engages the same issues, represents the same kind of stage in a mainstream of musical development as that of Schoenberg, Stravinsky, Webern, and Berg, and that its eventual originality is thus most fruitfully and justly gauged in the light of its shared connections, as "competitive" rather than as insular. If this music has already outlived its most skillful imitations, it is because the only satisfactory imitation must be total duplication, for the attributes of the surface are structurally comprehensible not so much as primitives from which the remainder of a composition may be said to derive, but as themselves derived from other dimensions of the composition. The "new sounds," it is now manifest, were less new as things in themselves than as new inferences from compositional premises.

This, in turn, affects the very mode of presentation of such a compositional premise, idea, donnée, which is, in its turn, a central characteristic of Varèse's style, for it involves the setting forth of a contextual, referential norm for an entire work. This crucial function is defined not only by the customary emphasis of priority, but by simplicity and—often immediate—repetition, repetition not of all dimensions of the musical idea, but exact repetition of one or more dimensions. By "simplicity," I mean brevity, the minimal motivic form in which the idea appears in the work, linearity rather than polyphony, and—often—a greater internal homogeneity than later forms of the "same" material. I shall refer to and recall for you *Octandre*,[2] because it is probably Varèse's best known and most widely performed ensemble work, as an instance of these characteristics. The

[2] Neither performed nor notated musical examples were available during the talk; to employ them here would prejudice the necessarily informal and general nature of the original discussion.

opening four-note statement, clearly articulated by a pause, and by immediate pitch and attack rhythm repetition (Varèse always regarded grace notes as on the beat), functions in the work much less as a total motive than as a unit of harmonic content, for, as the work unfolds, these initial four notes are interpreted as representatives of an unordered collection of four pitch-classes, to within transposition. This collection, not insignificantly, is one of the simplest all-combinatorial tetrachords, simplest in the sense that it is one of the two such tetrachords generated by a single interval. At the outset, this tetrachord is presented by temporal proximity (immediate succession), equally clearly, the dominant motive of the work, extracted from the tetrachord by spatial proximity (registral association, in a reasonably unambiguous sense of the slippery word "register") appears throughout in its initial ordering, under customary transformations. The three-note succession G-flat-E-D-sharp is verified immediately by twofold repetition, and a disjunct transposition (still stated within, and registrally extracted from, the tetrachord) and then stated explicitly by direct succession, conjoining spatial and temporal proximity, by the entrance of the clarinet as an "answer" at the "fifth above." The prominent foreground thematic role of this succession in the rest of the work is perfectly clear: in the trumpet and horn at the end of the first movement, divided between the two highest instruments (flute, with the first note, and clarinet, with the following two, this division into one and two corresponding to the linear division of the motive in the original tetrachord) on the first of the reiterated chords of the second movement (eight statements beginning with the first measure after rehearsal 5), and in the trumpet throughout the sixteen measures of the "repeated" chord in the third movement (where the F-sharp that completes the tetrachord is heard in the lowest note of the chord).

The ordered, tritone-transposed return of the initial tetrachord at the end of the first movement ends with the elision of the fourth note, clarifying the origin of the three-note figure of the piccolo which opens the second movement as the tritone pitch-class transposition of the first three notes of this terminating tetrachord, and—therefore—as a duplication of the opening three pitch-classes of the composition, reordered as a retrograde. The chord-forming entrances which follow the piccolo on the clarinet and trombone present the same trichord, now in the initial ordering. This trichord, the only possible three-note extraction from the tetrachord other than the forms of the previously discussed three-note thematic unit, is a primary articulative and unifying element in the second and third movements, and suggests why these two movements are performed without separation. The final chord of the second movement, which is the chord of maximal registral dispersion in the entire work, includes the pitch-classes of the opening tetrachord of the first movement as the highest four notes, and those of the closing tetrachord of the movement as the lowest four notes, with immediate succession thus transformed into immediate simultaneity, again, in its own way, the horizontal and the vertical. The tetrachord is stated linearly, early in the third movement, as the theme for imitation in the oboe, but now reordered so that the original three-note theme, inverted, is presented by linear, rather than by spatial, proximity; at this point, too, the pitch dyad F-E returns in the registral placement it occupied in the opening tetrachord, and—finally—occurs in thirteen consecutive measures in the last section of the movement, until the piccolo takes over these pitch-classes as a trill. The final sound of the composition is the trichord that opened the second movement, sounded as a simultaneity and transposed to the level presented linearly by the double-bass at the beginning of the third movement.

If I have spent what may appear to be a disproportionate amount of time identifying some of the modes of occurrence and adaptive transformations of the pitch content of the assumptive source, I have done so in order to attempt to show the structural basis of certain of Varèse's style characteristics. An analogy with spoken, or printed, language may serve to clarify the issue. If one were to ask: how large a sample of an unfamiliar "natural" language would have to be observed before phonemic, or graphemic, constraints could be inferred and employed to predict language events with an accuracy reasonably reflecting the redundancy of the language, obviously the answer would have to be that the sample would have to be large. But, if an "artificial" language were constructed, of but few phonemes and a limited number of possibilities of concatenation of them, then a small sample should suffice. The Varèsian opening statement is such a sample; its repetition is a reiteration and an emphasizing of the relevant elements in defining a work's constraints. Also, and most important, it is of such a character as not to suggest that it is itself an instance of a familiar "language" system, whose associated constraints would then be inferred, mistakenly and, for the coherent hearing of the rest of the work, disastrously.

Varèse, like Webern, directs one's ears to the structural and associative relevance of every dimension of the musical event, not, as does Webern, by isolating the event, by framing it with silence, above, below, before, and after, but by isolating the singularity that such initially defined determinacy can bestow upon the event, even in the most elaborate of vertical complexes, and the most varied of linear configurations.

If immediate repetition, as reinforcement, characterizes the Varèsian opening, it also and therefore characterizes the means of continuation, of achieving delineation and contrast within a single dimension, and total climax. But even at its most strikingly extreme, as at the entire 21-measure moderato section of *Intégrales*, only one measure is totally repeated and but once, and—at the conclusion of the section—a two-measure unit is immediately repeated twice (I overlook the probably erroneous change of the dynamic indication of the first piccolo on the first repetition). From such parsimony with regard to total repetition could be inferred the almost total abstinence from conjoined, all-dimensional repetition as "architectonic," the determinant of external "form" patterns. In this Varèse reflects, and probably antedates, the contemporary concern with "polyphonic" rather than phased repetitions. In his case, this is achieved far less often by holding one factor (say, the rhythmic) fixed, while another (say, pitch) is altered, than by employing different periods of repetition in individual—usually, instrumental—lines; the result is different ensemble rhythms, dynamics, simultaneities, etc. associated with individual component repetitions. Even where this specific procedure is made impossible by the medium, as in *Density 21.5*, the principle is still maintained. There are, I believe, no two identical measures in *Density*. The durational succession associated with the attack points of the initial three pitches occurs, in the same metrical orientation, only at two further places in the work, and at those places is associated with the opening interval succession also, but the pitch succession is altered in each case by transposition. The transposition choices, in one sense, reflect traditional criteria of similitude, in that they are the two which secure maximum pitch-class identification (beyond identity) with the initial statement; but in a further sense, the choices are "serial," in that the order of occurrence of these transpositions reflects the pitch-class ordering of the initial three-note succession. Obviously, neither this nor any other work of Varèse's is serial in any extensive sense, or even much beyond the sense in which traditional works are thematically "serial." And in the single instance of *Density*, where it might be observed that the ordered motive is not further embedded in an unordered collection, the serialism represented by the motive and its transpositions is combinational, not permutational, pitch-class serialism. That Varèse is not a "serial composer" is, clearly, not to be construed as a normative statement, but it is an important reminder that one of the fundamental aspects of the musical revolution in which Varèse was so primary a figure is that it was a struggle to create a world of musics, not a struggle between one music and another, serial and nonserial, tonal and "atonal." It is this that conveys the impression that what the dominant composers of Varèse's generation shared in common was a lack of, an avoidance of, communality.

Linear repetitions create a rhythm of durations between such repetitions, so that there is also the sense in which repetitions of different periodicities in simultaneous instrumental statements create "polyrhythms," and in which the individual rhythmic lines constitute a partitioning of time units corresponding to the partitioning of smaller units by pitch repetition in the individual line, or by repetition of simultaneities in the ensemble. These analogies suggest means of rhythmic linearization and delinearization as a mode of rhythmic development, while still not involving the intricate and largely unresolved questions of rhythmic relatedness in terms of related transformations, for such means are identity transformations, or—perhaps more informatively—they are transformations among dimensions rather than within a single dimension. Even so, the perception and, correspondingly, the verbal formulation of such interdimensional rhythmic relationships are complicated by the dependence of protensity perception not only upon duration but upon other dimensions of the musical event. Now we know how dangerous and, often, indefensible it is to speak of the "same rhythm" when the associated pitches are different or different in number or different in contour or associated with different dynamics or associated with different timbres. Therefore, Varèse is one of those composers, and the tribe has increased many times and in many ways in the past thirty years, whose music has necessarily directed our attention to the inadequacies of our analytical concepts with regard to rhythm, by decreasing compositional rhythmic redundancy, by increasing the number of rhythmic configurations, and the dimensions in which these configurations are made to appear.

Although it is probably the voluminous, strident sonority, dominated by broad registral dispersion and acoustically "unconventional" proportional ranges within the dispersion that is the primary association with the name of Varèse in the mind of the casual listener, in this respect, as well, he is more parsimonious than would be guessed by even a less casual listener. In all of *Octandre*, there are only eight locations, associated with twelve nonidentical chords, and constituting only some thirty-five measures, where all eight instruments are sounding. Here, again, there is the avoidance of conjoined repetition: in no two of these chords is the very ordering of instruments from top to bottom the same, although in each of these chords the lowest note is heard on the double-bass. Therefore, the effect of different "harmonies" is by no means dependent entirely on the explicit pitches presented by each instrument, but most importantly, on the strikingly different spectra associated with these instruments, individually, and in all constituent combinations, as a result of the different registral placement of the "fundamental" in each instrument and the different registral relations among the instruments. It is clear that, for Varèse, the invariant aspect of an instrument, in some important sense, the timbre of an instrument, is to be identified with its formant, that fixed, "amplificatory," resonance region of an instrument, which operates upon the spectrum of the input sound, resonating, according to the characteristics of the formant region, those partials whose frequencies fall in this region, and—thereby—attenuating those whose frequencies do not. So, only when a specific pitch (not just pitch-class) has been assigned an instrument can we speak of the spectrum (and, to this extent, the timbre) associated with the particular event. The distribution of pitches in a chord, although the pitch-classes are contextually derived, taken together with associated dynamics, is determined by the degree of resultant density (the relations among all the component frequencies passed by the formant region) desired, or—given a desired dynamic level—a distribution is chosen that makes such a dynamic level attainable, which is itself a matter of the relation of input spectrum to formant characteristics. Crescendi, such as those in the *très vif* section of *Octandre*, produce not what can be most accurately described as a change in loudness of a fixed sonority, but a continuous alteration of the number, relations, and densities of the partials of the total spectrum; the percussion instruments themselves constitute timbral resonance regions sliced out of the frequency continuum. The performance instructions required for such controlled results place the performers in the most responsible and demanding of roles, that of reproducing with the greatest possible accuracy and precision the most explicit and subtle of specifications.

Such concern with and structural utilization of the timbral consequences of dynamic, registral, and durational values approach the condition of nonelectronic "synthesis," and if the presence of such procedures suggests one of the many musical dispositions that led Varèse to the need for the electronic medium, then his eventual experiences with and composition for that medium seem to have "fed back" into his instrumental procedures. The synthetic separability of the attack and "steady-state" portions of the event (or, in the case of the percussive sound, the attack and decay portions) suggested the analogous construction of instrumental sounds combining constituent instruments into a resultant instrumental totality. For example, at the beginning of *Déserts*, the eventual "steady-state" G of the piccolo and F of the clarinet are compounded with an attack provided first by piano, chimes, and xylophone, then by chimes, xylophone, and high and low cymbals; then this latter attack is associated with "steady-state" continuations in muted trumpets, and—finally—an attack of chimes and vibraphone is associated with a "steady-state" in, again, piccolo, but an octave higher, and flute. Throughout, the piano provides a continual decay. In this way, too, percussion instruments of "indeterminate pitch" acquire temporary, local pitch by collocation, just as, conversely, instruments of definite pitch serve, on occasion, primarily as vehicles of rhythmic projection.

I eagerly anticipate detailed discussions of Varèse's music, which concern themselves with the analysis of total progression, the motion toward and from points of conjoined climax, by means of the transformation of rhythmic components, particularly in the sense of the number of attacks per unit time, the pitch content and range of extrema, the dispersion and internal distribution of the elements of similitudes, the total spectrum, and other compound concepts, for the possibility of such discussion, if it is to be more than mere translation from musical to verbal notation, depends upon the formulation of scales to measure degrees of similitude applicable to such concepts. Or, assuming that temporal progression and proximity define, in Varèse's music, his assumption of relatedness in these respects, to what extent can such contextually defined norms of relatedness provide, in the course of a work, unambiguous adaptive scales?

IN ACCORD with Varèse's strong feelings on the matter, which correspond to my own, I have tried to pay homage to Varèse the man by honoring the man's music. But, in conclusion, I shall allow myself a few personal words about Varèse, the colleague. Although, for chronological and geographical reasons, I was unable to profit directly from the International Composers' Guild, of which he was a cofounder, we all have profited eventually, if indirectly, from that remarkable pioneer of organizations for the performance of contemporary music. But I have been privileged to observe Varèse as the colleague of, the champion of, and—most consequentially—the enthusiastic audience for his younger colleagues, and as the eternal musical youth, pursuing and shaping the future at the Bell Laboratories and at the Columbia-Princeton Electronic Music Center.

As composers, as informed listeners, we can all express our deep gratitude for Varèse the composer; those of us who were fortunate enough to have known him dare now to express our further gratitude, our great affection for him, as colleague, as friend, as a man.

"OPEN RATHER THAN BOUNDED"

CHOU WEN-CHUNG

"SOUND AS living matter"[1] and "musical space as open rather than bounded"[2] are the central ideas of Varèse's philosophy. To understand their implications and ramifications is to understand the man, the composer and his legacy. These ideas, nurtured by a fertile imagination and generated by a vigorous sense of life, constitute the essence of his music and also the strength behind his lifelong "fight for the liberation of sound" and "crusade for new instruments." They were first conceived early in his student days in Paris in the middle of the 1900's. Thereafter, he continually made known his beliefs, particularly after his arrival in this country. In 1916, Varèse was quoted in the New York *Morning Telegraph* as saying: "Our musical alphabet must be enriched. We also need new instruments very badly. . . . In my own works I have always felt the need of new mediums of expression . . . which can lend themselves to every expression of thought and can keep up with thought." And in the *Christian Science Monitor*, in 1922 he added: "What we want is an instrument that will give us a continuous sound at any pitch. The composer and the electrician will have to labor together to get it. . . . Speed and synthesis are characteristics of our own epoch. We need twentieth century instruments to help us realize them in music." In 1924, Varèse wrote in the *Daily Mail* and the *Evening News*[3] of London: "We need to make a new and simpler approach to music. The development of the art has been hampered by certain mechanical restrictions which no longer need prevail. . . . Just as the painter can obtain different intensity and graduation of colour, musicians can obtain different vibrations of sound, not necessarily conforming to the traditional half-tone and full tone, but varying, ultimately, from vibration to vibration. . . . We are waiting for a new notation—a new Guido d'Arezzo—when music will move forward at a bound."

During his first decade in America, Varèse was busy with composing and introducing new music. But as soon as the activities of the

[1] Unless specified otherwise, all quotations are from Varèse's lectures.
[2] Gunther Schuller, "Conversation with Varèse," pp. 34–39, above.
[3] June 14, 1924.

International Composers' Guild ceased in 1927, he began seriously discussing with René Bertrand, inventor of the Dynaphone, and Harvey Fletcher, then Acoustical Research Director of the Bell Telephone Laboratories, the possibilities of developing an electronic instrument for composing. From 1932 through 1936, Varèse repeatedly applied for a Guggenheim Fellowship for the following proposed studies: "To pursue work on an instrument for the producing of new sounds. To inspect other new inventions in certain laboratories in order to discover if any of them could serve my new sound conceptions. To submit to the technicians of different organizations my ideas in regard to the contribution which music—mine at least—looks for from science, and to prove to them the necessity of a closer collaboration between composer and scientist."[4] In 1940, writing about the use of *organized sound* for films in *The Commonweal*,[5] Varèse observed: "We now are in possession of scientific means not merely of realistic reproduction of sounds but of *production of entirely new combinations of sound*, with the possibility of creating new emotions, awakening dulled sensibilities. Any possible sound we can imagine can be produced with perfect control of its quality, intensity and pitch, opening up entirely new auditory perspectives." Incidentally, it is this interest in the "weaving together of the disparate sonorous and visual elements which will make of a film a unified whole" that has given us the third electronic work by Varèse, the electronically *organized sound* for the sequence on the *Good Friday Procession in Verges* for the film, *Around and About Joan Miró* by Thomas Bouchard; however, this did not come to pass until fifteen years later (1955-1956). Meanwhile, Varèse made whatever modest experiments he could and worked on several projects,[6] notably *Espace*, for orchestra and chorus, and *Astronomer*, a stage work, both involving ideas that would require electronic means for their realization. Some of his ideas for *Espace* finally found their way into *Déserts* and *Poème Électronique*.

It is now a historical fact that recognition of Varèse came too late for him to fully realize his goals. Therein lies the tragedy. Still, the fantastic vitality and unswerving determination with which he struggled to disseminate his beliefs and the near-hysterical furor he caused in the musical world[7] point to the fundamental role his ideas played

---

4 The application was continually rejected.

5 December 13, 1940.

6 None of them were completed.

7 Witness the tremendous array of dispatches, reviews and debates in the daily papers and the periodicals long before the time of *Déserts*. The following review by William J. Henderson, in the *New York Herald* of March 11, 1923, seems to have described more the general reaction toward Varèse at that time than what happened after the premiere of *Hyperprism*: "It is a tremendous achievement to create a piece

in bringing about the present stage of development in music. All that he fought for is now either taken as a matter of course or soon to be realized. His teaching is so fundamental that many, who are now continuing in a tradition unthinkable without Varèse, are either unconscious of his influence or unaware of their own past opposition to what he vehemently expounded.

Next to his quest for a new medium and a new notational system to *liberate* sound from any and all *mechanical* limitations, the growth and interaction of *sound-masses* in space through a continual process of *expansion, projection, interaction, penetration,* and *transmutation* represent the most significant part of his thinking, equally applicable to *Poème Électronique, Déserts, Intégrales, Ionisation* or *Density 21.5.* Judging from these scores, it seems that a *sound-mass* refers to a body of sounds with certain specific attributes in interval content, register, contour, timbre, intensity, attack and decay. *Sound-masses* seem to emerge out of the *expansion* of an *idea*—"the basis of an internal structure"—into the sonic space. The sense of *projection* of *sound-masses* obviously depends on the source location of the emission as well as the independent movement of each *sound-mass* as opposed to the others. When such *sound-masses collide*, the *interaction* tends to bring about *penetration*, during which certain attributes of one *sound-mass* are transferred to another, thus causing *transmutations* to take place and changing the attributes of each *sound-mass.* Elsewhere this writer has attempted to demonstrate with brief analyses the meaning of Varèse's terminology as applied to specific examples;[8] suffice it to say here that this concept of *organized sound* accounts for the immense sense of growing organism in all his music.

In conceiving his music as "sound set free" yet "organized," Varèse had made original and fundamental contributions toward present-day concepts of rhythm, dynamics, timbre and form, not in his electronic works of the 50's but in his works for conventional instruments of the 20's and the early 30's. He thought of rhythm as "simultaneous interplay of unrelated elements that intervene at calculated, but not regular time lapses"; and yet rhythm was to him "the element of stability, the generator of form" (e.g., *Ionisation,* Nos. 11-12). His concept of "sound as living matter" not only brought about the use of a totally

---

of music that incites riot . . . it remained for Edgard Varèse (to whom all honor) to shatter the calm of a Sabbath night, to cause peaceful lovers of music to scream out their agony, to arouse angry emotions and to tempt men to retire to the back of the theatre and perform tympani concertos on each other's faces. This is a big triumph. The name of Varèse will go down in musical history as that of the man who started something."

[8] Chou Wen-chung, "Varèse: A Sketch Of The Man And His Music," *The Musical Quarterly,* April 1966.

independent intensity for each individual tone but also that of a continually varying intensity within the duration of the tone (e.g., *Intégrales*, No. 7). He consistently explored the intrinsic values of the
extreme instrumental registers and systematically employed the registral characteristics as an integral element of his sound-masses (e.g.,
Octandre, I, Nos. 2-3). In his use of percussion instruments, he
added to the composer's resources a profuse variety of new timbres
and of modes of articulation and termination. He elevated the percussion instruments to a truly independent position by integrating
their sound into his sound-masses according to their associative pitch
registers as well as their vibratory and articulative characteristics
(e.g., *Arcana*, Nos. 14, 16). His need for a "continuous flowing
curve" led him to the use of sirens, theremins and martinots (e.g.,
Amériques, Ionisation, Ecuatorial)[9] to produce "trajectories of sound"
in the shape of a parabola, a hyperbola or a spiral. Such trajectories
are often suggested by conventional instruments as well (e.g., *Intégrales*, Nos. 3-5). As for form, he compared it to the phenomenon
of *crystallization* and regarded it purely as "the consequence of the
interaction of attractive and repulsive forces" evolved out of "an idea."
Thus, to him form was "a resultant—the result of a process," rather
than "a pattern to be followed, a mold to be filled" (e.g., *Déserts*).

But Varèse's contribution extended beyond his ideas and his works.
Among the most important composers of our century, he was by far
the most aware of other composers and active in behalf of their music.
His devotion to this cause began in 1914, when he gave the first
concert performance of Debussy's *Le Martyre de Saint Sébastien* with
the Czech Philharmonic in Prague. The program, consisting entirely
of contemporary French music, was to have been the first of a concert
tour of the principal cities of Europe introducing new music of the
day. The tour was canceled by the outbreak of World War I. In
1919, the New Symphony Orchestra was founded in New York for
him, again with the express purpose of performing new music. But
after a single pair of concerts in Carnegie Hall featuring Bartók's
Deux Images and Debussy's *Gigues*, among other works, he was again
frustrated—this time by the critics, performers and audience.[10] Un-
daunted, two years later, Varèse founded the International Composers'
Guild. During its six years of existence, the Guild presented fifty-six
composers of fourteen nationalities, most of whom were introduced to

9 In the published version of *Ecuatorial*, two martinots are specified instead of the
theremins in the original version.
10 Because of hostile reaction toward the music, the board of the orchestra re-
quested Varèse to change his announced programs for the season. Varèse refused,
and resigned.

this country for the first time. More than half of these composers remain prominent today. To read their names is to review the history of music of the first half-century: from Bartók to Ruggles, Chavez to Satie, Honegger to Szymanowsky, Kodály to Vaughan Williams, Malipiero to Wellesz. Particularly interesting among the American premieres were: Bartók's String Quartet No. 2, and Improvisations on Hungarian Peasant Songs for piano; Berg's *Kammerkonzert*; Hindemith's *Kammermusik No. 3*, and Suite 1922 for piano; Milhaud's Sonata for flute, oboe, clarinet and piano, and *Saudades do Brasil* for piano; Schoenberg's *Herzgewächse*, *Pierrot Lunaire* and Serenade; Stravinsky's *Les Noces*, *Renard* and *Histoires pour Enfants*; Webern's *Fünf Sätze* for string quartet, and *Fünf Geistliche Lieder*. Among the world premieres were Ruggles' *Angels*, *Men and Mountains*, *Portals* and *Vox Clamans in Deserto*; and Varèse's own *Offrandes*, *Hyperprism*, *Octandre* and *Intégrales*.

The Guild was the first organization of its kind and scope in this century. In six years of bitter struggle, it shook the musical world into an awareness of new music and created an atmosphere tolerable for serious composers. Not satisfied with his work in America alone, Varèse formed with Busoni the Internationale Komponisten-Gilde in Berlin in 1922. He established affiliation with the Collective of Composers in Moscow through Arthur Lourié in the same year, and with Casella's Corporazione delle nuove Musiche in the following year. And, according to a document of the Guild, "Edward Dent and Adolf Weismann were at that time[11] planning the formation of the International Society for Contemporary Music, and paid tribute to the International Composers' Guild by adopting, in formulating the directives of their yet unborn organization, the Guild's ideas and aims as stated in its by-laws and manifesto." In 1928, a year after the dissolution of the Guild,[12] Varèse founded yet another organization, the Pan-American Association of Composers, to give performances of works by composers of North, South and Central America. The Association's concerts took place not only in the United States and Latin America, but also in Europe. Among other things, it introduced the

[11] Summer, 1922.

[12] In a letter to the daily papers and periodicals, on November 7, 1927, Varèse wrote somewhat sardonically: "It is a satisfaction now to see that the great orchestral organizations are following in our footsteps and are beginning in their turn to present the contemporary works of *all schools and tendencies* (italics mine) to a public now enlightened or at least compliant. . . . The International Composers' Guild can only live in the exhilarating atmosphere of struggle. It therefore retires at the approach of the official laurel wreath, holding itself in readiness at any time to respond to a new call to battle."

music of Ives (*Three Places in New England*) and Ruggles (*Men and Mountains*) to Europe.[13]

These little-known facts of another facet of Varèse's career, as performer and organizer, again demonstrate his tireless struggle in behalf of composers and new music. Throughout his life, he was ever ready to fight for individual composers' "right to make music with any sound and all sounds" regardless of their "isms" or schools.[14] In every respect then, Varèse's influence was "open rather than bounded."

[13] Nicolas Slonimsky, conductor, Salle Gaveau, Paris, June 6, 1931.

[14] In the International Composers' Guild manifesto of 1921, Varèse declared that it "disapproves of all 'isms'; denies the existence of schools; recognizes only the individual."

A VARESE CHRONOLOGY

CHOU WEN-CHUNG

1883[1] Edgard Varèse born, December 22 in Paris, son of Henri Varèse, engineer. Spent childhood in Paris and Villars, village in Burgundy, where the Cortots, his mother's family lived.

1892? Family moved to Turin, Italy. Fought to study music against wishes of father, who was preparing him for engineering career.

1900? Giovanni Bolzoni, director of Turin Conservatory, took interest in him, gave him private lessons.

1903 Left family, returned to Paris to pursue musical studies.

1904 Admitted to Schola Cantorum. Studied composition with d'Indy; fugue with Roussel; Medieval, Renaissance, early Baroque music with Charles Bordes.

1905 Admitted to master class of Charles Widor at Conservatoire.

1906 Founded Choeur de l'Université Populaire at Faubourg Saint-Antoine. Piano version of *Rhapsodie romane* performed at a *Rénovation esthétique* concert.

1907 Received *Première Bourse artistique de la ville de Paris*, at recommendation of Massenet and Widor. Disappointed with musical climate of Paris, left for Berlin toward end of year. During Paris years, composed following orchestral works: *Trois pièces*, *La Chanson des jeunes hommes*, *Le Prélude à la fin d'un jour*, *Rhapsodie romane* and *Bourgogne*, which was completed in Berlin. The manuscript of *Prélude à la fin d'un jour* was with Leon Deubel, whose poem inspired the work; lost after Deubel's suicide.

---

[1]Varèse's birth date has been a matter of confusion. His French passport gives the date as December 22, 1885, which was used in all documents and biographical references until his death. But as quoted in Fernand Ouellette's *Edgard Varèse*, a birth certificate from the *Préfecture de la Seine* gives the date as December 22, 1883. On December 14, 1969, Wilhelm Schluter sent this writer a copy of another birth certificate from the *Préfecture de Paris*, giving the date as December 24, 1885, which he obtained in preparing for the entry on Varèse in the new edition of Riemann *Musiklexikon*. Since Varèse himself once said to Mrs. Louise Varèse that the 1883 date was correct, it seems to this writer that, pending further scrutiny of the pertinent records in the municipal government of Paris, the 1885 dates have to be regarded as erroneous.

1909   Met Romain Rolland. About this time befriended by Rodin, Debussy, Busoni, Richard Strauss, Karl Muck, Hugo von Hofmannsthal. Founded Symphonischer Chor in Berlin.

1910   *Bourgogne* performed by Josef Stransky and Blüthner Orchestra, December 15, Berlin.

1914   Conducted Czech Philharmonic in Prague, January 4, in program of contemporary French music, including first concert performance of Debussy's *Le Martyre de Saint Sébastien.* During Berlin years, composed following orchestral works: *Gargantua* (incomplete), *Mehr Licht, Les Cycles du Nord.* Collaborated with Hugo von Hofmannsthal on opera, *Oedipus und die Sphynx* (incomplete), 1908-1914.

1915   Having served in French Army and been discharged due to ill health, arrived in New York on December 29.

1917   Conducted performance of Berlioz' *Requiem* at Hippodrome, April 1, "as a memorial for the fallen of all nations."

1918   Conducted Cincinnati Symphony Orchestra, March 17. Began work on *Amériques?*

1919   The New Symphony Orchestra founded in New York especially for Varèse for performance of new music. Opening pair of concerts given at Carnegie Hall, April 11 and 12.

1921   Founded International Composers' Guild. Worked on *Offrandes.*

1922   First Guild concert, February 19. *Offrandes* premiered by Guild, Nina Koshetz, soprano, Carlos Salzedo conducting, April 23, New York. Completed *Amériques.* Worked on *Hyperprism.* Founded with Busoni Internationale Komponisten-Gilde in Berlin. Guild established affiliation with Collective of Composers in Moscow. Learned that all his pre-war manuscripts, stored in Berlin warehouse, burned in fire, except for *Bourgogne*, which he later destroyed himself in a fit of rage.

1923   *Hyperprism* premiered by Guild, Varèse conducting, March 4, New York, causing riot in audience. Worked on *Octandre.* Guild established affiliation with Casella's Corporazione delle nuove Musiche. Six Guild members, Arthur Bliss, Louis Gruenberg, Leo Ornstein, Mrs. Arthur M. Reis, Lazare Saminsky, Emerson Whithorne, seceded from Guild to form League of Composers.

1924   *Octandre* premiered by Guild, E. Robert Schmitz conducting, January 13, New York. Worked on *Intégrales.* Visited London and Paris.

1925   *Intégrales* premiered by Guild, Leopold Stokowski conducting, March 1, New York. Began work on *Arcana*.

1926   *Amériques* premiered by Philadelphia Orchestra, Stokowski
conducting, April 9; performed in New York, April 13.

1927   *Arcana* premiered by Philadelphia Orchestra, Stokowski conducting, April 8; performed in New York, April 12. Visited
Paris. Announced dissolution of Guild. Explored with René
Bertrand and Harvey Fletcher possibilities of developing electronic instrument for composing.

1928   Founded Pan-American Association of Composers. Left for
Paris.

1930   Began work on *Ionisation*.

1932   Applied for Guggenheim Fellowship to "pursue work on an
instrument for the producing of new sounds."

1933   *Ionisation* premiered by Pan-American Association, Nicolas
Slonimsky conducting, March 6, New York. Worked on
Ecuatorial, for which Leon Theremin built two instruments
to Varèse's specifications.

1934   *Ecuatorial* premiered by Pan-American Association, Chase
Baromeo, bass, Slonimsky conducting, April 15, New York.

1936   *Density 21.5* composed January, premiered by Georges
Barrère, February 16, New York. Visited Santa Fe.

1937   Gave classes in composition and orchestration, Arsuna School
of Fine Arts, Santa Fe. Founded Schola Cantorum in Santa Fe.

1938   Visited San Francisco and Los Angeles. Approached sound
studios for use of their facilities.

1940   Returned to New York.

1941   Founded New Chorus.

1942   Reorganized and renamed chorus The Greater New York
Chorus, specializing in early music.

1943   The Greater New York Chorus gave first concert, April 24.

1945   Turned down offer of *Légion d'honneur*.

1947   *Étude pour Espace* performed with Varèse conducting, New
Music Society, April 20, New York.

1948   Gave seminar in composition, course on twentieth-century
music at Columbia University during summer session.

1949   Began work on instrumental sections of *Déserts*.

1950   *Octandre, Intégrales, Ionisation* and *Density 21.5* recorded,
Frederic Waldman conducting, issued by EMS as first
volume of projected "complete works" of Varèse. Project
suspended after death of Jack Skurnick, owner. Taught at

Kranichsteiner Musikinstitut's Internationale Ferienkurse für Neue Musik in Darmstadt.

1951   Harold Burris-Meyer wrote Magnecord Inc. providing specifications for equipment to be adapted for Varèse. During these years, with support of Burris-Meyer and others, Varèse approached various institutions and firms with no result.

1953   Ampex model 401A tape recorder presented to Varèse anonymously. Began work on electronically *organized sound* interpolations for *Déserts*.

1954   Invited by Pierre Schaeffer to complete work on *Déserts* at Studio d'Essai of Radiodiffusion française. *Déserts* premiered by Orchestre National, Hermann Scherchen conducting, December 2, Paris.

1955   Began work on electronically *organized sound* for *Good Friday Procession in Verges* sequence in film, *Around and About Joan Miró*, by Thomas Bouchard.

1956   Completed *Verges*.

1957   Began work on *Poème Électronique* at Philips Laboratories, Eindhoven, Holland.

1958   *Poème Électronique* presented during Brussels World's Fair in pavilion designed for Philips by Le Corbusier, as musical part of a "spectacle of sound and light," with images provided by Le Corbusier. *Dans la Nuit* projected at completion of *Déserts*, interrupted by *Poème Électronique*, later abandoned.

1961   *Nocturnal* (incomplete), premiered by Composers' Showcase, Donna Precht, soprano, Robert Craft conducting, May 1, New York. Worked on *Nuit* (second version of *Nocturnal*).

1965   Died November 6, New York.

ROGER SESSIONS

In Honor of His Sixty-fifth Birthday

ANDREW IMBRIE

It has frequently been observed that Roger Sessions' musical idiom is undergoing a gradual development. A transition has been traced from the early diatonicism of the First Symphony and the Violin Concerto through the First Quartet and the *Pages from a Diary* to the chromaticism of the Second Symphony. His subsequent adoption of the twelve-tone technique (in part or throughout, depending on the work) has been duly noted and pondered, despite the absence of fanfare to accompany it. This event takes on the aspect less of a latter-day conversion than of an absorption and an acknowledgment; and it has raised scarcely a ripple on the surface of his intensely personal style. For Sessions, indeed, the mastery of the row is a matter of technique, not system: a point of view consistent with his lifelong respect for the former and distrust of the latter.

Sessions' position in our musical life is unique. Not so long ago it was the custom among apologists for this or that middle-of-the-road composer to protest that he "goes his own way," "is not taken in by fads or slogans," and the like. That Sessions is not just another such mugwump is demonstrated by the forcefulness and profundity of the impression made upon us by his music, and by the way his words have troubled our conscience, deepened our understanding, and, in sum, given us pause. Far from ignoring the various fashions, movements, and theories which have influenced composition and pedagogy during his creative career, he appears to have been *against* them all. Thus it has been difficult to state exactly what he is *for*. In an age of musical revolution he has simply evolved.

Yet his rejection of formulas has not taken place without the most painstaking search for any valuable insights that might accompany them. Whether it be the conventional use of Roman numerals in harmonic analysis, or Hindemith's derivation of musical logic from acoustical laws, or Krenek's insistence on serialism as the cornerstone of the new music, or Schenker's concept of the *Urlinie*, Sessions has extracted from each in turn those elements which seemed vital and illuminating before subjecting the rest to a withering blast. His criti-

cism has remained consistently on the highest level, and has therefore
repeatedly had the effect of bringing us face to face with those ultimate
paradoxes without which art would become mechanics. And it is
perhaps through paradox that we can best approach an understanding
not only of Sessions' aesthetic position (if indeed he has one) but
perhaps even of his music as well.

His ideas, as expressed in criticism and teaching over the years,
lend themselves best to illustration by antitheses. We weigh the
alternatives of system and technique, theory and practice, convention
and tradition, subconscious and "super-conscious," pattern and song.
The acquisition of technique must be systematic so that, through
mastery, the system may be intuitively overthrown, and a new vision
achieved. But the vision is implicit in the work, and cannot be ab-
stracted from it. It inheres in the specific contours as much as in the
underlying impulses—or rather, it inheres in the tensions between
the former and the latter. Thus theory can never be more than a codification of specific procedures, and its chief usefulness is pedagogic.
Nor can theory ever serve as a criterion for the judgment of significance or quality, either before or after the fact. In his critique of
those theorists who have claimed for their systems a more lofty import,
Sessions has in each case diagnosed symptoms of internal contradiction: in Hindemith the intensification of the conflict between acoustics
and psychology; in Schenker, of that between structure and its embodiment; and in Krenek, of that between an imposed and a "natural"
order, the latter being interpreted in the cultural and psychological,
rather than in the purely physical sense.

Both in this last and in other connections, Sessions has insisted
upon the continuity of traditional responses to musical events, even
when new contexts have radically altered their significance. Since this
is one of the most controversial tenets to be found in Sessions' writings, it may be well to quote him directly. He has alluded to the
problem at several different times during his career, and his thinking
in this matter has undergone a progressive refinement. To some it
may appear that he is slowly retreating before inexorable historical
forces, while clinging to a forlorn hope. To others it may appear that
these same forces, while stimulating his resourcefulness of strategy to
the utmost, are at last powerless either to solve the mystery or to
defeat the truth. In 1933 Sessions confidently hails the end of the
age of musical experimentalism:

It is hardly necessary to point out that the art of Schönberg has
vital connections with the past. . . . The music may in fact be

regarded as pre-eminently a development of . . . chromaticism, and the "twelve-tone system" as, in great part, a bold effort to formulate directive laws for its further development. "Atonality," if its real and not its superficial meaning be understood, is merely another name for that chromaticism and not, as the term would seem to imply, a negation of the necessity for fundamental acoustic unity, based on laws which are the inevitable consequence both of natural phenomena of sound, and the millennial culture of the Occidental ear. "Tonality," in the old, cadential sense, scarcely exists in any music of the present day, and where it can be said to exist in essence its nature has been so widened and modified as to render it unrecognizable to a composer of the last century. But the ultimate foundations on which the older tonal system was built, since they are inherent in the physical phenomena of resonance, remain unchanged; they can be enormously extended but scarcely modified.[1]

In the same article, while criticizing what he labels as the "Alexandrian" state of mind of the Schönberg school, he insists that the music itself is "fundamentally unassailable."
Again, in 1937, we are told:

While contemporary conceptions of tonality are far from being the same as those of a half-century ago, musicians have nevertheless returned to the principle of a tonal, or, if you will, an acoustic center, around which tones and harmonies group themselves in clear relationship and in their various ways recognize the hierarchy of consonance and dissonance as it is furnished by the natural properties of the tone itself. . . . Tonality in the broadest sense is an inevitable product of the physical properties of tone. . . . As for Schönberg's own "twelve-tone system," in which an additional set of relationships is, as it were, rigorously superimposed on those derived from the phenomena of resonance . . . its ultimate value will depend not on any question of abstract merit but on its efficacy as a vehicle for the imagination of those who use it.[2]

But of course it is the elusive nature of the relation between acoustics and perception which gives rise to further explanations. In his subsequent article on the newly published *Unterweisung im Tonsatz* of Hindemith we find the following:

Hindemith assigns too great an importance, in the construction of a musical theory, to the physics of sound. . . . The musician as such

[1] "Music in Crisis," *Modern Music* (hereafter abbreviated *MM*), January 1933, p. 72.
[2] "New Musical Horizons," *MM*, January 1937, pp. 63-64.

is interested not in the objective nature of sound, but in the effects which sound produces and may be made to produce, and . . . physics can be useful to him primarily as a confirmation of effects observed, never as a point of departure, or as an adequate explanation of effects which are the manifest result of centuries of cumulative musical experience.[3]

The latter part of this statement gives a clue to the understanding of what might otherwise seem a contradiction in Sessions' critical position: on the one hand he seems to welcome and to desire a return to music based on the "natural properties of tone," while at the same time taking Hindemith to task for his overemphasis on physics. Sessions' concept of the "natural" is further amplified in his article on Krenek's *Über Neue Musik*:

> In a remarkable passage Krenek demands not a *natural* (*Natur-gegebenen*) but an intellectually determined basis (*Geistesbe-stimmten Voraussetzungen*) for music. This writer's antipathy for the twelve-tone system is expressed precisely in these terms, provided that by "nature" is understood not physics but the response of the human ear and spirit to the simplest acoustic facts. He is profoundly out of sympathy, therefore, with the conception which Krenek boldly avows, of music as an abstract system, like geometry. On the contrary it seems to him that its human meaning . . . lies ultimately in the fact that such elementary musical phenomena as the fifth and the measurably qualitative distinction between consonance and dissonance, are psychological as well as physical facts, out of which a whole language has grown, and which in music based on the twelve-tone system seem often more powerful binding forces (*Relations-Momente*) than those inherent in the system itself.[4]

In Sessions' later writings, we find similar ideas expressed, with changes in emphasis. As his own musical idiom approaches more nearly that of the dodecaphonists, we hear less about consonance and dissonance; and we find, of course, a gradual re-evaluation of the twelve-tone technique itself. Regarded as a system, its value is still, in Sessions' opinion, sharply restricted; regarded as a technique, its practical possibilities are great. In the last chapter of his textbook *Harmonic Practice* he discusses the problem of formulating contemporary practice:

[3] *MM*, November 1937, p. 60.
[4] *MM*, January 1938, pp. 126-127.

What is needed is a new and far more inclusive description of the various relationships between tones, and of the means by which the "musical ear" discriminates, selects, and arranges these relationships. . . . The twelve-tone system, for example, provides a possible answer to one aspect of this question, by offering a basis of organization through an ordered selection of relationships. It deserves the most serious study from this point of view; the heat of controversy has obscured the real nature of the system, of the function which it performs, and of the relationship of the composer to it. Like any other technique . . . it demands mastery, and the transition from calculation to spontaneity can come only as mastery is achieved. . . .

The twelve-tone technique, however, does not provide the answer to the question of how the ear perceives, coordinates, and synthesises the relationships involved, nor does it attempt to do so. Its nature is essentially practical; and when it is used by composers of imagination who have really mastered it, the experienced listener will inevitably be aware of what may be called "tonal areas" or "tonal centers.". . .

Such quasi-tonal sensations are simply evidence that the ear has grasped the relationships between the tones, and has absorbed and ordered them. It is a mistake to regard such sensations as connected exclusively with the tonal system as such. The intervals, and their effects, remain precisely the same; two tones a fifth apart still produce the effect of the fifth, and, in whatever degree the context permits, will convey a sensation similar to that of a root and its fifth, or of a tonic and its dominant. A rising interval of a semitone will produce somewhat the effect of a "leading tone," principal or secondary, and so on. . . .

Mention has been made . . . of "tonal areas" perceived in so-called "atonal" music. The attentive ear is aware not only of such "tonal areas" but of contrasting ones. If, however, such contrasts—akin in principle to contrasts of key in "tonal" music—are to be given precise technical definition, the areas themselves must be defined, in terms of the elements which produce them, the role which each of the twelve tones plays in setting them up, and the means by which the sense of the tonal area is shifted or destroyed.[5]

Here we have the crux of the matter: the inherent tension between those elements of design postulated for each work by the composer, and those traditional responses the listener brings, and always must

[5] New York: Harcourt, Brace, 1951, pp. 406-408.

bring, to his experience of any music whatever. True, it is always possible in any given instance for a composer to inhibit these responses, by providing a context that will not permit them. But if he attempts to do so totally, and on principle, as it were, the expenditure of energy required is enormous and the cost prohibitive.

> "Atonality" implies music in which not only is the element of what is defined as "tonality" no longer a principle of construction, but in which the composer deliberately avoids all procedures capable of evoking "tonal" associations. Actually this is virtually impossible. . . .[6]

One further quotation will illustrate Sessions' intuition concerning the limitations of serialism as a form-engendering principle:

> Once the initial choice has been made, the series will determine the composer's vocabulary; but once the vocabulary has been so determined, the larger questions of tonal organization remain. My own strong feeling is that, while these questions must certainly be answered in terms not alien to the nature of the series, it is not serialism as such that can ever be made to account for them. I do not mean at all that I am opposed in principle to the idea of basing the structure entirely on the series itself, as Webern and others have tried to do. What I am saying is that even in structures so based, the acoustical effect seems to me to derive in the last analysis not from the manipulation of the series as such, but from the relationships between notes, as the composer has by these means set them up. . . . The series governs the composer's choice of materials; only the composer's ear and his conception determine the manner or the effect of their usage.[7]

From the foregoing, one can perceive the central role of tradition in Sessions' thinking. Yet it is clear that he is hardly a "traditional" composer in the "traditional" sense. The reason for this is not hard to find, and it can best be suggested by stressing the difference between tradition and convention. Sessions has always warned his pupils against the attempt to apply abstract conceptions to their concrete problems in composition. To put it in another way, he has drawn their attention consistently and exclusively to those problems which arise from the music, and has refused to accept rationalizations which appeal to ideology. To give a somewhat broader meaning to the term

---

[6] "Problems and Issues Facing the Composer Today," *Musical Quarterly* (Hereafter abbreviated: *MQ*), April 1960, p. 164.
[7] "To the Editor," *The Score and I.M.A. Magazine*, July 1958, p. 63.

"convention," one might include under it all *a priori* choices which are made in order to conform to a stipulated aesthetic position, and which therefore give rise to the symptom of style-consciousness. This critical attitude applies equally to the once fashionable nationalistic "Americanism," to the aesthetic of "Neo-Classicism," or to today's fashions in "pre-composition." (It does not, however, apply to the mere use of a row, which is to be regarded as raw material, and whose usefulness for the composer is practical rather than philosophical.) In each case we are dealing with a mode of thought imposed on the musical material from without, an essentially *uncommitted* choice between alternatives whose validity does not depend on that material. For Sessions, the act of composition is, in this sense, profoundly un-"calculated": it is a deed, a gesture, although in its execution the highest intellectual and intuitive powers may be brought to bear. The way in which tradition (as opposed to convention) operates through the composer is complex, and has been discussed at length in Sessions' writings. Suffice it to say here that the conscious acquisition of systematic technique, derived from the study of the works of the great masters, goes hand in hand with the subconscious accumulation and association of aural impressions received from all conceivable sources; when the composer matures, his acquired technique has been assimilated into what Sessions calls mastery, and exerts its formative influence at what he calls the "super-conscious" level. This mastery may be extended, and indeed must be, by a lifetime of increased refinement and further acquisition; but the style that results is not *chosen*, any more than an individual's handwriting or gait is chosen. From this conviction, by the way, springs Sessions' strong antipathy to the teaching of harmony or counterpoint as a study of this or that "common practice period." For him, rather, the purpose of such teaching is to instil a thorough mastery of the musical "facts of life"—of "how notes behave."

The end-product of all this training and absorption, as they interact with the composer's own sensibilities, his personality, and his "vision," is the composer's "ear," which governs all his choices; and to these choices he is deeply *committed* through personal involvement. The moment that his choices become dictated by a calculated exclusiveness, the music runs the danger of becoming conventional. A composer must come to terms with everything old and new—but the terms are always his own. In this way he achieves *style*, as opposed to "*a style*." For, after all, "the style is the man."

The values that Sessions teaches, therefore, might be described as traditional values divorced from their conventional misapplications:

those very values, which, paradoxically if you like, are most clearly applicable to the most profoundly "revolutionary" masterpieces of any time. Sessions insists, first of all, on the integral nature of the musical experience:

> We teach and study harmony, counterpoint, and instrumentation; and in speaking of music we isolate as it were a number of other elements: melody, rhythm, line, meter, tempo, dynamics, texture, articulation, and possibly other matters. We frequently speak of these things as if each of them were a separate and independent element, and as if a total musical impulse or impression could in actual fact be adequately analyzed as the sum and interplay of these elements, each proceeding according to its own laws. But surely it is our thinking that is in all essentials highly artificial. These elements are not even *ingredients*, but rather dimensions, facets, or aspects of an integral *musical* experience, and are inaccurately conceived in any other terms. . . . Each one of these various aspects derives its function from the total and indivisible musical flow— the *song*. . . . The point that I wish to make is that music can be genuinely organized only on this integral basis.[8]

Hence both the usefulness and the limitations of musical analysis. We learn about watches by taking them apart, but they will not work until put together. Just as the "elements" of music are interdependent, so are the "processes" involved in composition: "Conception and execution are really inseparable, and in the last analysis identical."[9] The same interdependence can be claimed for the basic structural principles of association, progression, and contrast; and also for the two opposing forces of line and articulation, which exist in a state of delicate equilibrium.

It is perhaps this particular kind of emphasis on indivisibility and continuity which sets Sessions apart most clearly from his contemporaries. In an era fascinated either by the motive or by "sonority," Sessions speaks most often about line. Those of us who have studied with him will remember with affection his tone of voice in speaking of "the large gesture," "the long line." Music which is deficient in this quality becomes monotonous or static:

> It is easy to see how the element of line, in every larger sense of the word, tended to lose its importance, even though it could not

[8] "Song and Pattern in Music Today." *Score*, December 1956, pp. 77-78. See also *The Musical Experience*, Princeton, 1950, p. 19: "The basic ingredient of music is not so much sound as movement."

[9] August Centeno, ed., *The Intent of the Artist*, Princeton, 1941, p. 132.

of course be abandoned altogether. In the works of Debussy, Scriabin, the Stravinsky of *Petrouchka* and the *Sacre*, the Schönberg of the middle period, we have, so to speak, the apotheosis of detail. Harmony, for instance, instead of being as it had always been, until the so-called "romantic period," an organic element in a flowing musical line and even—so to speak—the determining framework of that line, has assumed more and more a purely coloristic function. According to the context it bears the weight of pathos, of suggestion, of evocation, and an infinite number of new colors and new nuances of relationship are brought into it; but it achieves its effect no longer through its organic flow and interplay with other musical elements but through the color and the dynamics of individual sonorities. Hence the static quality of some of Debussy's harmonies, a single harmonic detail often serving as the basis of an entire section or even an entire work; hence the monotony of Scriabin, who attempted to found a whole musical system on a single complex chord; hence the static quality of so much of the early Stravinsky where—as to a lesser extent in Debussy—the harmonies shift rather than flow.[10]

This is not to imply that line is a quality which the composer consciously and deliberately "sets up." It is, on the contrary, quite often in the background (both in the ordinary and in the Schenkerian sense): moreover its meaning is laden with ambiguity, particularly when one attempts, as Schenker does, to abstract it as a formal principle:

Every composer is aware through his own experience of the reality of a "background" in his musical construction that goes beyond the individual traits of melody and harmony which constitute the most immediately perceptible features of his work. He is conscious, that is to say, of a type of movement which takes place gradually and over large stretches, and which embodies itself in the need which he feels, say, at a given moment, for such and such a high note, or for this or that particular harmonic or melodic intensification. This is in a very real sense one of the most essential features of the composer's impulse and is far more than a part of an impulse toward "design," in the usual sense of the word. But the composer, too, will recognize the fact that musical line is, in its full significance, an extremely complicated affair, and that a single note may be fraught with a hundred implications and embody a

[10] *MM*, January 1937, p. 61.

hundred relationships within a given work. Most intelligent musicians, moreover, will realize that a musical impression is an integral thing, and that the various terms in which it is described and analyzed are, however useful and necessary, abstractions of a decidedly approximative nature.[11]

Edward Cone has remarked: ". . . the best analysis is the one that recognizes various levels functioning simultaneously, as when a tone resolves once in the immediate context but turns out to have a different goal in the long run."[12]

This is a point which he proceeds to illustrate by highly suggestive references to details from works of Schönberg and Sessions.

The keynote of ambiguity is struck again, and in a different way, by Elliott Carter in a recent review of Sessions' Violin Concerto:

This brief survey of some of the themes of a work whose main feature is a wealth of long, beautifully shaped singing or rhythmic lines and figurations that move in very broad sweeps is not intended to state whether such an over-all unification of the themes was striven for by the composer or not but simply to examine the score, and to point out a tissue of connections which must strike the listener at once since it seems to operate not only on a large scale but also in the joining even of details, and of one small phrase with another. . . . There are obviously many degrees of similarity possible between phrases controlled by the same directional motif, and when directionality is used with other kinds of remote relationships such as imitation of outline, ornamentation, and simplification, directional inversions, etc. the play of these could be likened to the use of metaphor and simile that results in the fascinating effects described in Empson's *Seven Types of Ambiguity*.[13]

Ambiguity of linear goal and ambiguity of motivic association can be joined with ambiguity of tonal reference, as indicated, for example, by Cone again in his review[14] of the Second Quartet. These ambiguities, as in the case of the literary ones pointed out by Empson, are far from being flaws in the structure of the work of art: they are, on the contrary, among the roots of it.

"Ambiguity" itself can mean an indecision as to what you mean, an intention to mean several things, a probability that one or other or

11 *MM*, May 1935, pp. 175-176.
12 "Analysis Today," *MQ*, April 1960, pp. 178ff.
13 *MQ*, July 1959, pp. 376-377.
14 *MQ*, January 1957, pp. 140-142.

both of two things has been meant, and the fact that a statement has several meanings. . . . The words of the poet will, as a rule, be more justly words, what they represent will be more effectively a unit in the mind, than the more numerous words with which I shall imitate their meaning so as to show how it is conveyed.[15]

The thing that makes ambiguity effective, however, the thing that differentiates it from arbitrary confusion, is our sense of the artist's mastery: of the basic unity of impulse, sureness of timing, resourcefulness in the exploitation of ambiguity itself. The artist must, in other words, inspire our confidence while stretching our credulity.

In studying the work of art with the purpose of understanding it better, it will be useful to gather evidence for the kind of consistency and mastery just alluded to, as well as evidence of those imbedded ambiguities which in some way modify the consistency and introduce tension into the design. We must at least try to find out a few of the ways in which the civilized listener is brought to a state of confident receptivity and alertness: a state in which predictability and unpredictability are balanced so that expectations can be frustrated without disappointment, or fulfilled without satiety; so that surprises seem inevitable; so that detail is exciting because of its context. In our investigations we must balance, too, those elements of design that are directly predicated upon the composer's choice of materials against those that depend on certain tendencies toward the ordering of experience which the listener may be expected to bring with him as part of his "listening equipment," whatever our ideas may be about the origin of these predilections or their desirability. Finally, we must not claim too much either for our method of analysis or for its results: having been shown the pitfalls, we would be foolhardy to do so. Self-assurance becomes us as composers—not as analysts.

I have chosen to examine the opening passages from two works of Sessions. The first, written in 1935, is undebatably in B minor; the second (1958) is consistently dodecaphonic.

The first phrase of the first movement of the Concerto for Violin and Orchestra (Ex. 1) ends at No. 1, and comprises those motives so vividly characterized for us by Carter in the review already referred to. We may distinguish three motives: a) the one which ascends in stepwise motion from tonic to dominant, using the diatonic B minor scale; b) the disjunct motive that follows, with its upbeat quality, its changes of direction, its introduction of material foreign to the scale

[15] William Empson, *Seven Types of Ambiguity*, New York: Meridian, 1955, pp. 8-9.

Ex. 1

at the climax, and its precipitous descent immediately prior to c), which is the cadential appoggiatura-motive. This feminine cadence is further extended by the imitative echo of the two flutes, which also serves two additional functions: to provide a delicate thickening of texture at the cadence (thus confirming the structural downbeat it creates) and at the same time to modify the finality of the cadence by suggesting further motion yet to be completed—this suggestion being made through the harmonic sense of "V of IV," and through the cadential stranding of unresolved dissonance. Considering the three motives in their mutual interaction, we should notice the distinctive shape of the complete phrase they generate, as well as the clear articulation of its separate parts. The phrase as a whole constitutes a single gesture, whose motion is initiated, brought to a climax and closed off by the three motives, respectively. While the first two are contrasted with one another not only by their inherent character, but also through instrumentation and mode of attack, they are welded together by the steadiness of the sixteenth-note motion and by the stepwise continuation of the line from F♯ to G♯. The subsequent disjunct motion is made possible through the gradual accumulation of energy initiated by the earlier ascent; but this energy is expended as the melody reaches its peak. The arrival of the high point, F♮, as introduced by C♮, has a disturbing effect on the tonality—an effect which is made especially dramatic by its conspicuous position, but at the same time made plausible through motive and line. In the first place, the disturbance has had its precedent in the lesser shock caused by the abandonment of the scalewise ascent at G♯; this note must eventually "go somewhere." An acceptable function for the G♯ in its immediate context was that of serving as a melodic "dominant" to the C♯, but a residue of dissatisfaction is left over: the scale still requires continuation. The isolation of the G♯ was further heightened, of course, by the interpolation of the low D before the C♯, even though the tritone thus formed effectively dissociated the D from the "mainstream" of linear motion. (The D is heard as a reminder of the D in the original diatonic ascent, and serves to link it to the low C♯ just before the cadence.) The high C♯, meanwhile, is now prominent by virtue of being the first tone not prepared by stepwise motion (except, of course, for the very first B), and thus sets itself up in opposition to the tonic. That this opposition has further consequences will soon become evident. The opposition is, however, made acceptable not only by the presence of C♯ in the key of B minor, but possibly also by octave transference from the lower C♯'s which precede and follow it, and of course by the "dominant" support of the G♯ already mentioned. This little motivic cell of a rising fourth is repeated in the climactic C and F, which are not separated from each other. They thus form an irreducible lump of foreign matter, smoothly inserted but acting as an irritant. The ear attempts to reconcile it with its context in two ways. First, by hearing the two tones as B♯ and E♯, we can interpret them as leading tones (by octave transference) to the F♯ and C♯ immediately following. This helps to palliate the sting (and explain its presence within the phrase), but the "suspension of disbelief" required of the listener in making this octave transference is considerable; and so the F remains "in our ear," forming another, stronger, opposition to the tonic, and requiring an eventual second resolution in its own register. The descent from the F is sudden, being accomplished by two leaps (the only exception to the rule that for this motive each successive interval changes direction). Enough energy is regained by this loss of altitude to carry the musical impulse through the expressive appoggiatura which concludes the phrase. The D♯ at the end of the phrase modifies the D♮ of the minor mode, and arouses the expectation of further upward motion on a slower, larger scale. The A in the alto flute resolves the G♯ mentioned above, and leads it back to G, which is then, also, abandoned at the cadence. The first flute, simultaneously, starts from the tonic in a new register of its own, and moves up chromatically to the C♮, which has two effects: first, that of giving renewed vigor to our impression of the C-F complex already introduced, and second, that of initiating still another stepwise line upward.

Thus we gain the impression of a clearly articulated musical idea, a gesture for which the requisite energy is furnished, and by which it is consumed, leaving, however, a residue of unfulfilled expectation. Tonally, two areas of opposition to the tonic have been established: the first being that of the C♯ with its "adjectival" dominant G♯, the second being that of the F with its C. On the linear plane, no fewer than five clearly distinguishable lines have been cast out: the first and lowest being the slow ground-swell reaching from the initial tonic through the low C♯ to the D♯ at the cadence; the second being the quick ascent from B to F♯ through the diatonic minor scale, and continuing through the G♯ to the A in the alto flute. The G♯ having brought us to this point, the G♮ now brings the curve of this line downward, having stopped short of completing the scale. A new thrust will be necessary in the next phrase to carry us beyond the A, which, by the way, thus achieves a certain prominence, and can be considered a third point of opposition to the tonic. The G will ultimately resolve to F♯, but not to the one which is being held over by the trombone, for obvious reasons of instrumentation and textural articulation (the staccato accent followed by the rest, for example). Meanwhile, the leap to the C♯, followed by the C♮, opens up a third possibility for linear motion, which at this point is left ambiguous by this chromaticism, and which will acquire shape and impetus only when the line is picked up later. The F (which initiates the fourth line) is alone in its register, and, as already mentioned, poses the most urgent challenge to the tonic. The direction of its ultimate linear resolution is left unspecified, while the fifth line is begun by the high B and C.

Ex. 2

Ex. 3

Space does not allow the continuation of a detailed verbal exposition of the ensuing phrases, and I must depend on linear diagrams to make the analysis clear. I have attempted to peel the first two phrases like an onion, to show the structure of the overlapping layers of stepwise movement. These layers are numbered. Ex. 2 shows them in their positions relative to one another, while Ex. 3 spreads them out separately. Since the second phrase is doubled in octaves throughout, I have shown only the upper lines in the diagram. Exx. 4 and 5 refer to the third phrase.

Before we proceed to these diagrams, a few descriptive remarks about the first three phrases in their general outline may be relevant. It will be seen that the second phrase begins with the first motive again, this time on D♯, where the cadence of the first phrase left off. The association between the opening motives of the two phrases is very strong, since one is the literal transposition of the other. Their respective harmonic functions are very different however, since it will be seen that no real harmonic area of D♯ minor is established. The E♯ has, of course, taken us beyond the expected subdominant, but, as the

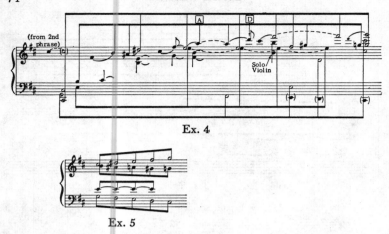

Ex. 4

Ex. 5

diagram will show clearly, this E♮ eventually arrives at the end of the phrase; it arrives, moreover, as a result of that much slower linear movement which I have already called a "ground-swell." This is the motion traced by the white notes with descending stems in Exx. 2 and 3 and designated line 1. (Other numbers, from 2 to 6, are similarly assigned to the remaining lines.) The second motive retains its identity not through literal transposition, but through its qualities of disjunctness, frequent changes of direction, steady sixteenth-note movement, upbeat character, breadth of span from high point to low, and steepness of descent immediately prior to the structural downbeat, which again supports the feminine appoggiatura-cadence. The original gesture is expanded to twice its former length; but this time the high point is the tonic. As will be seen in the diagrams (line 6 of Exx. 2 and 3), this high B temporarily resolves the earlier C♮, but serves also as the springboard for the later ascent to C♯. It is the third phrase which accomplishes this by means of further upbeat movement based on the second motive alone. The masculine downbeat at No. 3, with its bare diminished fifth on the second degree, in a high register, is thus heard as the goal of the three phrases, which can be said to encompass the elaboration of the motion from I to II in B minor. Increase of tension as this goal is approached is accomplished in several ways: for example by the overlapping of the second and third phrases (compare the separation of the first from the second), by the dramatic ascent of the third phrase (compare the downward tendency of the first two phrases), by the thickening of texture, the liquidation and compression of the motive, and the crescendo. The opposition between tonic and supertonic is, by the way, one of the most important form-engendering principles of this movement. Foreshadowed in miniature by the first independent C♯ in the first measure, the tritone on C♯ appears now as a point of dramatic tension for the ushering in of the solo violin; ultimately this same tritone is heard at the final cadence of the first movement, leaving the tonic still challenged.

It will now be necessary to explain the symbols used in the diagram, Ex. 2. White notes are used for the outer voices, which move on a larger scale; black notes are reserved for the inner voices. By "voices" I mean those underlying structural lines already alluded to, whose identity is upheld by stepwise movement. Obviously, these are to be distinguished from the real voices of the surface texture, in which disjunct motion arising from motivic activity will cause them to skip, inevitably, from one underlying "voice" to another. It is, of course, the tension between these two levels of melodic activity which, as one aspect of the musical content, engages our interest and attention. Both white and black notes of these structural lines are equipped with stems; and the beams joining the stems serve to connect all the notes that comprise each line. Dotted beams connect with notes belonging to the next phrase, which will be represented in Exx. 4 and 5. A dotted tie indicates that the repetition of a given tone acts as a reminder of its earlier appearance, and connects it with what comes next. Numbers enclosed in squares refer to the lines as separately shown by corresponding numbers in Ex. 3. Letters (pitch designations) enclosed in squares or rectangles indicate the position of contrasting areas articulated or elaborated. Arrows and brackets are used in conjunction with these wherever necessary to clarify the exact location or extent of such areas. Notes without stems act primarily as melodic dominants or leading-tones to subsequent notes, with which they are slurred. Slurs may also be used to connect two notes having stems, thus indicating that the first note may have the dual role of carrying its own line, while at the same time functioning as dominant support for a note belonging to another line. Notes in parentheses show, in cases of octave transference, the position the notes would have occupied in the original register. Unattached stemmed notes with single flag act as grace-notes or appoggiaturas. The high C♮ of line 6 is designated "NN," or neighbor-note, although it also has the effect of providing impetus for the later ascent to C♯. Finally, the chord accompanying the A of line 3 serves to emphasize the A, its root; but in addition, its components C♯ and E anticipate the future linear roles of these notes.

As to the lines themselves, a cursory examination of Ex. 3 will show a strong family resemblance between them. Except for 6, they all begin by ascending to a high point, after which they curve downwards. The high point in each instance is approached by half-step and left by whole-step, thus becoming melodically tonicized. The device of approaching a melodic goal by over-reaching it and returning to it is already foreshadowed by the small linear motions at the beginning, which I have designated as i and ii, and which serve the additional function of facilitating, for the ear, the separation of the two upward scale motions of lines 1 and 2. It is interesting to note that, beginning with i and ii and continuing through 1, 2, and 3, each line reaches a step higher, culminating in G♮; and that 4, 5, and 6 have as their respective goals either this G♮ or the C♯ which together constitute the *II* tritone, which, as we have seen, is the chief opposition established by this introductory section. Thus we can divide these lines into two groups, of which the first leads to the point of opposition, and the second elaborates it. As if to mirror this differentiation of function, each line of the first group is characterized by a strong initial ascent, while the lines of the second group are not. In fact, line 5 articulates its descending tendency in the actual music by means of two successive octave transferences, which the ear accepts this time without effort, because this device expresses so exactly that tendency to downward movement at the end of the phrase, and because the ear is led so carefully downward by the statement of each note involved, both in the old and in the new register.

It remains for me to comment briefly on the outcome of the two ambiguities established in the first phrase: namely, the ultimate direction taken by the C♯ which initiates line 4 and that of the F♮ which initiates line 5. In the first case, the C♮ that follows immediately (and acts as dominant to the F) necessitates the restatement of the C♯ in the second phrase, which then of course proceeds up to the D. But the force of the C♮ is still present, and may well account for the prolongation of that tone which now takes place, and also for the insistence on the simultaneous sounding of the C♮ with the C♯, before the former finally resolves to the B. Thus, while the roles of the two chromatically opposed tones become clarified, the conflict between them is intensified. In the case of the F♮, the enharmonic ambiguity is exploited even more directly: a plausible resolution to E is provided in the second phrase, immediately followed by an equally plausible resolution to F♯ (considering the F♮ as E♯). This F♯ is prepared by the appoggiatura G, whose entrance actually precedes that of the E, so that the two possibilities, are, so to speak, locked together, and the ear accepts the two simultaneously. In the last analysis, the G appoggiatura is given added importance because of the fact that it initiates the stepwise outlining of the G-C♯ tritone.

The third phrase brings the lowest voice (line 1 in Exx. 2 and 3) from the E to which it has arrived at the end of the second phrase, to the final tritone (Ex. 6). The ear can follow a path back to the C♯,

Ex. 6

thus forming a big "cantus firmus" whose shape has been made familiar by the lines already discussed; or the ear can follow a line up to the G, thus forming an uninterrupted scalewise progression. In either case, by this means and by the help of subsidiary voices, the E is liquidated, and the characteristic tritone of *II* is made vivid both by melodic elaboration in contrary motion, and by its final harmonic presentation at the cadence in bare form without third.

Exx. 4 and 5 should be almost self-explanatory. Ex. 4 shows the notes in their actual register, and Ex. 5 shows the underlying voice leading with octave transference eliminated. The upward transferences at the beginning of the phrase are facilitated by the motivic symmetry, and by the doublings, which, however, are only suggested in Ex. 4 at the beginning. The big transference from the low C♯ to the high D♯ at the outset is much facilitated by the ear's retention of the high C♯ from the end of the previous phrase. The entrance of the solo violin repeats the movement B-C♯ (established by the three phrases as a whole), but this detail I have not included in Ex. 5. Ex. 6 is a much simplified representation of the linear movement of the entire passage.

Besides the tritone which forms the goal of the passage, and which also concludes the movement, two other important contrasting harmonic areas are set up through tonicization at the linear climaxes: that of F with its dominant C, and that of D with its dominant A. The conflict between C and C♯ can be interpreted as that between the upward and downward scales of D minor, or as that between D minor and its relative major. These possibilities are all exploited to the full in the central part of the movement. The opposition to B minor reaches its highest degree of intensity just before the return to the tonic at the cadenza, and culminates in a complex chord (Ex. 7) which could serve as dominant to either D minor or F major. The C♯ is missing, having been worsted by the C♮, which, in the ensuing passage, ultimately resolves to the tonic B, while the B♭, re-interpreted as A♯,

Ex. 7

also resolves to B in contrary motion. This resolution is handled in an indirect manner, being greatly prolonged by the characteristic technique of "horizontalization" (the C, for example, first serving as the point of departure for the recapitulation of the very first motives), but when it finally does arrive, it does so as a deceptive cadence, which in turn launches the violin cadenza. This whole passage deserves the closest study; the elegance of the effect cannot even be hinted at here.

The foregoing analysis has depended upon the assumption that the ear tends, wherever feasible, a) to follow stepwise motion, and b) to expect this motion to have a goal consistent with the context as established. This context is the result of the operation of two forces: 1) the assumed tendency of the ear to select those relationships which, for scientific or historical reasons, for better or for worse, are accepted as simpler; and 2) the imposition by the composer, through compositional selection and emphasis, of relationships which, in their interplay with each other and with those under 1) above, must be understood as characteristic of the individual work. The analysis has assumed, moreover, the interdependence of the musical elements; so that the manipulation by the composer of texture, dynamics, meter, rhythm, motive, or articulation can be shown to be relevant and necessary to the embodiment of the harmonic or linear design (or the other way around, the line or harmony being necessary to help explain a given motivic transformation or metrical downbeat, for example).

In turning to the opening passage of the first movement of Sessions' Quintet (Ex. 8), I shall continue to make the same assumptions. Just as Schönberg in adopting the twelve-tone technique did not abandon his preoccupation with "developmental variation," just as Stravinsky in doing the same thing did not abandon his manipulation of "ontological time" to produce an effect of "euphoria or dynamic calm," so Sessions may be supposed not to have abandoned the "long line."

Ex. 8

Ex. 8

The row on which the music is based is given in Ex. 9, in the four forms in which it appears in the opening melody: namely, O, RI, R₆, I₆. It will be seen that this is a hexachordal, or "semi-combinatorial" row, a fact which clearly determines the choice of the inverted row-

Ex. 9

forms used here. It will also be seen that O begins on F♯ and ends on B, while I₆ begins on B and ends on F♯, and that the same reciprocal relation obtains between RI and R₆, which are bounded by F♮ and C♮. From this we may conjecture that the tritone transposition was chosen for this reason; and this conjecture will take on added credibility if it appears that, for example, phrase articulations are handled so as to coincide frequently with these terminal points. Moreover, certain properties arising from the ordering of the tones within the row will also be seen to contain possibilities for motivic or harmonic-associative exploitation; for example, the grouping F♯-D-C♯ (1, 2, and 3 of O) associates with C♯-F♯-D (2, 3, and 4 of RI). Consequently, the complementary groupings A-F-B♭ and B♭-A-F are also present. As to the structure of the original form of the row itself, we may briefly examine it to determine whether it will yield implications of a quasi-"tonal" nature, as suggested by the deployment of those relationships that the ear might be predisposed to select. From this point of view it seems hardly necessary to point out again the "dominant-tonic" relationship of the terminal tones of the row, especially when the first three notes (already important in another connection, as we observed a moment ago) are diatonic elements of the key of B minor, and when the next-to-last note is the leading tone. Against this implication, however, the F immediately preceding exerts a powerful subversive influence, which is not sufficiently explained away by considering it a dominant to the leading tone. And it is F, of course, that forms the basis for the contrasting implications of the complementary forms of the row.

It may be expected, then, that the composer will have taken advantage of these properties of the row and its forms as chosen at the beginning, that an initial presumption of B minor will be challenged by its tritone, and that the group of phrases ending with the melodic statement of I_6 will in some sense be heard as moving to the dominant (especially since, as happens to be the case, the following phrase begins with the original form of the row transposed up a fifth). (The use, in this connection, of terms like "B minor," can be justified only if understood in a generalized sense. The presence of contrasting centers exerts its influence on the way the "key" is heard; and exerts it constantly: so that "B minor as modified by its tritone, etc." would be more accurate. Even this, however, falls far short of being truly descriptive, and I can only once more allude to the passage from Empson already cited.)

Further than this I shall not pursue the study of the row or its derivatives. Such things as the techniques of row-manipulation for purposes of accompaniment can easily be ascertained by the time-honored method of note-counting (for example, the reciprocity of melody and accompaniment at the beginning as it is maintained by interchanging the groupings into which the melody has been divided by articulation: thus, if the first four notes are called A, the second two B, the third three C, and the fourth three D, it will be seen that A is accompanied by C and D; B by A and C; C by B, D, and part of A, and D by A, B and C).

I shall proceed, rather, to the examination of the melodic line in the first violin up to m. 25, in the effort to come to a better understanding of the effect produced when the raw material of the row is embodied in the actual pitch-registers, rhythmic values, textures, dynamics, and so on. I shall then briefly discuss the first few measures of the accompaniment, indicating in a summary fashion the direction of its subsequent movement. This separation of melody and accompaniment is convenient for purposes of analysis, because a differentiation already exists within the texture. Unlike the Violin Concerto, which begins with an orchestral introduction acting as upbeat to the entrance of the solo violin, the present work begins with a leisurely exposition of a long melody with gently pulsating accompaniment. The bass line discreetly acts as a foil to the melody by reflecting its general character and mode of articulation, without recourse to imitation, yet without assuming an obtrusive character of its own. The manner in which the bass moves toward the cadence at mm. 24 and 25 will be discussed later.

The principal melody, then, falls into two large phrases, the first ending with the B in mm. 8-9. This part is expository in nature, giving the impression of a clear and delicately balanced internal organization: the second, beginning with the highest note of the first and continuing initially in the same vein, but gradually becoming more animated, is expansive in character.

The expository part of the melody is, as we have seen already, divided into four short groups, which together form a unit. The first group, the longest, starts an upward movement, the second completes it, the third and fourth bring it down again in two stages to the cadence. It is appropriate that the longest grouping be employed to initiate this motion, and the shortest be used to express its climax. The balance of the two intermediate-sized groups serves to achieve an equilibrium at the close. This balance is further stabilized by the association of the falling sevenths terminating each of the two groups, while on the other hand the expressive accent on the B♭ differentiates it as cadential. The crucial position of the two-note group at the top of the arch gives it somewhat the function of a keystone: it provides a high point in its first tone, and in its second resolves the upward thrust of the first group. At the same time, the falling sixth from the first tone to the second prepares the ear for the cadential motive of the falling seventh characteristic of the last two groups. The third group can thus be heard also as a kind of relaxation and free expansion of the second by means of the unobtrusive addition of a halfstep and an increase in the size of the falling interval. To this formation the last group then gives renewed definition through tightened rhythm and bolder contour. The finality of the cadence is, of course, weakened by the same expressive accent that identifies it, appearing as it does before the downbeat. The entrance of the cello *after* the downbeat weakens it metrically still further, but at the same time adds weight to it by its effect of thickening the texture. Thus the entire statement is linked to what follows, as well as separated from it, by the interplay of accent, texture, and metrical placement. Line, too, plays its part, on the one hand by defining a clear curve, but on the other hand by linking the high point of the first large phrase to the initial tone of the next.

The linear diagram of this part of the melody, shown in Ex. 10, emphasizes the role of the B minor area. The tonic of this key is outlined in the lowest register by the first two and last notes of the melody, thus acting as a foundation. The triad is, however, challenged by the F♮, which in turn is supported from a distance by the high C, clearly retained because of its climactic position. The E immediately following the high C is clearly the goal of the C♯ and D♯; but how does it function? As subdominant of B or as leading tone to F? Does the G♯ resolve to the A by octave transposition, thus tonicizing it in cooperation with the E, or is the G♯ really an A♭ pulling down to the F via the G? (If the former be the case, then the G could have an effect analogous to a natural seventh added to the root A, to which the G♯ resolves. This "natural seventh" would then resolve to the F, and the A to the B♭.) These possibilities are shown in Ex. 10 by

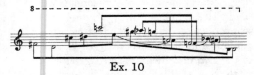

Ex. 10

means of beams connecting the stems. The beams below the notes join the notes whose relationships support B minor: those above the notes connect the ones supporting F. White notes are used this time to indicate the position of the components of the opposing triads. In view of the initial impression made by the first four-note group and the confirming cadence, one tends to hear B minor as outweighing its opponent—especially in view of the dependent position occupied by the F when it arrives. B♭ might be advanced as a candidate for a secondary tonal center, but its strength is vitiated by the powerful E and A which terminate the two preceding phrases (the D♯, forming part of a clear stepwise line to E, cannot without great difficulty be heard enharmonically as a subdominant), and by the quality of the accent placed upon it, which is, as we have seen, expressive rather than metrical, and in this context causes the B♭ (A♯) to press for resolution to the B♮. The acceptance of octave transposition by the ear is, as in the case of the Violin Concerto, facilitated by the general downward motion of the phrase-ending. Nevertheless, again as before, the notes that resolve in a different register leave a residue of unsatisfied expectation, which can serve to lead the ear forward to the ensuing phrases. Actually, the elimination of some or all of the octave transpositions postulated by the present analysis would strengthen the impression of B minor (see Ex. 11) while at the same time, of course, destroying the character of the melody.

Ex. 11

Ex. 12 is a diagram of the entire violin melody which cadences

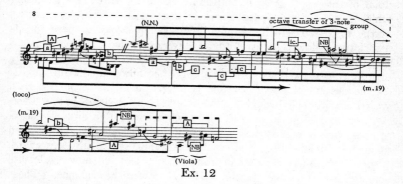

Ex. 12

at m. 23 on the F♯, as modified by the F♮ in the cello. (The two notes are interchanged in m. 24.) Measure 23 is also the point at which the first viola brings in the first motive again, a fifth higher. This occurs on the downbeat of that measure, while the cadence of the previous phrase is syncopated. This forms a clearer cadence accent than the previous articulation already discussed, emphasized as it is by simplification of texture and slowing down of harmonic rhythm; yet a dovetailing of the phrases is effected not only by overlapping of cadence with initiating motive, but also by the continuation of the F in the cello across the bar-line and its resumption of the repeated-note pattern relinquished by the second violin. Ex. 12 attempts to portray the means by which this cadence is prepared by the lines of the second big phrase. The three goals represented by this important point of articulation are: 1) the cadential F♯ in the first violin, 2) the F♮ that modifies it, and 3) the C♯ in the first viola. This C♯ can be understood as the fifth of the dominant, and it forms also a strong association with the first statement of the melody (m. 1), where it appears in close proximity to its "root," and where it initiates a line in its own register. (Compare the accidentally similar role of the C♯ at the beginning of the Violin Concerto.)

In Ex. 12 I have used white notes to bring out the highest and lowest lines formed by the melody. These lines are shown as directing the movement of the melody toward its goals, while the inner lines are more ornamental in nature. They also, however, have a structure that supports the outer lines. It will be seen that the prevailing high point for the first half of the big phrase is B. The C♯ at the beginning is a neighboring tone to this, although it also serves to prepare the entrance of the C♯ in the viola at No. 23 by providing a still higher point of reference. It is, in addition, part of the three-note grouping which has been mentioned above in connection with the properties of the row, and which is undoubtedly being exploited here for its associative value. This grouping I have bracketed and marked "a." Finally, the C♯ may also be heard, especially in retrospect, not as a neighboring tone, but as the structural beginning of the line to F♯.

The descent of the upper line is interrupted just before its goal, which is withheld throughout the octave transfer down to the lower register, and supplied only at the cadence itself. The high A and G at m. 17 are, in other words, repeated in mm. 21 and 22, and resolved at m. 23. Meanwhile, an alternative A♯ and G♯ are thrust upward, having been hinted at first in mm. 17 and 19, and now made into something of a climax (at m. 22) just before the cadence. (These are identified by *NB*.) On one level they can be heard as ornamenting the cadential line, but on another level the meaning of these two notes will become clear when they, and their two immediate predecessors in m. 21, are compared with the viola melody which is to follow. This four-note motivic grouping, the last two notes being interchanged, forms a strong association, and is another binding force for the articulation of the phrases. This four-note group, together with its first appearance at the original register, is bracketed and labeled *A*.

The lower line moves from the initial F♯ at m. 1 through a prolonged E and a D to the C♯ of the viola melody, and needs no comment.[16] The manner in which the subsidiary lines elaborate and support these motions should be clear from the diagram. A tonicizing motive that consists of double neighboring tones converging by half-step on their goal, and the inversion of this motive, are labeled *c* and *ic* respectively.

[16] The prolongation of this E not only provides subdominant emphasis to balance the dominant at the cadence, but also bears out the implication of the E at the climax of the first phrase, which achieved its initial importance by serving as goal of the first linear movement (C♯-D♯-E). The constellation B-D♯-E which appears prominently during this prolongation (especially at m. 19) is related to "a" by inversion, since it constitutes the first three notes of the row-form I_6. Its instability of contour, however, prevents it from being heard as clearly motivic, in the sense that "a" is so heard.

The motive of the leap of a major seventh is labeled *b*, and achieves prominence because of its appearance at crucial points: the cadence of the first big phrase, the transposed and inverted appearance at the beginning of the second, and its final appearance in m. 19 as the vehicle of the octave transposition of the structural line.

Notes with dotted stems are to be interpreted as chromatic passing tones, while the interrupted bracket whose broken halves are terminated by dotted lines indicates that the motive *c* is interrupted and completed after an interpolation. Finally, the subsidiary diagram, Ex. 13, shows an enharmonic re-spelling of the cadential movement,

Ex. 13

to emphasize the relationships supporting F. In this case, the F, not the F♯, is interpreted as the goal; and again, the ambiguity is part of the integral impression. Ex. 14 attempts to summarize the lines

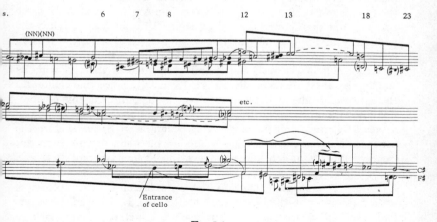

Ex. 14

formed by the accompaniment. After m. 11 the inner parts are not continued, and the outer parts are given in outline only, details being omitted. A more detailed diagram of the bass movement at the cadence is given in Ex. 15.

The upper part of the accompaniment moves chromatically from

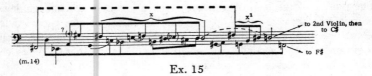

Ex. 15

B to the C♯, but is inflected by a new line beginning at m. 12, which descends from F, ultimately to the C at m. 20, which again illustrates the ambiguity. In relation to the goal of C♯, the C can be interpreted as B♯, but the line from the F gives it independence. The inner parts emphasize B♭, by descending from F to that point and remaining there. This B♭ is also shown as part of the bass line, where it is extensively tonicized, but ultimately is seen, with the preceding G♯ (m. 4), to converge on the A, which ultimately prepares the D at the cadence. This D is also foreshadowed by the D at the first cello entrance at m. 8. The resolution of this D to C♯, by the way, does not take place immediately, but is withheld until the second, foreshortened appearance of the motive in the first viola at m. 25. It, too, therefore, acquires some independence, especially in view of its extensive preparation by the bass. In this connection, note the treatment of the bass motion A-G♯-F♯ (mm. 12-14), which is repeated in m. 15 by the groups of two notes in triplet-meter. The A is repeated in the same register, but the G♯ and F♯ are transferred up an octave. Thus the ambiguity of the goal of this line is suggested: that is, the tension between the immediate goal of D, to which A is the dominant and starting point of the line, and the ultimate goal of the C♯, with its starting point G♯. Note finally, in Ex. 15, how the bass line elaborates the approach to the D (x) and then recalls the outline of this elaboration by means of the little figure in m. 21 (x¹), which now also serves as a tiny reminder of the area centered on B, just before the cadence. This has the effect, in my opinion, of enhancing the dominant force of the F♯, and helping to place the D in its perspective as a subordinate region.

These remarks and diagrams make no pretense to completeness or to infallibility in the interpretation of events. It is hoped, however, that they will prove useful in suggesting a method of approach to this music. Further study is indicated, particularly of the relation between melody and accompaniment, here discussed only in terms of their respective long-range goals. The details are subject to many more interpretations than the ones given here; the tracking down and accounting for their myriad implications would require the labors of a Sisyphus. For "a single note may be fraught with a hundred implications and embody a hundred relationships within a given work." In this attempt at exegesis I selected those relationships which seemed most clearly to suggest forward motion on a larger scale, toward goals which, either through the ear's prejudice or the composer's insistence, seemed most evident and audible.

The question will be raised whether the ear can retain and sort out a simultaneity of complexities such as those suggested here. One can only answer that the music is convincing, that it moves forward, and that its arrivals at and departures and from the phrase divisions carry conviction and seem to provide the requisite degree of contrast and continuity, movement and associative power, formal logic and expressive eloquence. These cannot be accounted for by row-manipulation alone; besides, the choice of register, dynamics, rhythmic values, etc., is clearly dictated by musical considerations which demand some method of study such as that suggested here.[17]

It is true that all the details of line manipulation are not consciously seized by the listener: but the broad design is apprehended, and a sense of the rightness of the details in relation to this design cannot but be intuitively felt. In listening to this music, one is immediately made aware of the presence of a forceful musical personality at work, who has full command over his resources. Here is unconventional music in the great tradition; here is pattern made to sing; here is movement in sound, expressing that which is noble.

"Is it not precisely the nature of art to transcend this fragmentary reality and to give it significance through synthesis—through the creation of a spiritual world in which 'the unattainable' in Goethe's words 'becomes event' and the fragments achieve a unity impossible in the real world? The significance thus attained is no doubt never a truly definitive one, but it is perhaps in still deeper sense the 'Innerste Ausdruck des Wesens' since it represents the creative embodiment of the most constant even if ultimately the vainest aspiration of mankind—that of transcending itself and approaching something like divinity. Is not art, therefore, significant precisely in so far as it is not fragmentary, and are not the greatest works of art those in which completeness, not so much of form as of range and depth and intensity, is most fully attained?"[8]

[17] Compare, for example, the studies by Brunswick (*MM*, May 1933, p. 182), and Cone (*MM*, April 1941, p. 159, and *MQ*, January 1957, p. 140).
[18] Roger Sessions (*MM*, January 1938, p. 128).

CONVERSATION WITH
ROGER SESSIONS

EDWARD T. CONE

CONE: Suppose we start out with something about your musical education. With whom did you study at Harvard?

SESSIONS: I took the regular course. I ought to go back a little behind that, though, because I started studying the piano when I was four years old. Then I went away to boarding school when I was nine. I didn't realize how much music meant to me until the summer of 1908 when, after having been at boarding school for two years, I began working at the piano with my mother again. That summer was a very decisive one for me, musically. I began to be tremendously absorbed in music. I was eleven years old at that time, and in the following year I began composing.

The year after that, 1910, I told my parents that I had decided to be a composer. I suppose they were a little anxious about such a decision and so, surreptitiously, they asked the advice of a lot of musicians, including Humperdinck, who was in New York at the time. My father was going to see Puccini but he didn't succeed. I heard, years later in Italy, that Puccini had told a story of having been asked to see the music of a young boy in America and to advise his parents whether he ought to go on with it. He paced the floor all night and decided he couldn't take that responsibility, so he called off the appointment. I don't know whether it was I or not but I assume it was, because Puccini did call off the appointment.

Incidentally, both Puccini and Humperdinck were in the United States for world premieres of contemporary works at the Metropolitan, which is an interesting historical fact. One was the *Girl of the Golden West* and the other one was a work by Humperdinck called *Koenigskinder*.

But the general report was favorable, and I was encouraged to study. But of course neither my parents nor I had any idea what was required. We asked some more advice and got some rather peculiar answers. Arnold Dolmetsch, whom I saw myself, advised me not to waste my time studying harmony but to study counterpoint, counterpoint, counterpoint. So since I couldn't get into a counterpoint course at Harvard without having passed harmony first, I studied some harmony over the summer, passed the harmony exam, and got into the counterpoint course.

CONE: Who gave that?

SESSIONS: Archibald Davison. And he was very good. The only trouble at Harvard was that in those days there was no thought of serious training for a professional musician. They were training cultured gentlemen rather than musicians. I didn't know this. I simply took the courses, and didn't take them, I regret to say, too seriously. I heard a tremendous amount of music during those years. I spent a lot of my father's money going to concerts and buying scores and all that sort of thing. I heard the Boston Symphony every week—sometimes two or three times a week—and I went to many other concerts.

Of course in those days one studied music by studying scores, by playing them on the piano, sometimes two-hands, sometimes four-hands. There were no records. So I did get really quite a knowledge of musical literature during that time.

But in my junior year, Edward Burlingame Hill, who was the member of the faculty that I knew the best, took me on a walk and said to me, somewhat confidentially—or I assumed that it was: "I want to tell you that we are not in a position here to give you what you need. I won't go into the reasons why." And he urged me very strongly to go after I graduated to France to study with Ravel.

CONE: What year would this be?

SESSIONS: That's the point. This was the spring of 1914, and so I didn't go to study with Ravel. Obviously I couldn't have. And in some ways I don't regret it at all. In fact I'm sure it was much better that I didn't; because in the first place I was eighteen years old, and I didn't know anything about the musical world except what I had gotten from going to concerts. I was quite shy—very shy, in fact—and I don't know at all how being precipitated into French musical life would have affected me. Anyway, it couldn't be, and so I followed the suggestion that I go to Yale and study with Horatio Parker. I liked Parker, and I had and still have great respect for him. The only thing is that the teaching at that time was not only extremely traditional but it was second-hand, so to speak, and also the general level was such that it would probably never have occurred to a teacher like Parker to give what he had it in him to give.

CONE: What composers, for example, were held up as the modern composers to emulate?

SESSIONS: They didn't talk much about modern composers. There was some interest in contemporary music, which meant Debussy and Strauss and oh, faintly shining on the horizon, Stravinsky and Schoenberg—Schoenberg a little more than Stravinsky, perhaps, although I'm not so sure. At that time the difference in age between Schoenberg and Stravinsky counted for much more than it does now. Schoenberg was an older man but a much more problematical one, perhaps; and furthermore, the whole trend in the United States was pro-French.

CONE: Was Parker himself pro-French rather than pro-German?

SESSIONS: No, not at all. But I wasn't very much aware of Parker's taste. He was a very sad man, really; this is the way I always think of him, as a very sad man, a very good musician, but very lonely. The day before Commencement, when I got my Bachelor of Music degree, I went to spend the evening with him. He was extremely nice and he said, "Well, don't ever spend more than four years in the same place. I'd have done much better if I hadn't spent so many years at Yale." Mrs. Parker said, "Oh, I don't think you would have composed any more." He said, "I didn't say I would have composed more, I said it would have been better."

I think he was discouraged and disillusioned; he had never been able to give to students what he wanted to give, and he'd sort of given up trying. He taught in an extremely traditional, conventional way, which wasn't always accepted very wholeheartedly by his students. But of course this was at a time when the traditional concepts of harmony were just dished out, without any critical examination of premises and without any explanations that would take one very far.

CONE: Did you do any free composition with him?

SESSIONS: Yes, sort of. And then we had a thesis. I started a symphony, and wrote one movement. That was my thesis, and I won a prize, the big prize at Yale, for it.

Then after I left Yale I got a job at Smith. We'd just entered the War. It was always a question as to whether I would be going or not. I was finally rejected because they were more fussy about eyes in those days than they have been since. But I went on writing this symphony. I had very big ideas for it when I got started; but I found that I didn't know really what I was doing, and I felt that I needed more teaching.

I didn't know exactly what I needed. I know that I started doing Cherubini's *Counterpoint*. It was strict counterpoint—perhaps not the best strict counterpoint—but it was strict and totally unlike anything. I had been taught.

CONE: How did you happen to find Cherubini? Did you find it on your own?

SESSIONS: I went to the library and looked around and here was a counterpoint book with the name Cherubini on it—a good name, after all. I studied the *Cours de Composition* by Vincent d'Indy. This seemed to be much more illuminating than anything that I had had. I didn't realize until later that it too was essentially very conventional, even if on a very different level. I mean, at least he looked at music. There was a long analysis, of a kind, of the *Hammerklavier* Sonata, which I studied very thoroughly. But the real reasons for things were still very elusive. And so I finally realized—this was in the fall of 1919—that I must have some advice.

There were other reasons. At Smith, the head of the department had already shown my symphony to Joseph Stransky, who was the conductor of the Philharmonic, and got him to agree to play it in Northampton and possibly in New York when it was finished. So I had an obligation of that kind; yet I realized that I probably ought not to finish it but should learn a little more about composition first, or at least have some absolutely first-class advice.

I wrote to Bloch in New York. I wrote to him because he was the only composer living in the United States at that time whose judgment I felt I could rely on, and whose advice would carry weight with the head of the department at Smith.

Meanwhile, I thought that I'd better get to know some of Bloch's music. It was just beginning to be published by Schirmer's and I sent for it and it arrived before I had Bloch's answer. (Things used to arrive very quickly in those days. If I ordered a work on Wednesday I'd have it on Friday, even in Northampton, Mass.) So I devoured these things, mainly his Psalms for soprano and orchestra, and for baritone and orchestra, and his First Quartet. I went down to see Bloch in a state of terrific enthusiasm; he treated me quite roughly. He sat me down at the piano and made me play the first movement of my symphony, and then he stood behind me and shouted the names of all the composers that I was influenced by. It happened that I knew that I was influenced by these composers so that, although I was a little disconcerted, I wasn't really fazed by it. It finally got so that I joined in with him just to show him what the situation really was.

Then he sat me down afterward and said, "Look, after all, every young man is influenced by other composers. But the important thing is that *you* must be there too. Now, you must make a big resolution: give up the symphony and work very hard for two years. And in two years you'll be able to do anything you want."

In order to get me started we analyzed the first eight measures of Opus 2, No. 1 of Beethoven, the F minor Sonata. And I must say that these ten or twenty minutes or however long it took to go through this were about the most important thing in my whole musical education, because of the way Bloch went at this. There was nothing very startling about it; but just showing how one thing led to another, how these harmonies, simple as they were, built up to an important rhythmic point, how the bass line went up the scale, how the motifs got shorter as the climax is approached—all this made sense for the first time. And I really, literally, thought to myself, "All that harmony that I studied does make sense after all."

CONE: Did he do any contemporary analysis at all?

SESSIONS: Not at all, no. We talked about Wagner, but we didn't do that kind of thorough analysis. His analysis was, generally speaking, along the lines of "classical form." And then later we talked about counterpoint. He didn't actually teach me any counterpoint, but he put me in a way to learn some counterpoint. He used Orlando di Lasso and other works of that period, which I knew already to a certain extent. I'd studied them by myself a little in connection with the d'Indy book.

At that first interview, Bloch had asked me, even before the "ordeal" at the piano, if I had ever studied the anatomy of music. He asked me if I had ever looked at music from the point of view of a conductor, or from the point of view of a composer. And his teaching showed me what he meant by that.

As you know, I later changed my ideas about the way to study counterpoint. I think certainly that it's very helpful and important to study composition by looking at works but I don't think that it's quite the right approach to deduce rules from these composers. Not that it's a bad approach—when I say it's not the right approach I mean that unless it's taught by a composer like Bloch, who was always a composer, not anything else, the issues can become confused.

CONE: Who put you on the track of Schenker's *Counterpoint*?

SESSIONS: This came much later. A very good friend and neighbor of mine in Florence named Victor Hammer, a German painter who'd known Schenker very well, told me about Schenker and I began reading his books. He spoke of Schenker with tremendous enthusiasm which I didn't quite understand. He was a conservative painter, and he and Schenker got together on that basis. I think what brought him and Schenker together was a general antagonism to contemporary art; but he persuaded me that there was something to be learned from Schenker, and I still think there is, provided one doesn't go the whole hog, Schenkeristically speaking.

CONE: To get back to Bloch, how long did you continue formal study with him?

SESSIONS: Well, I didn't have very much money. I was teaching at Smith and getting the princely salary of fifteen hundred dollars a year as an instructor and I married on that salary. So I went down from Northampton whenever I collected enough money to pay him, which I must say I did regularly. He always told me I was one of the very few of his pupils who always paid their bills regularly, which surprised me a good deal. But the lessons were very, very important to me. Two years after I went to him, I moved to Cleveland as his assistant. I didn't study formally after I got to Cleveland, in the fall of 1921, but I showed him my work.

After that first year in Cleveland I began to be once more very much aware that there were other composers in the world besides Bloch. During the summer of 1922, the orchestral scores of *Petrouchka* and *Le Sacre du printemps* were published, and I got to know them for the first time, though I had known the four-hand arrangements for nearly ten years. Do you know that four-hand arrangement of *Sacre*? It's very curiously printed. It doesn't give any indication of what the music is really like. I played it with Edward Burlingame Hill in 1914, so I had known it to a certain extent for all that time; but I was never sure that I understood it. When the orchestral score came out I realized that I did understand it. I mean, it was what I had hoped it was; and that had an enormous influence on me. Bloch didn't like that at all, for a number of reasons, some of which I can understand very well—from a human point of view; I don't understand them from a musical point of view. Of course the fact that I had this big enthusiasm didn't help matters at all. I could never sell Stravinsky to Bloch at that time. It came by itself many years later.

CONE: Were the atonal works of Schoenberg beginning to be known here then?

SESSIONS: Well, after all, I played for myself, at the piano, Op. 11 and Op. 19. I had heard the Five Orchestral Pieces in the fall of 1914 in Boston, and I was impressed to the point where I wanted to know them better. But they were much less accessible than Stravinsky was at that time. You understand that I had had no chance actually to hear any of these pieces except the Five Orchestral Pieces and the Quartet, Op. 7. I felt there were very beautiful things in both of them, but for the moment I thought they were beyond me—although I do think that *The Black Maskers*, which I wrote the winter after my experience with the score of the *Sacre du printemps*, has a certain influence of Schoenberg too. Of course, I was never quite totally sold on either Stravinsky or Schoenberg; but I felt for the moment that Stravinsky was the nearer to me of the two.

CONE: Were you already becoming aware of your own contemporaries at this point, of people like Copland and Piston?

SESSIONS: No, I didn't know anything about Copland or Piston until I went to Europe for the first time in 1924. I had a letter from Bloch to Nadia Boulanger.

CONE: Is this the source of the story that you studied with Nadia Boulanger?

SESSIONS: The fact that I went to see her quite often in Europe and I met people at her house—I suppose that's the source of it as much as anything. Actually I did have an idea at one time that I'd like to work with her, but she refused on the ground that I was a pupil of Bloch and didn't need to study with her. She was very scrupulous in this matter.

CONE: Can we go back a bit and discuss a subject that there's quite a bit of interest in today: the Copland-Sessions concerts? I say "interest today" because a great many people have heard and read about these concerts; but very few of us know how they were started, why they were started, and what was actually played at them.

SESSIONS: I have to say really that Aaron played much more of a part in this than I did, mainly because I wasn't living here, although when they actually started I was. I spent six months here in the spring of 1928, and during that period the first Copland-Sessions concert took place. Aaron lived in New York and for that reason was more active in organizing them. He found people who were interested in subsidizing and supporting them; my function was to give him moral support more than anything else. That's the most I can claim.

CONE: Did he choose most of the music?

SESSIONS: Not without consulting me, but of course when I went back to Europe that became more cumbersome. Three years later I said, "I think you should get somebody else to go on with this because I'm not doing my share."

CONE: They went on for three years?

SESSIONS: Yes. I suppose I'm partly responsible for the fact that they did stop.

CONE: Do you remember what pieces were played? Were they mainly American compositions?

SESSIONS: I think mainly, yes. My First Sonata was to be my contribution. Unfortunately I didn't finish it in time, but two movements were played in a first version; and Aaron's Pieces for String Quartet were played at the same concert. Then later on *The Black Maskers* was played in the original version.

CONE: Was that originally scored for chamber orchestra?

SESSIONS: Yes, it was scored for, I guess, five woodwinds, four brasses, piano, percussion, and strings.

CONE: This reminds me of another series of concerts which you sponsored just before or during the early days of the last war. How did that series come about?

SESSIONS: This was a joint venture of Mark Brunswick and Edward Steuermann and myself. I think those were about the most successful series of concerts of contemporary music that I was ever involved in. The three of us didn't always agree as to the works that were to be included, but we worked on the assumption that an unrelieved evening of contemporary music was less effective than contemporary mixed with other music. The plan of each concert was two contemporary works and between them some little-known work of a past composer.

CONE: Yes, I remember some Berlioz songs, "Nuits d'Été" probably, and the third "Leçon de Ténèbres" of Couperin.

SESSIONS: Also *En blanc et noir* of Debussy, and *The Hanging Gardens*. I believe we did the first American performance of the Stravinsky Concerto for Two Pianos. We did the *Lyric Suite*, I know. I remember my First Quartet was played at one concert, and the "Diary" pieces were done at another, and then there were some pieces of Steuermann's. I think there was some Bartók. And then the Scotch Songs of Haydn, "An die ferne Geliebte" of Beethoven which at that time was hardly ever performed.

CONE: I would like to ask you something about your own teaching in relation to your composing. I might start off by recalling something that Stravinsky said or wrote somewhere, that he thought it was a mistake for a composer to teach, that it inhibited his composition in some way. Would you like to comment on that?

SESSIONS: I don't quite see his point. After all, a great many composers of all kinds have taught. Bach taught, Haydn taught, Mozart taught. He had a quite well known pupil called Süssmayr. I don't know whether Beethoven taught.

CONE: Well, what Stravinsky was actually talking about is the situation of a composer in a university. He felt that the atmosphere of the university was not conducive to composition.

SESSIONS: I suppose he may have been talking a little out of his European background, where composition isn't taught at the university. I do have some thoughts on this subject, since I have been involved in it for the last thirty years, especially at Berkeley and at Princeton. But there's never been a moment in my teaching when I didn't feel completely free to do what I thought was necessary under the circumstances. I think this is the main point. If one can teach at the university on the same terms as one would teach anywhere else, then I don't see that there's any problem.

Lately though, I have felt that perhaps there is a problem at the university. This has nothing to do with Princeton as such or with Berkeley as such. I have felt that a conflict of a certain kind, a kind of hidden conflict, could arise, owing to the fact that the traditional basis of the university is the training of critics rather than composers. And I have felt that the emphasis on theory in the literal sense of the word, and on what goes under the general heading of musicology could lead to confusion in students' minds. Whether this is a phase in the working-out of the whole situation, or whether it's an unavoidable aspect of it that can't be changed, I don't know.

CONE: Do you find that the students you have now, as opposed to those you had ten to twenty years ago, are more likely to confuse the theoretical and scholastic approach with the purely compositional?

SESSIONS: I've found some who do, maybe because it's a different type of student that comes to study music now at the university. It may be a feature of the "compositorial explosion," so to speak. There weren't nearly so many people studying composition even thirty years ago as there are now. And so, by and large, one doesn't have so many exceptions nowadays as one used to. Numerically, perhaps, but not proportionately. Everything is more diffused. There are many more universities teaching composition.

Furthermore, the postwar movement in composition, in certain quarters, anyway, has laid much more stress on a certain kind of theoretical teaching in the purest sense of the word "theory." What we called theory in my day was simply harmony and counterpoint, which is not theory at all, it's craft. I think the danger today is that instead of craft, we have more and more theory, you see. I think that on the contrary the most important thing is to lay the overwhelming emphasis on craft. Craft can't arise out of theory, but I think theory, if it has any use at all, must arise out of craft.

I go back always again to what Bloch said: "In two years you'll be able to do anything you want." I think this is what craft really is. It's the aim of craft. The danger I see today among some young composers is that they learn to write one piece and keep on essentially writing one piece all their lives. They learn certain clichés and formulas; and if they ever had the independence and the imagination to want to do something else, they couldn't. When I say "do something else," I don't mean something less far-out at all; but without a very solid craft, and the self-confidence and assurance it brings, they are helpless. I've known cases of composers that are really quite well known, and not only American, who have found themselves in precisely that kind of dilemma. They felt that their music was becoming cliché-ridden, wedded to certain *procédés*, as the French would say, and found themselves caught in a trap. It's like a man who wants to write a book in a language that he hasn't fully learned. There are certain things that, when it comes to really fully expressing himself, he can't say.

CONE: Once, many years ago, you very cryptically remarked to me: "You really shouldn't be teaching students counterpoint; you should be teaching them moral philosophy; and unless you have that in common, you can't really teach them counterpoint."

SESSIONS: Did I say "moral philosophy"? The phrase sounds very unfamiliar. I think that I would say perhaps artistic philosophy. But I think they have to learn counterpoint anyway! I do find, in recent years especially, that the most important thing I can give my students is a certain attitude, which is very much that of a good craftsman. They should have music—that is, tones and rhythms and harmonies, all the materials of music—completely at their disposal. And then of course the necessity of being very serious—of putting everything they have into their work.

CONE: Well, these are moral attitudes, after all.

SESSIONS: Yes they are, just as in everything else. What I'm saying doesn't apply to music alone.

CONE: As far as your own compositions are concerned, do you think of them in terms of a division into any specific "periods"?

SESSIONS: Well, I haven't ever thought of it in precisely those terms. This is a little difficult to apply to one's own music. It's much easier to apply to somebody else's. But I suppose, perhaps, I do. I know for instance that after I had written *The Black Maskers* I went through a phase of appraisal. I was aware that there were some things that I wished I had been able to do in it, perhaps, that I hadn't been able to. I wanted to gain more flexibility in harmonic movement, for instance. This ties in a little with the period in which I wrote it. Of course some of my reflections, as I look back on them, seem quite unfair to this piece now. But one is always looking at it from a very personal point of view. I was a little disturbed that part of its interest seemed to be in the fact that it portrayed interesting states of mind; and I wanted to cultivate more solid virtues in my music. I suppose that was the way the whole neoclassic movement of music at that time presented itself to me, though I never thought of myself as being a devotee of neoclassicism, as such.

CONE: No, but I think the First Symphony and the First Sonata have often been referred to as neoclassic.

SESSIONS: Yes, they have, and those little organ pieces that I wrote at that time too. Naturally I was identified as that, from the outside much more than from the inside. As a matter of fact I felt in my First Sonata I began to move away from it, much more so in my Violin Concerto. Perhaps I moved away from it even more than I was aware of, as I look back at these works.

CONE: I think I've heard you refer to the Violin Concerto as a turning point.

SESSIONS: Perhaps, yes, although my First Sonata might be called a turning point too. And then with my First Quartet I was really very much surprised and even slightly dismayed to see myself writing the kind of music that I had to write but which was very different from my idea of myself at the time.

Another demarcation was a pause of four years between *The Trial of Lucullus* and my Second Quartet, although as I look back at my Second Symphony and my Second Piano Sonata I can see the connection very well. But at the time I felt the Second Quartet was a departure in my music.

Then my Quintet, written in 1958, I felt was a departure, too. I used the twelve-tone system in a much more thoroughgoing way than I'd used it before, although parts of my Solo Violin Sonata are pretty strictly twelve-tone. I think I became more aware of the full resources of the twelve-tone system from then on.

CONE: Do you look on your movement toward the twelve-tone system as a gradual one? Did you see it coming?

SESSIONS: Oh, very gradual. Other people saw it coming before I did. I remember Milton Babbitt asking me, after he saw my Second Sonata, "Do you realize you're on the brink of the twelve-tone system?" But it was a very gradual development. I'm very glad it was.

CONE: Can you, looking back, see why it should have occurred, why it was inevitable?

SESSIONS: Oh, I suppose so. I think that I was tending in that direction all the time, from my First Quartet on, perhaps. But I remember a talk I had with Dallapiccola in 1952. He spoke of having come to it very gradually himself, and I said, "I doubt whether I ever will use it. After all I'm fifty-five years old, and it's a little late in the day for me to turn around and adopt an entirely new technique." Of course it was in the following winter that I wrote my Solo Violin Sonata! As a result of the fact that the opening theme contained twelve different tones, and seemed to go naturally on that basis, I caught myself using the twelve-tone system.

I wasn't going to say anything about it to anybody. But when Andrew Imbrie saw it for the first time, he looked at it and counted, "One, two, three, four, five, six, seven, eight, nine, ten, eleven, twelve." Then he read it and he said, "But it's still your music." I said, "Well, of course, it's still my music. If it weren't my music I wouldn't have any business to do that."

Of course I've always felt that much too much has been made of the system as such. Naturally, no system is in itself nearly so important as some of the proponents of serialism have wanted to make it.

CONE: I remember before you were writing twelve-tone, you often used to say that not only did you hear all of your own music as tonal in a certain sense but also that you heard even Schoenberg's twelve-tone music as tonal in a certain sense.

SESSIONS: Yes, if I could extend that remark a little, I'd say it still—you've got to remember—*in a certain sense*. I had this out with Schoenberg once, too. Well, I can't say I had it out, exactly. I told him that the first movement of his Fourth Quartet suggested to me at moments the key of D minor. He said, "Yes, but it's not D minor at all. What you're hearing are relationships between the notes and you associate that with tonality, but that isn't all tonality is—it's a great deal more than that." I got his point immediately. Of course he was right.

The only thing is, there are people who think that in order for a piece to be really atonal you should not be able to hear any tonal relationship between the notes. I think such hearing is unavoidable. The minute you know a piece you hear these relationships, and of course if one's been brought up on tonality the temptation is to define them in tonal terms, although such definition holds only on the most primitive level. I might have said to Schoenberg, "But your first notes are D, C♯, and A." (We didn't carry the conversation this far, obviously, because I knew what he meant.) He could have said, "Well, haven't I got a right to have a row beginning with D, C♯, and A?" These things are unavoidable. There's no row possible in the world that one can't hear tonally.

CONE: I suppose what he meant was that if you're speaking of tonality in the proper sense of the word, you're referring to a system which exists outside the individual piece in question, whereas in his pieces, whatever feeling of key is evoked, appears only by the internal relationships of that piece alone.

SESSIONS: Yes, of course, but in a sense that is true of all music.

CONE: But if you hear the Ninth Symphony in D minor, you're quite properly relating that piece to a lot of pieces in D minor, because they have certain progressions in common. Schoenberg's Quartet does not have any of these progressions in common with classical pieces in D minor.

SESSIONS: Exactly. I think really the point is, is tonality the basis of the structure of the piece? But I object to the absolute distinction that some people make between tonal music and nontonal music. I don't think that there is a clear distinction. You can say that such and such a piece by Haydn is tonal and that such and such a piece by Schoenberg or Webern is not tonal; but there are an awful lot of pieces between! Where does the one thing end and where does the other begin? What real sense does this distinction make, except for the fact that you can talk about certain music in terms of keys, and that you learn a very great deal about these pieces if you do talk about them in terms of keys? You can't talk about certain other pieces in terms of keys and learn much about them. In other words, I think these are useful classifications and only their utility or nonutility is the criterion of their validity.

CONE: What about the question of cadences in music of this kind? One can certainly find convincing cadences in twelve-tone music.

SESSIONS: You've got to have cadences, otherwise you don't have any articulation. I would insist that the cadences in classical music are very individual too. I'm not denying that there is a basic pattern; but there is much more than that in a cadence in, let's say, *Falstaff* or the C♯ Minor Quartet. The individual aspects are what give the music its life.

CONE: What takes the place of the harmonic definition of a classical cadence?

SESSIONS: I think a lot of things. The movement of the outer voices, certainly. The rhythmic flow, sometimes the curve of the line, sometimes something in the instrumental scheme or in the sonority. A composer today must himself be aware, and then cause the listener to be aware, of a close of some kind, a rhythmic articulation at this point. There are innumerable ways of doing that, of course. After all, in classical music, you can have IV, V, I in the middle of a phrase and yet you know that it's the middle of the phrase.

CONE: In other words, the rhythmic aspects are probably more important in defining a cadence than the harmonic.

SESSIONS: I would say all the aspects together. But one can never tell in advance what will work in a specific place. One can only tell what *has* worked. Then, if one has pupils, one can say to them, "Something of this sort *might* work."

CONE: You said that in the case of the Violin Sonata, you arrived at the row simply by realizing that the melody at the beginning was indeed a row. Is this the way you arrived at most of your tone rows?

Or do you sometimes compose them in advance with certain structural characteristics in mind?

SESSIONS: I never do that. In fact, I don't really see the sense in doing that. I might to this extent: after having had an opening musical idea, I might still work on it from the standpoint of row structure. So perhaps what I said before is not strictly accurate. I'm not sure that it was entirely accurate in the case of the Sonata. I just don't remember. I almost always work with a symmetrical row, or a row which can easily be modified in such a way that it becomes a symmetrical row, and I tend to work, first of all, with trichords. For instance, an original musical idea was the basis of the row in *Montezuma*. It is, in the very first measure of the piece, divided into trichords. Now, you can pair these trichords. There are three possible combinations: you can group I and II together, or I and III together, or I and IV together. If you take I and III together, or I and IV together, you can generate a complete symmetrical row. If you take I and II together, the row isn't symmetrical. This gives a lot of leeway. However, a good deal of that I discovered in the course of the work. I forget just at what point I became aware of what I was doing.

CONE: But actually your sketches go back many years before you were working twelve-tone at all.

SESSIONS: Exactly.

CONE: Then you must work out a row primarily with its thematic possibilities in mind, rather than its combinatorial or structural possibilities.

SESSIONS: I don't see the sense of the latter at all, because if one has a conception of the work as such, that must arise from something that has some character at the beginning. Otherwise it's a question of finding a nice row, and then writing a piece as a result of the row. This I just don't get at all; I can't see that much can result from that.

CONE: Well, couldn't you see how Berg, for example, might want an all-interval row and therefore worked out one to use in writing the *Lyric Suite*?

SESSIONS: Oh yes, but I think he had a conception of the *Lyric Suite* beforehand. I am very chary of the concept of "pre-composition." I think the composition starts, or it should start, with the beginning. I don't quite see looking for a good row without some idea of what it is going to be good for. This idea of pre-composition suggests precisely that. Now here's a good row, what am I going to do with it? Well now, by what criteria is this a good row? I don't think there is any such thing in the abstract. I think that some rows are good for one thing, and others are good for something else. One has to find a row that's good for what one wants. In that sense it's got to come out of some musical impulse.

CONE: Do you see yourself as, so to speak, writing twelve-tone compositions from here on, or could you as easily slip out of it as you slipped into it?

SESSIONS: Well, of course, you might say—and I suppose a lot of people would agree—that there are moments when I slip out of it. I wouldn't agree with that myself, and I don't see that one can essentially "slip out." But I think that one's relation to it can change; in fact, I think it's almost bound to, provided one goes on writing new pieces all the time. I would feel very uncomfortable writing essentially the same piece a second time. However, one can easily get to the point where the row in a certain sense isn't necessary any more. I think Schoenberg very often did. But the row is still there, and it's one of the resources one has.

CONE: You mean it's not necessary in detail?

SESSIONS: No, it's not necessary in detail. I don't think it should be, any more than, or still less than, the key in tonal music is always necessary. There are frequently places even in classical music where the key is in the background rather than in the foreground. I've talked a great deal about the beginning of Beethoven's Opus 59, No. 3. For many years this was supposed to be vague. Well, of course, it isn't vague at all—it's only vague from a very, very pedantic conception of the key; it's not vague for a minute musically. It doesn't, so to speak, "express" anything vague. But any deviation, such as you find constantly in classical music, from the key in its most literal form, is a departure from the key. I feel that many things can be done in twelve-tone music, with even more simple justification than that, that are not strictly under the primitive rules of the system.

CONE: I am going to ask you a question which I will phrase in such a way that it applies to Schoenberg; but, as you will realize, it could probably also be applied to your own music. But perhaps you will feel a little freer about answering it if I apply it to Schoenberg's music: what is your reaction to the criticism that you often read now in certain advanced circles that Schoenberg's twelve-tone music is really a kind of mixed bag, and that he is still trying to apply a new harmonic system to an outmoded rhythmic and formal structure? (By formal I mean phrase-structure, rhythm in the largest sense, not just the fact that he may use sonata-form.) Does Schoenberg employ nineteenth-century methods from which the post-Webern school has since freed twelve-tone music?

SESSIONS: I could say a great deal about that. Naturally I've thought about it a good deal, and I'm perfectly willing to answer it in relation to my music, too. In the first place I would say that this raises criteria which are completely irrelevant. I don't think historical, much less pseudo-historical, criteria are artistic criteria at all. Secondly, I would say that Schoenberg didn't ever use the sonata-form in any real sense of the word. I think the sonata-form has been given very rough definitions that have very often missed the essentials. In fact, one of the essentials of the sonata-form is tonal structure. It is an absolutely ironbound, built-in condition of the sonata-form; if you don't have the tonal structure, you don't have the sonata-form.

CONE: What about the whole question of the general phrase-structure, the rhetoric, so to speak, the fact that his music is still built on antecedent and consequent, on cadential phrase-structure, and so forth, which, as you know, many present-day composers are trying to get away from?

SESSIONS: This seems pedantic to me. Antecedent-consequent phrase-structure means you have two phrases in an idea. And why is it worse to have two phrases in an idea, or more "nineteenth century," than to have one phrase in an idea?

CONE: Then the answer might be, "Let's have no phrase."

SESSIONS: Then you don't have any articulation. Of course this depends on one's definition of a phrase. I think a lot of these things are based on a confusion between generalities and particulars.

The confusion lies in the application of historical, or quasi- or pseudo-historical criteria to matters that are strictly artistic. I think this is part of a general lack of security nowadays. People want to find justification and explanation for everything. This would be my answer in a nutshell. I would like to be much more precise about these things, but the things themselves aren't very precise. Who is to say with authority what belongs to the nineteenth century and what belongs to the twentieth century?

Remember one thing: Schoenberg was a giant, and therefore he is hard to place in any historical category. Webern, to my mind a much lesser figure, is for that reason much easier to handle. I think that is why he is in higher favor among certain circles now.

CONE: Have you yourself ever serialized any other aspects of your music than pitch?

SESSIONS: Not really, no. There's one place, in one work of mine, where I did this for fun and in a rather satirical spirit. I won't say where it is.

Quite seriously, of course, any composer can do anything of this kind or anything else he wants to do as a specific case; but as a principle it makes no sense at all. To try to serialize rhythmic elements is possible, but as a very special case. It's more of a tour de force than anything else, like some of the pieces in the *Musikalisches Opfer*—a game, which a very great master like Bach could play very well! So well, in fact, that the result is more than a tour de force.

CONE: Will you tell me, not for publication, where you have done this?

SESSIONS: Of course. It's. . . .

June 16, 1965

TO THE EDITOR

ROGER SESSIONS

THE QUESTION of the education—or, as I would prefer to put it, training —of the composer is, in my opinion, today much cluttered up with a quantity of extraneous matter which tends to confuse or even to obliterate the central issue. A good part of this confusion may certainly be traced back to a traditional system of teaching which had not only become frozen in its essentially cut-and-dried treatment of materials, but had also and with still graver consequences, taken its basic assumptions so much for granted that they had finally become desiccated to the point of sheer abstraction, devoid of relevant content.

Consider, for example, the word "form" as it is often still used, both in theory and in practice. Fortunately the practice has remained in many cases superior to the theory. Nevertheless, "form" is still much too often conceived in terms of "forms," either frozen from the distant or immediate past, or postulated for the (strictly speaking, nonexistent!) "present," or "future," as a *Ding an sich;* all too seldom is it conceived as an outgrowth of musical ideas themselves, in their immediate and dynamic aspects, and the growth of these ideas in the mind and will of the composer.

Many times, for instance, I have been asked by young and inexperienced composers whether a given formal scheme, thought out and planned in advance of its eventual musical content, will "work." But such a question can only be answered by the composer himself, in terms of specific musical material and the way he treats it—it makes no sense whatever in any other terms at all. If it is really a musical idea—one which has its origin in tones and rhythms concretely imagined and "heard"—it may have some value to him, and in that case it is up to him to realize it in such a manner that it does "work"; otherwise the scheme itself is, to say the least, premature.

This brings us already to what I have elsewhere referred to as the central issue,[1] which is that of craftsmanship. This is a better word than "technique," in my opinion; the latter, through many associations, is too easily confused with the idea of gadgetry, which is precisely the opposite of genuine craftsmanship. In any case, craftsmanship is nothing more nor less than the ability to cope, successfully and with assurance, with any

[1] See "Conversation with Roger Sessions," above.

108

problem with which a composer may be confronted. This would seem so obvious as to be hardly worth saying. While no analogy is perfect, the analogy with the knowledge of a language in which one aspires to be a writer is as nearly apt as an analogy can well be. One cannot expect to achieve "style" on any level whatever unless one can speak as well as write easily and fluently, and above all with precision at all levels; and no amount of rationalization can possibly gainsay this necessity. A composer, like a writer or anyone who makes, constructs, discovers or creates in any field whatever, needs to acquire precision, fluency, and resourcefulness in the highest degree. Only on that basis can he move with assurance in any direction he may choose, and recognize—through experience—the technical problems he will have to face, and discover the means of solving them.

All this is, or should be, obvious enough; but we are today surrounded by such a tropical luxuriance of verbiage that it is sometimes difficult to see through the foliage to the bare facts of life. The point is that an art is, first of all, and to an overwhelming degree, a craft; and that a craft is mastered through prolonged practice—not through theory or "learning" in the usual sense.

So, what can be taught, and to what elements do the above remarks apply?

Obviously, the aptitudes on which ultimate quality depends—imagination, invention, vitality, daring, temperament—cannot be taught; and while a teacher can and should certainly communicate attitudes toward music, and no doubt will communicate enthusiasms which he himself feels, his primary function is not that of teaching his pupil to write "great" or even "good" or "interesting" music. This of course cannot be taught, and such an aim could easily, and often does, interfere with the primary task of the teacher, which is purely and simply that of teaching him to write: that is, to use the materials at hand with precision and assurance. He is teaching *composition,* not literature or aesthetics or, in any real sense, theory; and in my opinion he can teach effectively only to the extent that he keeps the goal of craftsmanship, and the practice by which this is developed, constantly before his own mind and that of his pupils. This has to be emphasized for a number of reasons, of which one important one is an all too prevalent tendency of today to crowd a number of disparate objects into one pedagogical package. If it is kept in mind that the single goal of instruction is the pupil's resourcefulness and independence (which can only be achieved through mastery) in the actual *handling of materials,* not that of learning rules or theories or imitating "styles," one need not concern oneself unduly about methods. The teacher's function is above all that of keeping before his pupil's mind the real demands of his craft, pointing out to him, as far as possible, the most efficient means by which he may learn to meet these demands; and then, following with helpfully critical attention his actual progress in meeting them. When, and to the extent that, the pupil begins to possess real security with his medium and the assurance that this brings, his teacher will become less and less a "teacher" in the full sense of the word, and more and more a (let us hope) understanding and sympathetic adviser.

To pass on to more specific matters: an aspiring composer must understand, from the beginning and always thereafter, that nothing he does or "learns" can be of any real value except insofar as he has formed the habit of complete accuracy of both outer and inner hearing. This applies, of course, not only to tones, but to note values, rests, articulation, rhythmic pattern, tone color, dynamic nuance—everything, in fact, that reaches the ear of the listener, and in terms of actual media, not of abstract ones. One of the most persistent problems, and certainly the most crucial one, that one encounters in teaching composition is sloppiness and lack of precision in this respect—a lack of what I have sometimes called "musical realism." No doubt this situation is today complicated by elements peculiar to the present period; but the problem itself is not at all a complicated one, and one would not even think of mentioning it if one were not quite frequently confronted with instances—sometimes neatly rationalized, but nevertheless patent—in which the composer's intentions, as indicated on paper, do not correspond to what one actually hears, or to anything that even an ideal performance could "bring out."

In regard to this point, careful meticulous training, beginning as early as possible, can certainly be helpful. But vital above all, in this as in many other areas, are the habits which the student must himself form. He must learn, that is, to reach the point where he will imagine, or in other words, "inwardly hear," musical sounds, rhythms, and the rest, with the utmost immediacy, precision, and vividness; where he will envisage musical symbols and musical concepts in these terms just as automatically as he translates a written word into the sound of that word as pronounced. Only insofar as he does this, do the symbols have any meaning.

To be sure, what we call the "musical ear" embraces a number of related but clearly distinguishable abilities, which may be unequally present in the same individual. A "good ear," in terms of musicianship, is not simply the ability to identify sounds, rhythms, and musical patterns accurately. It is not simply the ability to read music and inwardly hear it. It includes also the ability to coordinate sounds and patterns of sound, even on a very far-flung scale; and, of course, for the composer, to conceive and construct them, with precision and clarity. This "inner ear" is of course the composer's principal domain, and eventually it can become almost or even in a sense wholly independent of the outer ear, as the obvious example of the late Beethoven demonstrates. A composer who is also a performer should understand very well what this implies. He knows that, as well as learning and knowing his own and other music from the inside, he has to study it as a performer, which means, in terms of precise hearing from the *outside*, as it were, as well. This means, in simpler terms, not only knowing exactly what he wants, but how to achieve it in terms of performance, which—and this is my real point— is not quite the same thing. The composer needs some experience in dealing with the actual process of projecting music, as well as hearing it inwardly. Certainly, for composers, the inner ear is, and must be, paramount; and the stories of composers—even very eminent, even great ones—who in conducting their own works fail to notice that the clarinet is playing in B♭ rather than the prescribed A, or that the cello in a given passage is playing in the bass instead of the tenor clef—such anecdotes are quite believable if not necessarily always true. They mean exactly nothing in terms of the aural capacities of the composers in question; they indicate only that at the precise moment involved the composer's attention is focused inwardly rather than outwardly, most likely perhaps on some other moment or phase of the performance itself. In a similar sense composers frequently develop the ability to remain quite oblivious of the sounds around them (even at less rewarding moments in the concert hall or the opera house!) and pursue their own musical trains of thought, inwardly listening to tones, rhythms, phrases, which have no conceivable connection with the live sounds being emitted all around them. There is nothing very mysterious about this, after all; most people are able to carry on a connected and even very serious conversation in a noisy restaurant or waiting-room provided their attention is not compellingly demanded elsewhere. In any case, I find it important for the composer to have at least some experience as a performer. This is simply a part of his training in artistic realism, of which I have already spoken.

There is little that a teacher can do in regard to the training of a composer's ear, beyond making clear the demands involved and stressing the fact that the necessary faculties are to be acquired only by practice and experience. No doubt certain "innate" qualities are in some degree necessary, or at least helpful. But the possession of these "innate" qualities does not in any sense presuppose or guarantee musical ability —nor can either the former or the latter be measured in terms of the other. All of the faculties I have described must be acquired by the composer, for they are the elementary "tools of his trade." They are still only "tools"; we must really grow out of the superstition that "genius" or "talent" can be determined or measured in terms of anything short of real achievement. But the composer cannot get along without the possession of these abilities, in the highest possible degree; and he needs to cultivate them to the point where they become, as it were, second nature.

The earliest stage in the composer's specific training must obviously consist in a thorough mastery of the elementary materials of which music is made, and a resulting awareness of the effects which can be produced by those materials. By "thorough mastery" is meant the ability to use them not only with precision but with ease and assurance; to be able to do with them whatever one chooses, and not to be limited in one's choice either by lack of fluency, or by imperfect awareness of every element involved, or by imprecision at any level whatever. Obviously I am talking about counterpoint and harmony, or in other words elementary practice in the "horizontal" and "vertical" dimensions, respectively. Let us not labor here the terms "vertical," "horizontal," or even "elementary"— they are quite sufficient for our present purposes. One begins with harmony and counterpoint as distinct disciplines because they represent— on the elementary level—distinguishable aspects of musical movement, and present, on the same level, distinguishable problems. They are more easily grasped at this stage if the problems proper to the one are for the time being eliminated as far as possible from the study of the other. These are exercises in ultimate precision. Not only is the habit of precision most easily formed in the early stages of any craft, but it is most easily and efficiently attained if one has only one problem to worry about at a time.

One might strongly emphasize, however, that the disciplines of counterpoint and harmony, for the composer or for any other practical musician, are not a matter of "learning the rules" or of studying "styles." It is a question of mastering a craft in the only way that a craft can be mastered—that is to say, through *practice*. Obviously, and not only for our time but for centuries past, the "rules" have been neither binding nor, as such, relevant, outside the elementary discipline itself. But within the discipline, they serve a twofold pedagogical purpose. First of all, they provide logical limitations to the materials involved, reducing to a minimum the exigencies of context, thereby confronting the student only with problems which he can handle easily and on a quasi-objective basis. Secondly, they accustom him to awareness of some of the most common pitfalls; at the same time they furnish him with ready means of avoiding these, and eventually, therefore, the means of recognizing the contexts in which they are no longer to be considered as pitfalls, and therefore not to be avoided. In other words, counterpoint and harmony are practical disciplines and can be mastered only through practice, both intense and prolonged. In no real sense can or should they be considered as "theory," to be "learned" in the usual sense.

Undoubtedly, however, they are today almost always begun at a much later age than they should be. The fact that there is no ready means in sight by which this situation can be improved is no excuse for ignoring the problem. By the time a young musician's tastes and predilections begin to take on a definite shape, he should have all of this behind him. As things are today, a very large number of our young composers begin this elementary training at a time when they have already gained —as indeed they should have done by the age of eighteen or twenty— a certain degree of sophistication regarding music and the musical world; but in all except the rarest cases they have acquired little or no awareness of what the composer's craft entails. In some cases they may have attempted composition of a more or less ambitious kind. They may quite possibly have worked seriously at an instrument and learned that real mastery demands years of practice and even drudgery for several hours a day, in order to gain an indispensable degree of precision and coordination. If a serious student of composition has gone through this experience, he should be able to grasp more readily the need for a comparable effort on the part of one who aspires to compose. After all, at least as much is demanded of one who makes music as of one who performs it.

Obviously, this parallel is not quite exact; it is quite true that the element of physical coordination is not in a direct sense a part of a composer's problem. But the latter on the other hand has plenty of other things to think about, if only because it is for him to discover and imagine, in the clearest terms, what the performer is later to reproduce. In terms of his own elementary training—his harmony and counterpoint—he is obliged to acquire the same degree of precision and ease that his performing colleague acquires with his scales, arpeggios, and other basic exercises.

The logical and the most effective time for all of these disciplines is as soon as possible after a young person begins to show any inclination toward music—which should mean, in childhood. A child has the time to take them slowly and absorb them gradually and will be induced by his budding interest in music to value the sense of achievement which they can give him. It is, on the other hand, very difficult for the eighteen- or twenty-year-old to understand why all this is necessary— and one can certainly sympathize, even while thoroughly disagreeing. If he has not already acquired the assurance and precision that only a real mastery of the elements can give him, he is in the position of one whose immediate aspirations have outstripped his equipment; and he may easily tend to shy away from, and to undervalue, all of those problems and situations—unfortunately often the most fundamental and

ultimately the most difficult—which he is not equipped to cope with
effectively. He is quite likely to resist both inwardly and outwardly the
drudgery, the boredom, and above all the time, involved in acquiring
what he needs. If it is brought to his attention that virtually every composer of significance has gone through this training as a matter of course,
he is still quite likely to remain unimpressed. He may easily waste a
good deal of energy looking for short cuts which, since this is a matter of
craft and not of theory or information or "style," simply do not exist.
His understanding is not encouraged or facilitated by the persistence, in
our country, of certain vestiges of a cultural colonialism, which lags in
recognizing the composer fully as a man of potential achievement "here
and now," romanticizes the nature of his gifts and therefore undervalues
both his real gifts and his craft, and consequently ignores what is required of him. I am not implying that these attitudes themselves per-
sist, but rather various preconceptions derived from them. The fact that
"success" of a temporary nature is sometimes achieved by works in
which the craft is imprecise and uncertain, compounds the situation.
The problem, however, remains. If the composer is to avoid becoming
—and remaining, at least to some degree—the slave of his own technical limitations, he has to learn to overcome them; and he can do this
most efficiently by beginning at the beginning.

I suppose it is fairly clear from the above that when I speak of
"counterpoint and harmony," I am referring primarily to "strict counterpoint" and what is known as "functional" or "traditional" harmony;
for it is only the materials generally understood under these terms which
fully satisfy the requirements that I have postulated. The usual arguments against such study may be summarized in a general way under
two headings: they are considered either a waste of time or part of a
hidden conspiracy to tie the student to the past. To the former of these
objections I have already given my basic answers; the latter deserves
some further comment. Obviously one of the main purposes of an
artist's education, and even in a broad sense the whole purpose, is to
liberate the student—assuming that he wishes to be liberated—from
"the past": not only his own past, but that of the craft of the composer
in general. The purpose is, once more, to help him to be the master of
his musical materials, not the victim of his own helplessness regarding
them.

Like many of the words in common and unfortunately careless usage
today, the word "tradition" has come to embrace offshoots of very
varied and often contradictory character, and a great deal of loose thinking results. There is no inherent reson why "tradition" should be an
unmitigatedly dirty word; one can counter Mahler's dictum *Tradition ist
Schlamperei*, which was eminently true in its original context, with

Picasso's "Well, you see, everyone has to have a father." One might even in this connection recall that the Oedipus legend is just as "traditional" as that of Orestes! In any case, the "present" is ineluctably the consequence of the "past"; and if a craft is to be learned at all, the beginnings will inevitably be found somewhere in the "past," whether that of yesterday, last month, or at any point previously. That is why I do not find the cited objection a serious one, even if it had not always proven wrong in fact. The crux of the matter is a structural, not a "historical" matter. It is quite true, for instance, that "strict counterpoint" corresponds, though very roughly indeed, with "sixteenth-century" or "Palestrina" counterpoint, and was invented, presumably by Fux in the early eighteenth century, as an introduction to the "learned" style. But its utility to the young composer of today, and to those of many years past, has nothing to do with any "style," learned or otherwise. It is simply a convenient and practical way of introducing a young musician to a set of problems with which he will be confronted, in increasingly refined form, throughout his career as a composer; and of presenting these problems to him at the outset in their simplest form. If it is preferable to so-called "Bach counterpoint," it is simply because the latter is founded on thorough-bass, on harmonic structure, which itself presupposed, in Bach's day, a mastery of voice-leading, as it were, in the abstract. The same is true, in even greater measure, of polyphony as actually practiced by any composer since Bach's time.

It is for this reason that some intensive work in what is generally known as "strict composition" and "fugue" is important to the developing composer. Of course, it is not really "composition" at all; and whatever we choose to call it, it should not be considered as essentially creative activity. The point is that what the student is doing in harmonizing chorales, writing "minuets," "rondos," "sonata movements," "fugues," "inventions," etc., is simply combining the results he has gained by systematic practice with elementary materials, into some kind of organic shape; he is not working in the "style" of Bach or of any composer, but simply, as it were, putting sentences, paragraphs, and topics together coherently and bringing his acquired craft into working order. "Composition," then, if you like, and even "style" of a kind; but of a category quite different from the styles of composers who were working with the total range of materials available to them, and pushing those materials, without inhibition, as far as the impulse toward real musical expression demanded. Style, in the real sense of the word, is after all predicated on this state of affairs; the composer is free to do anything he wishes and to follow his musical impulses wherever they may lead him. The student of "strict composition" is obviously not doing anything of the sort; he is learning to handle materials constructively, and with real fluency.

No doubt, a genuinely gifted composer will reveal his gifts in everything he does; experience has abundantly shown me that, even in strict counterpoint exercises, a real composer will somehow produce results of a kind that those written by an ungifted one, however correct, do not. This will be still clearer in the case of exercises in "strict composition." Some compositional element will inevitably be present, certainly, if it is present in the musical nature of the pupil; and a sense of "style," or consistency, already present in the mere choice of materials, is certainly to be cultivated. The work done should be, in other words, presentable in every respect, here as everywhere else. But at this stage the student is first of all solving specific problems; and his energy must, once more, be directed primarily toward gaining fluency and assurance in his craft.

One must, of course, emphasize strongly that, here as everywhere else, it is not a question of what a student has "taken" or "studied," but of what he can do. In this connection one must obviously refer back to the individual teacher, who should be in a position not only to judge the student's prowess, but to adapt his teaching to the latter's real need. I do not at all rule out the possibility of a method of teaching through which a student could learn his craft by means other than those I have indicated. I would still insist, however, that a composer in the fullest sense of the word is one who has the whole range of known musical possibilities within his comparatively easy grasp, and who therefore is free to choose to do whatever he likes, with full assurance. If the student is lucky enough or perspicacious enough to pursue his studies in close contact with a teacher who is both a real master of his craft and genuinely interested in his student's work, the precise means or methods of teaching are of little or no importance. While the principle of apprenticeship, on which the training of young artists and musicians was based for many centuries in the past, has virtually ceased to exist in present-day or even relatively modern times, I think it still represents the most valuable and efficacious kind of training a young composer can have; and I find certain educational tendencies of today a matter of concern in this respect. I shall return to this subject presently, as it seems to me of increasing importance as a student's development progresses.

Subject to the qualifications at which I have just hinted, it seems clear to me, both logically and practically, that the study of counterpoint should precede that of harmony. While "harmony" for me not only means training in the use of "chords," but eventually includes everything which has to do with the relationships between tones, it must presuppose some ability to handle voices; furthermore, it seems to me that, unlike the discipline of strict counterpoint, it can and should be pursued up to the point where the materials involved begin to pose the questions with which our own century has been confronted—which means, up to the point where "harmonic" problems begin to merge with questions of style and composition. Harmony should, even from the beginning, be so taught as to embrace questions of form and movement, as well as to accustom the pupil to clear and precise application of his knowledge of voice-leading to situations more complex and qualified than those he has encountered in his strict contrapuntal studies. Eventually the point will come where the terms "harmony" and "counterpoint"—essentially abstractions, adopted consciously for legitimate pedagogical purposes, but nevertheless quite artificial—no longer serve any useful purpose. They must at this point give way to consideration of a total musical context, and to a large extent one created by the pupil himself. This brings us to a new set of problems, which I shall try to discuss in some kind of order.

It is at this point, for instance, that the question of "atonality" begins to be acute, and a precise critical examination of its implication is in my opinion quite indispensable. The disadvantages of both the term and the concept have been repeatedly pointed out; and it is curious that, in a period like ours which prides itself on its scientific approach to intellectual problems, a term which has the built-in imprecision of any purely negative concept—which originated as a journalistic term of reproach, and was taken over as a slogan—should have persisted as a concept even though the term itself has become obsolete. As I and others have pointed out elsewhere, the fuzziness of the concept is matched by a lack of clear definition in the prevalent usage of the term "tonality."

To be sure, the controversy itself is by this time essentially obsolete. I do not remember whether the term "atonality" was current as long ago as 1911, but the idea most certainly was; and I would not even be discussing it here did I not feel that, for purely pedagogical reasons, it still must be clarified. The essential point is that "atonality" not only came *after* "tonality" but that it was the result of developments inherent in the very nature of tonality itself.

There is in fact a very fundamental point at issue here; and it is, again, not at all a matter of "history" in the usual sense of the word. "Tonality" is not a "closed" system; both its dawn and its twilight were long, drawn-out processes, in which exact lines of demarcation are necessarily arbitrary, and exist, if at all, only in the realm of theory. For theoretical purposes, however, it has often been regarded as a closed system; and in this issue lies both the original motivation of the term "atonality" and whatever rationale it can be logically claimed to possess.

Though this raises both intellectual questions and questions in the realm of criticism, which are far from being always clearly faced, it is not that which is relevant here. The line of development, as far as the musical vocabulary is concerned, is clear enough. The adoption of the tempered system, the proliferation of even sharper harmonic contrasts, the increasingly bold use of "harmonic alteration" and the gradually developing "independence" of the resultant combinations: not only did these and other pertinent developments take place under the sign of tonality, they were the result of impulses inherent in that principle itself. For the crucial aspect of tonality was not simply or perhaps even primarily the discovery and exploitation of functional relationships within the key, but the possibility of shifting these relationships from one locality to another, thus achieving a new dimension of contrast, and thereby a vastly larger area of musical operations than had hitherto been possible. It is in fact the reaching out of the musical ear for this constantly larger area, both in terms of extension and of expressive intensity, that has led to the "technical" developments in question. This is all abundantly documented—as is the massive raising of eyebrows in certain quarters, at each successive stage of the process.

Now, obviously I am not attempting to maintain that "tonality" as hitherto defined is, or should be, still with us. I am emphasizing the *continuum* of which the principle of tonality, as applied rather than as ever formulated, was a phase, as was also the development beyond tonality. The *continuum* is nothing more or less than that of ever-accruing auditory experience; and the problems at issue are to be resolved by the development of the musical ear alone, not by hypothesis and theory, and least of all through sloganizing. In other words, I feel that at this late date nothing but wasted time results from laboring these principles as such. I find it futile and misleading to argue, for instance, whether one is "hearing" "tonally" or "atonally"—still less, whether one *should* "hear" in this or that manner, or to concern oneself with what are sometimes called "tonal references" in manifestly non-tonal contexts, or to identify other than strictly harmonic matters with "tonality" or its absence. Any conceivable succession or combination of tones can be heard as "tonal," in virtually any sense one wishes, if one provides it with the proper context, either in one's imagination or otherwise. The only relevant factor is the actual context of the passage in question and the specific use the composer has made of it. It is of course the task of the composer to make his contexts quite clear, and that of the listener to become aware of the inner logic of the music—in its own terms, and not with reference to something outside the music, unless such reference may clearly impose itself as the result of an evident intent on the composer's part.

To sum up: tonality and "atonality" are not opposing principles in any sense whatever, but successive phases in the evolution of the Western musical ear, the latter being the clear product of the development of the former. But while tonality constituted, over the course of nearly three centuries, the principal basis of musical design, no such claim can be made for "atonality" for the simple reason that, as a purely negative concept, it possesses in itself no constructive implications.

It is quite obvious, however, that strong constructive elements are manifest in the best of the music which we call "atonal." But their clear and adequate theoretical formulation lies still in the future. I am of course not forgetting the possibilities inherent in the serial principle, as well as other developments; but these developments and possibilities, for all the verbiage that is constantly expended on them, remain still in the empirical phase of development. The solution of the problem is, in other words, to be achieved by the composer only on the basis of a sure instinct and a solid background of musical experience—of a total awareness and mastery of the means at his disposal. Of course this has always been true; the composers of the past were not thinking in terms of theoretical dogma any more than are those of today. What they and their contemporaries did possess were general terms in which everything that went on in their music could be more or less adequately discussed. Even this was much more true of certain periods than of others. I doubt whether it was really true, for instance, in the time of Monteverdi. Today we can—and do—discuss procedures, but we have not yet found the terms in which we can adequately generalize about musical effect.

I have dwelt on this subject at considerable length in order to illustrate some of the pitfalls inherent in the present vogue of "analysis" as an independent and self-contained musical discipline. Having as a teacher insisted and even fought for the importance of close and accurate observation of what actually transpires in the course of a piece of music, I cannot, I suppose, be suspected of opposition to analysis as such. In practice today, "analysis" often seems to go far beyond this, not only into the realm of purely speculative dogmatism and even snobbery, but into that of a kind of virtuosistic intoxication with detection for its own sake, often regardless of the relevance or even the actual existence, from a musical standpoint, of what is "discovered," or, in current analytical jargon, "heard" by the analyst. A little experience is quite sufficient to show that one can "hear" anything that one sets out to hear.

Naturally I am calling attention to a problematical aspect of "analysis" as it is sometimes practised, and not aiming barbed shafts at musical analysts either in general or, so far as I am aware, in particular. I am, however, expressing a strong and fundamental conviction regarding the training of the young composer. He can derive vast benefit from learning to observe how music is put together by a master craftsman, provided he be encouraged to make his own observations—certainly, with some guidance from an experienced teacher: to observe, for in-

stance, contrasts of greater and lesser importance; the articulative elements which throw these into relief; the rhythmic structure in terms of
motifs, phrases, and larger sections, or whatever elements go into the
making of the music in question—anything, in fact, that the composer
has clearly indicated and which seems clearly relevant to the structural
flow of the music. Above all, he must learn—once again—to be aware
of these things *auditorily,* and to discriminate by auditory absorption, so
to speak, between what is most essential and what is less so, or non-
essential, irrelevant, or merely problematical. What he has to gain by
this, of course, is not only intimate knowledge of the works in question,
and a keener sense of what it is really to know music, but a sharpened
sense of musical consequence, movement, and structure.

"Analysis" which goes beyond this may certainly be of interest to
him, as to anyone who cares for music. However, it is of the utmost importance that he never become confused in regard to the basic difference between the creative and the analytical process. This unfortunately
has to be emphasized today because of a very prevalent tendency to
seek a kind of pseudo-security in a process of constant "rational" justification and to dismiss, under the term "intuitive," whatever is not
immediately explicable in such terms. Thus I have known instances in
which young composers have wasted considerable energy in trying to
produce an *Urlinie* according to prescriptions derived from the theories
of Schenker; or who have been seriously disturbed to find themselves
writing music which seemed right to them according to their own
musical instincts, but which they could not check according to what
they had been led to regard as criteria. It cannot be too much emphasized that the only genuine security an artist can find is in the knowledge of what he wants, in terms of his art, and in getting it, by whatever means he has at his disposal. It follows that first of all he has to
learn to trust his own ear, his musical instinct, and his musical imagination, as developed by experience, as the court of final appeal. By no
other means can he discover his own criteria, or can he develop the
boldness which is a *sine qua non* of significant artistic achievement. The
basically analytical, rationalized approach to composition is the essence
of academicism, whether of the "left" or of the "right," and the result
can scarcely be other than academic, timid, and sterile.

Of course I am talking here about basic attitudes, not passing a
priori judgments; and basic attitudes in art are often very elusive,
sometimes even to those who hold them. My point is, I hope, clear; it
is simply that a student of composition should not be allowed to forget that
his primary task is to discover his own musical identity, to discover the
music which he, in the most direct and immediate sense, wants to bring

into existence. He should therefore not be encouraged to make demands on himself which are essentially dogmatic, premature, or otherwise irrelevant to that process.

I cannot in fact refrain from reiterating here that the ultimate goal of a composer's musical training is to liberate his talents and his creative personality, not to indoctrinate him to or from any specific point of view. His craft must be such as to allow him the freedom to pursue with assurance any direction he himself may choose to take; and his teacher should be neither surprised nor disturbed if, in the process of self-discovery, the pupil seems sometimes or even frequently to shift his direction. This does not happen in all cases, of course; but it can be a normal sequence in any process of growth. The teacher's role then becomes one which challenges his powers of tact, discretion, and sympathetic imagination to the utmost; for there is little he can do other than to make available to his younger or less experienced colleague whatever he himself has learned, keeping the exigencies of fully adequate craftsmanship before the latter, while exerting no pressure whatever on him to go the same way, or to prevent him, as the case may be, from going in a directly opposite one. The crux of the matter is that music, first and above all, must have a *face,* and unless it is going to remain at best in the category of the merely "typical" or "generic" its face can be none other than that of its creator. I am deliberately avoiding the word "style" which is very frequently misused to apply precisely to the "typical," and often in the most superficial sense—*Die Zauberflöte,* we are sometimes told, is a "hopeless" mixture of "styles"! Needless to point out, it possesses at every moment the unmistakable features of Mozart. While I would willingly concede that to cite the mature masterpiece of a Mozart in the midst of a discussion of the composer's process of self-discovery has its problematical aspects, I can think of no clearer illustration of my meaning at this point. What I have called the "face" which music should possess is the result of imagination, craft, experience, and above all involvement (obviously in Mozart's case, all in a supreme degree). It is not at all a matter of "techniques" or "genres," or the like. Neither is it a matter of "avoiding influences," which cannot in any case be avoided, or even of striving for "novelty" or "originality" as such. These, if they become major preoccupations, are essentially desperate measures which at the very best can never work except in the most temporary sense. What constitutes a "face," "personality," "character," or originality in any sense whatever derives from positive elements, qualities that are present in the music, and not from negative ones. It is a question of fully digesting everything—including "influences," which are always present—and making it wholly one's own.

The application of all of this to the teacher is obvious. In my opinion, no one can possibly be a good teacher of composition if he attempts or wishes to mold the style of his pupils in any way further than that of helping them to envisage and become aware of the problems in their own work, and if necessary suggesting lines along which the solutions might possibly be found. In such cases it is indispensable that the ultimate solution be at least as satisfactory to the pupil as to the teacher. Otherwise, the problem has not been really solved, nor has the pupil really learned anything.

At the same time, I still believe that the best training a composer can have, certainly at the "advanced" but quite possibly at every level, will be that derived from close association with a single teacher. This mode of study is not particularly in vogue today, for a number of reasons too involved to discuss here. But a young composer who is in the early stages of his development is almost certain to derive more benefit from association with an older colleague who takes a real interest in him, and with whom he can talk freely and informally about his own problems, about music and musical questions in general, and about many other matters not so obviously connected with music, than from almost any other single source. Experience of this sort is likely to teach him far more about the actual process of composing than anything he can learn in a classroom; for obviously this kind of contact between teacher and pupil is so much more immediate and so much less constrained by the inevitable limitations of classroom work. This is no doubt also true of other subjects than music; but once again the analogy of instrumental or vocal study occurs to one. The more individual and fruitful dialogue, and even to some extent collaboration, that a young artist can have with an experienced older musician, the better. I believe also that in general it is better that the greater and more important part of a young musician's study should be done with one rather than with several teachers. For one thing, less time will be wasted in "adjustment"; for another, I believe more is learned, in the early stages of a composer's development, by reacting strongly and profoundly to one personality—whether *for* or *against,* and generally a mixture of both—than by the ultimately much less challenging process of dealing with advice—often conflicting—from various sources, and most likely coping in depth with none of them. However, this last observation, like most generalities, is subject to obvious qualification, and at any point in a discussion of this kind it is plausible to stop and demand whether a real musical gift will not instinctively seek and find the soil that offers it the most nourishment. I am sure that many a musician who has acquired a reputation as a teacher finds himself frequently asking himself what his teaching really consists in, and questioning whether it has not been simply his good fortune to have had gifted and stimulating young musicians around him.

It may have been noticed that I have said nothing regarding systematic instruction in the serial technique or in other methods or techniques in present vogue. My omission has been intentional; I don't feel that this is a part of a composition teacher's business. In this I am in full agreement with the point of view of Arnold Schoenberg, who always insisted that such methods are for the composer, young or old, to discover for himself. Since the time during which Schoenberg was teaching, years have passed, and many arguments have been heard, both pro and con. The key word on the subject seems to me to have been said by Schoenberg himself. On being told by Darius Milhaud, just after the Second World War, that the dodecaphonic technique was much in vogue among the younger French composers, he replied with the question "Do they succeed in writing some *music* with it?" In other words, I believe that, as a matter of course, a teacher should encourage his students to familiarize themselves with the works of composers who have used the dodecaphonic method, as with all music of the last half-century, and adopt it themselves as they see fit. But they will find their own ways best if they do this as the result of their own inclinations toward music and the urge—call it curiosity, or involvement, or what you like—to gain from music whatever experiences it has to offer. Naturally the teacher should be ready to help them in any direction they desire; but his overriding preoccupation should be with musically convincing *results,* not with methods. Perhaps the essence of the matter is that by the time the young composer has arrived at the point where he can think of using the materials and methods of today, he has gotten well beyond the stage of exercises in "strict composition," and must be encouraged to make his own explorations and his own decisions.

I have also said nothing thus far about the necessity for a knowledge of "musical literature." Certainly such knowledge is an essential part of the equipment of every composer, young or old, and, in fact, of every full-fledged musician. But I might just as well add that every musician —and composers above all—of real distinction whom I have ever known has been a man or woman of outstanding general culture. Such knowledge is not the result of training, but of profound inclination. As someone once remarked, "one does not *memorize* a work like the Eroica Symphony, one *knows* it." A knowledge of musical literature should be a matter of course, "not," as has also been said, "of courses." Knowledge in depth, moreover, is what really counts; one does not know a work simply by hearing it a few times, or even by having "analyzed" it; one must have taken it into one's inner life, experienced it, and reacted vitally to it, strongly and repeatedly, to the point where it has become, as it were, a part of oneself. If a would-be composer has not had this experience with quite a considerable amount of music, it is difficult to imagine that he will accomplish much. But this is something that no kind or degree of instruction can give him; it is an inherent habit which he must have acquired spontaneously and as a by-product of the kind of musical involvement he needs to have if he is eventually to create anything of significance. To be sure, this to some degree presupposes opportunities, economic and otherwise; but the strong inclination must be there.

What I have outlined indicates the requirements, as I see them, for a composer who has set no limits on what he wishes to achieve. Obviously, many composers have achieved considerable "success" and reputation on palpably less than what I have outlined as minimum requirements. In a very few cases I would certainly be among the first to acclaim these achievements as significant in the most real sense. I suppose the case of Mussorgsky is the most striking of these. The stories one sometimes hears about Schubert (and some of his well-intentioned friends!) and Wagner, for instance, are quite baseless; neither of them was at any moment helpless in any sense of the word. But the whole history of *Boris Godounov* and the various revisions it has undergone, as well as the specific type of weakness one frequently finds in Mussorgsky's other work, is as good an illustration as I could ask—above all because of his enormous gift— of what I have tried to convey here. Obviously there have been many musicians of far greater "competence" than Mussorgsky whose contribution to music can in no way be said to match his. But it is of no value whatever to point out, for instance, that Rimsky-Korsakoff's version of *Boris* robs the work of much of its character and its musical force. This seems to me quite evident, and I cannot imagine disagreement from anyone who has witnessed the opera in a version closer to the original. But this would be true even if Rimsky's musical invention had been the equal of Mussorgsky's. Only Mussorgsky himself could have really "improved" his work. What is relevant here is that one finds Mussorgsky at certain points helpless; if he had not been, there would at no time have been any question of "revising" his work. It would have been completely realized, totally "itself," as are at least a number of his smaller works, and not to be tinkered with by any musician in his senses. The point is that Mussorgsky's craft *was* defective, and the only relevant, if unanswerable, question is what he might have achieved if this had not been the case.

A COMPOSER'S INFLUENCES

ERNST KRENEK

To ASCERTAIN and evaluate the influences that might have caused a creative artist to orient himself in certain directions and to make decisions that would determine his own course as well as that of his art (provided he is himself in a position to emanate influence) is a difficult task, because the presence or absence of influence is, like all matters of history, not verifiable through experiment. Faced with the evidence of what has happened, we will never know what might have happened if some elements contributing to the actual result of the process had been different. Although it may appear obvious that certain phases in a composer's growth were caused by influences to which he was exposed, we can never be sure whether he would not have turned in the same direction without those circumstances.

Within the narrower realm of the *métier,* of technical procedure, it is, on the whole, possible to trace influence with a far greater degree of certainty than it can be when dealing with matters of style and general orientation. All of these aspects will most frequently coincide in the case of the apprentice who is obviously influenced by the master from whom he not only learns his craft, but who also is the most vividly present model of achievement asserting itself with authority. One usually recognizes as a good teacher one who does not try to impress his own image upon the receptive minds of his students; I, for one, have always tried to maintain this goal in my own teaching, although I could not always prevent my students from imitating some of my idiosyncracies. But influence is not only passively received, it is also, consciously or not, sought after. The beginner, however, will sooner or later try to branch out in a direction different from that prevailing in his teacher's studio.

In my own case, I remember that during my third year at the State Academy of Music in Vienna (1918) I came upon the *Lineare Kontrapunkt* by Ernst Kurth. It had probably been received by the school library as a reference copy and passed on to my teacher, Franz Schreker, as concerning his department. He admitted having never looked at it and, at my request, let me borrow it. I read the disquisition of the Austrian-Swiss musicologist with rapt attention, and it turned my entire musical orientation inside out. I was fascinated by the notion that music was not just a vague symbolization of *Gefuehl* instinctively conjured up into pleasant sounding matter, but a precisely planned reflection of an autonomous system of streams of energy materialized in carefully controlled tonal patterns. Thus, when I moved to Berlin two years later, I was ready to be further "influenced" by the "radical" tenets of Busoni, Schnabel, Erdmann, Scherchen, and others whose orientation was related to Kurth's basic philosophy; and the concatenation of influences ultimately led me to the "progressive" movement of atonality. I reported this to Dr. Kurth when I was introduced to him in Berne another two years later and was surprised to find that he was shocked by such an interpretation of his trend of thought. Kurth, it seems, had had nothing more in mind than a novel exegesis of the Bach style and had very little esteem for our "new" music—which may serve as an anecdotal footnote on how the concept of influence is seen from the angle of its generator *malgré lui,* who may be totally unaware of and even unsympathetic to what he happens to be generating.

Within these same limits of technical manipulation separated from its external meaning, influence may also be the fruit of challenge. More frequently than he might care to admit, a composer is tempted to try his hand at a new technical procedure, not because he has noticed that it was particularly productive of material success, but rather the opposite: he is attracted by its esoteric traits, whose mystery he craves to share with the initiated. Here it might be useful to distinguish between influence and motivation, which may interchangeably act as cause or effect. When a composer is motivated to turn to an advanced technique by the challenge confronting him, he will expose himself to the influence of the originators and practitioners of that technique. On the other hand, the influence emanating from a strong personality may motivate a composer to direct his creative efforts into similar channels.

In reality, it is hardly possible to maintain such neat distinctions. When I decided, in the late Twenties, to make use of the twelve-tone technique, the factor of challenge as described here was certainly a very important motivating element. But there were others. Few transformations of compositional style and technique can be fully explained without considering influences from far outside the field of music. Thus, when in 1924 or so I turned from the atonal style I had adopted so eagerly a few years before, first to the neoclassical posturing of the Baroque concerto, and shortly afterwards to the neoromantic attitudes displayed in *Jonny spielt auf* and the song cycle of the *Reisebuch,* the first move was touched off by the exhilarating experience of Stravinsky's *Pulcinella* and by my contacts with the seemingly carefree, unspeculative, straightforward music of my French contemporaries. Needless to say, I was moved to take note of these characteristics in the first place because I was inwardly ready to be swayed in a similar direction and only waited to find a proper influence. The second step was more gradually prepared by my discovery, through my great friend, Eduard Erdmann, of the marvels of Franz Schubert.

In neither case was a purely technical challenge decisively significant. These moves were retrospective and led to a revival of traditional procedure. The motivating influence came from the outside world; the increasing awareness of the problematical position of modern music in contemporary society generated a desire to reassess the social function of music. A preoccupation with sociological matters dominated the Twenties and produced a neoclassicism based on the illusion that a return to the stylistic characteristics of Baroque music would somehow restore the happy rapport between music and its recipients that had supposedly existed in earlier times. Undoubtedly, the contemporary attempts to integrate jazz elements into "art" music were prompted by the same desire to establish music as a vehicle of widely intelligible communication. The diligent exploitation of folkloric materials that was pursued among all tribes civilized enough to notate a five-eighths bar was dedicated to the same purpose, as were the numerous species of *Gebrauchsmusik,* from the melancholy recorder exercises for Boy Scout bands to the heroic marching songs of socialist realism, and, on a much more sophisticated level, the dramatic essays of Brecht and Weill, in which communication was meant to induce action.

This raises the question of the influence of politics on music. Since music as such does not denote concrete objects or concepts, as pictorial or literary representation does, but attaches itself to extra-musical content only through verbalized marginalia such as titles, mottos, programs, or sung texts, music free of such connotation is on the whole left alone by politicians who eagerly scrutinize literature, painting, and sculpture for tokens of subversion. This does not mean that the composer remains, or wishes to remain, unaffected by political developments. Direct influence from that quarter may be relatively trivial, perhaps driving a composer into exile when he becomes aware that the bloodhounds are closing in on him, not because of a few dissonances too many in his latest opus, but because he has expressed himself in words against the master of the hunt. The indirect influence may be more considerable.

To return to my personal experience: the awakening of my interest in the twelve-tone technique, which was internally plausible as a result of both my exhaustion of the resources available from manipulating neoclassical and neoromantic clichés, and my discovery of the challenge offered by the new technical procedure, coincided with my increasing disgust over the rise of totalitarianism. Seen in this light, my adoption of the musical technique that the tyrants hated most of all may be interpreted as an expression of protest and thus a result of their influence. The case was slightly more complicated, since I linked my bid for artistic freedom with a reassertion of my faith in the dogmatic systematism of the Roman Catholic Church, in which I grew up. I spent much intellectual effort on constructing a sort of mystical affinity between the *philosophia perennis* of the Aquinate and the universalism of dodecaphonic organization. Thus my first work in the newly acquired technique was the opera *Charles V*, explicitly anti-Nazi, pro-Austrian and Catholic. My most uncompromising twelve-tone works of that period, the Sixth String Quartet and the Piano Variations, were written in 1936 and 1937.

Personal influences, perhaps of particularly high significance, are even less susceptible of precise definition than other impulses, because they result from contingencies that vary unpredictably from one individual to the next. Analysis will bring them into line with the over-all image of a personality. But this is a kind of historical interpretation whose validity is debatable. If accepted, it will be called "objective."

If this passage has a relativistic appearance, this probably reflects a basic trait of my mental make-up. In my formative years at the end of World War I and through most of the Twenties, I shared the skeptical attitudes that prevailed after the collapse of the old order, and to which I have returned to some extent, but on a different level, in recent years. The most durable influence on my thinking at that time came from Karl Kraus, the Viennese poet and satirist, whose one-man magazine, *Die Fackel*, I began to read in 1917. A true satirist, he was never committed to any established philosophy, political or otherwise. He attacked right and left with beautiful impartiality and equal vehemence, not, however, out of blasé, aimless spite, but because anything entangled with the contaminating realities of modern civilization was found wanting when measured by his very simple, but exceedingly demanding ethical standards. At that time I was mainly impressed by the splendid isolation of a great mind dwelling in aggressive disdain above the jungle of controversy and dealing out brilliant invective as he went. While Kraus's unsurpassed dialectical prose has strongly influenced my German writings, his relation to music was limited to boundless enthusiasm for Offenbach, so that no direct influence could transpire in that field. But his philosophy of language and poetry was close to my thinking about the autonomy of music, which remained intact even during the period of heteronomous *Gebrauchsmusik*. In maintaining both, apparently contradictory, tendencies, I found support in the German philosopher and musician, T. W. Adorno, who stressed the relevance of social criticism as much as he promoted independent, advanced musical thinking. Musical autonomy, though not in a progressive sense, was also emphasized by the little known, but very original Swiss theorist and philosopher, E. G. Wolff, with whom I had been associated for many years.

The question of the extent to which external circumstances and environment influence creative activity has special relevance, since so many noteworthy composers of our time have had to live through protracted periods of formidable social upheaval, or to emigrate to foreign countries. At face value, traces of such influence are surprisingly faint, especially when such crises and transplantations occurred during a composer's maturity. Without external evidence, it would be just as difficult to determine whether Schoenberg had composed his Fourth String Quartet in Europe or in America, or Webern his Second Cantata before Hitler or during the war, as it would be to infer whether a work by Beethoven was written before or after Napoleon's downfall.

On the other hand, whenever we observe nuances in a composer's style that might be ascribed to his changed circumstances—such as various gestures of compromise in works by composers who settled in America —we are again confronted with the unanswerable question of whether these might not have occurred anyway as a result of intrinsic development. At any rate, instances of changes so drastic that they clearly indicate extraneous influence are very rare.

The intransigency characteristic of my own management of the twelve-tone technique during my preoccupation with religious absolutes culminated in my *Lamentatio Jeremiae Prophetae,* which I composed four years after coming to America. This work was influenced by the war situation insofar as it was written with utter disregard of practicality of execution, since performances then appeared to be even less likely than usual. (After fifteen years, the work was found still very difficult, but feasible.) Whether the subsequent relaxation of my compositional technique and of my general frame of mind was prompted by inhaling the American intellectual climate, or a natural reaction against former attitudes (a backswing such as I had experienced before) is really not determinable.

Since before my immigration to America I had not been active as a teacher, it might be wondered whether ten years of intense academic work here have influenced my creative work. Undoubtedly, the study of music history has left visible traces in some of my works, since I derived various ideas for novel treatment of the tone row and for basic serial manipulation from insights gathered in historical research.

Perhaps a more subtle connection between contemporary music and the academic life is the obvious influence of scientific attitudes on composers. In some circles the attachment to science has become a sort of status symbol, and strenuous efforts are made to demonstrate its existence; but the evidence produced is frequently dubious and sometimes even faked. We are reminded of Oswald Spengler's prediction forty years ago that the true representative of our age will be the engineer and that the artist will become obsolete. Perhaps some artists fear that he was right and attempt to demonstrate that they really are engineers, in order to be assured of a *raison d'etre*.

At any rate, the very nature of the twelve-tone technique and its further development into serialism inevitably leads to a mathematical style of reasoning, and the operation of electronic sound apparatus induces scientific and technical interest. Whatever the inspiration derived from such studies, it is different from the romantic adulation of the grandeur of machinery that the futurists inaugurated. The fact that we are able to fill the heavens with containers of complicated gadgetry is impressive, but far less fascinating than the mysterious theory that made it possible. The composer dreams that the image of the universe as outlined in the concepts of Einstein's relativity, Heisenberg's principle of indeterminacy, Planck's quantum theory or Schroedinger's wave equations is somehow reflected and sublimated in his complex serial manipulations of musical atoms, although they do not require much beyond junior-college mathematics.

If the composer's inclination to depend on precise computation and strict over-all control is the tribute for protection exacted by Science, his attitude may be interpreted as a desperate surrender of his prerogative as a sovereign creator relying on the powers of imagination, a reduction of its infinite possibilities to the trivia of verifiable fact. But just as modern science seems to approach areas where the hard and fast relationships of old are transfigured into referential patterns having unforeseen properties, music organized under the influence of such thought processes moves on to new imaginative potentialities which might not have been visualized without experience of the scientific influence.

CONVERSATION WITH
AARON COPLAND

EDWARD T. CONE

E.T.C.: There is a frequently quoted legend to the effect that the name Copland originated on Ellis Island, when an immigration officer misunderstood your father's pronunciation of Kaplan. Is that true?

A.C.: I'm not sure I know the real answer. My father did not come directly from Russia to the U.S.; he probably didn't have enough money to make the trip all the way, a typical situation in those days. In such cases Scotland, especially Glasgow, was a known stopping-over place. You had enough money to get from Lithuania (where he started) to Glasgow, and then you got a job there and earned enough money to go on to the U.S. So my father was in Scotland for about two or three years.

In 1964, when I was conducting in Glasgow, I noticed that there were more Coplands in the telephone book spelt without an *e* than with an *e*. One of the reasons, it seemed to me, was that *o* in Scotland is pronounced like *u*. They don't say Scotland, they say Scutland. And they would say Cupland, not Copland. In Glasgow everybody called me Cupland; and to this day David Adams, who is the European head of Boosey & Hawkes, and who is Scottish, always refers to me as Cupland. Now if you pronounce the name Kaplan in a Jewish or Russian way, you get almost exactly the same sound, and I suspect that the transliteration was made there in Scotland, and that my father simply took the spelling they gave him.

E.T.C.: Then the story about the immigration officer is a myth?

A.C.: I guess it is—I might have started it myself. This idea about Scotland only struck me when I was told there, "Your name isn't spelt peculiarly from our standpoint; it's more usual than the other way."

I might add here that nobody in our family ever, to my knowledge, mentioned the name Kaplan to me. The first time it occurred to me that the name might originally have been Kaplan was when I went to visit my grandfather, who was the last of the family to be brought over. Of seven children, my father had been the first to come, and he gradually brought over all the others, one at a time. His parents were the last to leave the old country. When I was taken to visit them, I was astonished to see on their name-plate the name Kaplan. At that moment I realized that this must have been the original name.

E.T.C.: Were you brought up as an Orthodox Jew?

A.C.: Well, my father was president of the oldest synagogue in Brooklyn —it used to be off Court Street, down near Borough Hall. I was born on Washington Avenue, possibly half an hour away, so it wasn't a question of going there every Saturday; but on the High Holidays, naturally, we went. Nevertheless I can't say it was anything more than a conventional religious association.

E.T.C.: Were you Bar Mitzvah?

A.C.: Oh, yes, it was a big affair! I never mastered Hebrew properly, though. I merely learned how to read it, with only a hazy understanding of its meaning. I'm sorry to say I can't speak a word of it today.

E.T.C.: What was Rubin Goldmark like as a teacher?

A.C.: He was top man of his time for composition,—everybody studied with him. With the founding of the Juilliard School he was named head of the Composition Department, although I studied with him before Juilliard existed. He was recommended to me by my piano teacher, Leopold Wolfsohn, with whom I studied for about four years in Brooklyn. When I was about seventeen, I decided that I needed harmony lessons. (I had begun by trying to study harmony through a correspondence course, but that didn't work.) When I went to see Goldmark, I realized that I was going to a highly recommended man who must be pretty good.

He *was* good—what he knew he knew very well indeed. *His* Stravinsky was Wagner: he had gone up and down the country giving lectures on Wagner's operas. But he had very little sympathy with or understanding for contemporary music, so that it would have been useless for me to hope to get anything from him on that score. We went through regular harmony and counterpoint. His be-all and end-all was the sonata-form. You hadn't finished your studies, he thought, until you could write a proper sonata in three movements with the first and second themes and developments all in the right places.

E.T.C.: Have you kept those exercises?

A.C.: Yes, I have. I have the Sonata still—it's awful. Just what you'd expect, and I knew at the time it wasn't very good.

E.T.C.: Were you writing your own music on the side?

A.C.: Yes, I was. I brought him my innocent little *Cat and Mouse* piece. He said, "I can't tell you anything about this. I don't understand how you go about it or what the harmonies are all about."

The Cat and the Mouse was rather like Debussy. It still sells rather well—about a thousand copies a year! Durand published it, a fact of which I was very proud. Monsieur Durand himself heard me play it at the graduation exercises at Fontainebleau that first summer. He came backstage and said he liked it and asked me to come to see him in Paris. And when I did, he took the piece. That was the first thing I ever had published, and the exciting thing to me was that it was Debussy's publisher who had accepted it. I still remember the thrill of that—you know, seeing that familiar Durand cover on my first published piece!

E.T.C.: At what point did you feel that you needed something that Goldmark couldn't give you?

A.C.: I had been thinking about France from the time I was eighteen or nineteen. In those days, it was clear that you had to be "finished" in Europe. You couldn't be "finished" in America. Remember that I was an adolescent during the First World War, when Germany and German music were very unpopular. The new thing in music was Debussy and Ravel—also Scriabin. (I was very Scriabin-conscious in those days.) It seemed obvious that if you went to Europe you would want to study in France. Also I had met an older fellow, a Johns Hopkins graduate named Aaron Schaffer, who had gone there just after the war, in 1918. (He lived in Baltimore and later became the head of the Romance Languages Department at the University of Texas. He died a few years ago.) He was a strong influence for France, because he went to study at the Sorbonne, and wrote fiery letters about all the wonderful things he was hearing in the concert halls. Germany seemed like that old-fashioned place where composers used to study music in Leipzig. All the new things seemed to be coming from Paris—even before I knew the name of Stravinsky.

E.T.C.: This seems to have remained a lifelong prejudice with you.

A.C.: I suppose it has sort of stuck. I did spend the summer of 1922 in Berlin, though. You know who told me to go there? Boulanger! She felt I should have some contact with German musical culture. The following year I spent the summer of 1923 in Vienna. In that way I tried to counterbalance my strong French orientation.

E.T.C.: How did you find out about Nadia Boulanger? You didn't go to her straightaway, did you?

A.C.: No, I certainly didn't. I had never heard of her. It was by sheer chance that I learned about the establishment of the Fontainebleau school. This was its first year, 1921. I read about it in *Musical America*, of all places. I was excited about the idea of having somewhere specific to go—after all, I didn't know anybody in France, and I was hesitant at the age of twenty to go there cold. The idea that a school was being started in the summer, just for Americans, made me think that in that way I might have the chance to get to meet more people. I headed for the school's office in New York so fast that they told me I was the very first student to sign up.

I was very lucky to have gone there. I studied with Paul Vidal. He was the Goldmark of the Paris Conservatory—the man to study with, it was said—but he turned out in fact to be another version of Goldmark. He was very conventional in his tastes. Also I couldn't understand his French. He spoke a kind of patois that was very hard to catch. (I had only high-school French at the time, so this was a real problem.) But they kept telling me about a teacher—

E.T.C.: Who was "they," other students?

A.C.: Yes, especially an attractive student harpist, Djina Ostrowska. (She died a few years ago, too.) When she enthused about her harmony teacher, I said, "I'm not interested in harmony, I'm studying composition." But she said, "Come anyhow, just to visit the class." And I did, finally. I remember Boulanger was analyzing something out of *Boris Godunov*. The enthusiasm with which she was doing it, the sense of her knowing the work cold—but mostly her enthusiasm, her relationship to music as an exciting thing—registered strongly with me.

Then Mademoiselle Boulanger did a very nice thing. She invited me to visit her in her home with the harmony class; in that way I got to know her better. At any rate, it suddenly struck me one day that here was the person I wanted to study composition with. (Looking back, I think it was a very brave decision, because I knew perfectly well at the time that there had never been any great women composers. This should have been a deterrent, but wasn't.) She wasn't teaching composition at Fontainebleau —just harmony (which was what she taught at the Conservatoire, the school and the Conservatoire being closely connected), so I studied composition with her privately when I settled in Paris in the fall. I remember bringing some piano pieces to her at the beginning. She said, "Why don't you make a ballet out of these?" I said, rather skeptically, "Do you really think I could?" But I did, and that turned out to be the main project during the three years I studied with her.

In addition I attended the Wednesday afternoon "déchiffrage" classes. We looked at lots of contemporary music at those meetings. The analysis wasn't detailed, it was a way of getting to know the work by performing it at two pianos or reading it from the score. The principal model she held up at all times was Fauré, and the idea of the long line: starting a piece at the first note and going straight on until the end in some connected fashion. We also looked at Debussy, and Stravinsky scores too, as soon as they came out (or sometimes before they came out, because she knew Stravinsky personally and borrowed the scores from him). No Schoenberg that I remember—no emphasis on the contemporary Germans. Don't forget that this was 1921. Twelve-tone music, of course, we didn't know about until 1924. I don't know when she herself first became aware of Schoenberg.

E.T.C.: How did she teach composition?

A.C.: I would bring her stuff that I was writing, and the exciting thing was that you had the feeling that her musical instinct was so sure that she could immediately point out the weak spot and tell you why it was weak, why it didn't seem to belong there, why it seemed to stop the flow, or whatever else was the matter with it. All that was very valuable: the sense that you were with someone who knew all the answers, who could relate them to general principles—and who was enthusiastic about what you were doing! *That* was the main thing. Mr. Goldmark had been a very nice man, but he lacked enthusiasm—it was just a job. To her it was an art, it was music, it was exciting!

E.T.C.: Did she ask you to do specific analysis on your own?

A.C.: I don't remember bringing in things I had analyzed. I remember hours of reading Mahler scores, painfully reading them at the piano—especially *Das Lied von der Erde*. It didn't matter how slowly you went, you had to go on!

E.T.C.: Did she give you any orchestration?

A.C.: Yes. I was orchestrating my own ballet, which turned out to be a 35-minute work in the end. It has never been performed in its entirety, but a 16-minute excerpt ultimately furnished the music for my *Dance Symphony*.

Just before I left France in 1924, she told me of her engagement to appear in America the following season as organ soloist with the Boston Symphony and also with Walter Damrosch's orchestra, and she asked me if I would like to write a concerto for her. I protested that I didn't know anything about the organ. "Oh, you can do it!" she said—she was always saying "You can do it!" Also, I had never heard any of my own orchestration, so I was very chary about what I might turn out. But she insisted, and so I did.

E.T.C.: Was it your influence that persuaded a number of other young Americans to go to Nadia Boulanger?

A.C.: I think it was. I wasn't literally the first American to study with her, but I was the first to study composition with her. Melville Smith had been studying organ with her, and I believe that Marion Bauer had studied harmony shortly before. Then there was Herbert Elwell. He had been with me at Fontainebleau but had hated it and "escaped" to London in the middle of the term—much to the distress of the Director! When he returned to Paris later in the winter, he went to Boulanger after hearing me enthuse. Roy Harris, Walter Piston, and Marc Blitzstein didn't come until later, after I had returned to the States. (Virgil Thomson learned of her through Melville Smith.)

Boulanger had been known as a teacher of organ and harmony and counterpoint, but the idea of studying composition with her was mine. I like to think so anyway.

E.T.C.: When you returned from Europe, how did you see yourself making a living?

A.C.: I thought I'd teach, like everybody else. In those days, one wasn't thinking about the universities, or even the conservatories. You would just send out cards to interested people and then hope for the best, which is precisely what I did. I took a studio on West 74th Street and waited for something to happen. I thought my announcement reading "recently back from Paris" would do the trick but unfortunately nobody answered!

By January I realized my position was getting pretty desperate. I went to see the writer, Paul Rosenfeld. (He was an important personality in those days, and I'm very sorry that he is forgotten as much as he is today.) I asked him if he knew some wealthy patron who would like to support a young composer for a year, and he mentioned Mrs. Alma Wertheim, a sister of Henry Morgenthau, as a possibility. She very kindly agreed to give me $1,000.

About four months later the Guggenheim Fellowships were established. They started with a preliminary trial year, during which time no applications were accepted; they chose candidates themselves, and they delightfully picked me to be the first Guggenheim Fellow in music. The fellowship was renewed the following year as well. I used to go to Europe in the spring, from April to September, returning for the winter in New York.

E.T.C.: Was it about this time that the League of Composers was started?

A.C.: No, that was founded in 1922, during my student years in Europe. You evidently don't know the whole history. That brings up something that I find very troubling: namely, that composers nowadays seem to have no sense of history whatsoever, and practically no interest in where they came from, or how they got here, or why we are where we are now. You can't imagine how distressing to me that is. It makes our younger men seem so primitive, like savages on an island who have no conception of how anything happened, and couldn't care less. It may have a healthy side to it, of course, but it seems to me somewhat poverty-stricken to have no curiosity at all as to your own historical background.

I remember once, when I was at Harvard in 1952 on the Norton Professorship, getting curious about the music of George Chadwick. I had always thought of him as being very German-oriented, but something I had recently read made me think that perhaps he had changed his mind during his later years, around 1910. I took out some of his scores from Widener. When I had one of them in hand, I noted that the last borrower had had it out in 1896! There's an alarming lack of curiosity today.

E.T.C.: Were you illuminated about Chadwick, by the way?

A.C.: I was quite surprised by how smoothly written his scores were. The technique was really first class. It wasn't very original, but it was certainly good music of its time. I don't think it would hurt us occasionally to hear some piece from that period. Who knows, there may be some dark masterpiece, rotting away, waiting to be rediscovered! But clearly it wasn't a very rich period, except for Ives, of course.

The Twenties, on the other hand, began something that carries over right into today, so that a little curiosity as to how it all began might be of some value to the young. It was Varèse who sparked the organization of our modern-music-performing societies with the formation of the International Composers' Guild. Soon there was a breakup on the board caused by some difference of opinion. The reason generally given is that Varèse didn't want to repeat premiere performances, while other members wanted to give second and third performances of things they liked. Actually I think it was more a clash of personality than anything else. Anyway, the splinter group called itself the League of Composers and was perhaps somewhat less radical in ideas than Varèse himself. Varèse and Carlos Salzedo (who was important to the development of new music here, from the standpoint of propaganda and performance) continued with their own ideas; the splinter group was led largely by Louis Gruenberg and, I think, Lazare Saminsky. They were greatly helped by Mrs. Claire Reis, who was the very active chairman of the League for more than twenty years. The establishment by the League of the magazine first called *The League of Composers Review*, and then renamed *Modern Music*, under the keen editorship of Miss Minna Lederman, was very important. It not only helped to keep everyone aware of what was going on but helped to develop writers. That was where Virgil Thomson began writing, where I began—where practically everybody began. (That's not quite true. My first article was published in *The Musical Quarterly*. It was a long study of Gabriel Fauré—naturally.)

The real critic of the movement was Paul Rosenfeld. He was in neither camp; he was a friend of both camps. But he had great admiration for Varèse. He wrote the first significant book on the American movement, called *One Hour with American Music*. It's very brief, but it states some basic things. The chapter on Varèse is still very readable. I wish that with all the reprinting of books in paperback somebody would have the bright idea of picking the best of Rosenfeld and bringing him out again. He did write in a kind of prose that was too highly flavored—that was his main weakness. But he was a sensitive fellow; and when his reaction was sound, he had insights which would bear rereading nowadays. Besides, it's always interesting to learn how the newer things seemed to listeners who were making contact with them for the first time.

E.T.C.: I remember his articles on Sessions's *Black Maskers* and on your Piano Variations.

A.C.: Yes, I thought at the time that he was very brave, for the Variations didn't get good criticisms from the press in general; it seemed from the standpoint of idiom and expressive character very odd and strange, and hard as nails.

E.T.C.: Do you see your music as falling into definite periods? I think of the Variations, for instance, as inaugurating a new one.

A.C.: Yes, different interests came along at different times, which resulted in music of different character. There was a distinct break around 1930 with the Variations. Why it came I can't tell you. The period of the Twenties had been definitely colored by the notion that Americans needed a kind of music they could recognize as their own. The jazz came by way of wanting to write this more immediately recognizable American music. It's a very unpopular idea now but seemed very much in the cards then. Don't forget that it was the Hungarianness of Bartók that seemed so fascinating: not only was he writing good modern music, but it was Hungarian in quality. Stravinsky was very Russian—a Russian composer, not just a modern composer. (No one could have forecast his neoclassic development.) I was just thinking along the line that seemed the ordinary line to think along, simply applying the same principle to America and trying to find an American solution.

There was a second thing working in me at that time, if I can analyze it myself. In addition to the sense of the Americanness, the need to find a musical language that would have American quality, I had also a—shall we say Hebraic—idea of the grandiose, of the dramatic and the tragic, which was expressed to a certain extent in the Organ Symphony, and very much in the Symphonic Ode, which very few people know nowadays. The Ode was a major effort, on which I worked for several years. It really seemed like a culminating work, so that I had to do something different after that. But I certainly didn't visualize doing a work like the Piano Variations! I think now, however, that the Variations was another version of the grandiose, except that it had changed to a very dry and bare grandiosity, instead of the fat grandiosity of a big orchestral work that lasted twenty minutes.

E.T.C.: Couldn't one say that in the Thirties, with the Variations and the Short Symphony, your music became more international in style?

A.C.: Perhaps, but nonetheless I like to think of them as being in some way American. Their rhythmic life is definitely American, and influenced by jazz, although there are no literal quotations. I wouldn't have thought of those rhythms, particularly in the Short Symphony, if I hadn't had a jazz orientation. When I say that I had a jazz orientation, most people think I mean that I played jazz. Actually I didn't play jazz at all. I did read popular music, of course, but I never could improvise in the jazz manner.

E.T.C.: How long would you say the new style lasted?

A.C.: Primarily through the Variations, the Short Symphony, and *Statements*. In *Vitebsk*, which preceded these works, the sharpness and dryness of the harmonies might fit into this period too. But I think of it primarily as a *morceau caractéristique*, a piece that just happened. I don't know why, except that I had heard the Jewish theme I made use of in a stage production of *The Dybbuk*, and liked it. After that, during the early Thirties, I went to Mexico. That explains *El Salòn Mexico* and my interest in Mexican tunes.

The late Twenties were rather rough going, as it was difficult to earn a living. By the fall of 1927 I had used up my two Guggenheim Fellowships but through Rosenfeld I inherited a course of lectures he gave on contemporary music at the New School for Social Research. He had tried lecturing for a winter and hadn't enjoyed it, not being a public speaker in any sense; audiences made him nervous. He asked me whether I would like to take over. I began talking to perhaps fifty people and found that you could earn money faster by talking to fifty than by talking to an individual student. So I fell into lecturing, without ever having dreamt that I was going to. Later I began to speak on the subject of music in general, which was the origin of *What to Listen For in Music*. I found the audience tripled as soon as I announced my subject as Music rather than Modern Music. So economically I was in a fairly good position up to about 1937. Then— I don't remember why, either the audience dwindled or I grew bored with lecturing—anyway, I gave it up. Perhaps the depression hit the audience. At any rate, the lectures ended, and those years between 1937 and 1939 were rather "grimmy."

Fortunately, toward the end of the Thirties, American composers began to interest entrepreneurs whose projects required music specially written for them. One of the first was Lincoln Kirstein, whose *Ballet Caravan* introduced American themes which demanded American music. The movie companies, especially those making documentary films about the American scene, began to feel the need of a music that would reflect what they were showing on the screen. I suppose my music was considered sufficiently American—I don't remember how some of them happened to come around to me, but they did. That provided not only a source of income but also the new feeling of being asked to write music for a functional purpose. Before that we wrote for ourselves; nobody was asking for it.

E.T.C.: I suppose this was the origin of what you have sometimes called your vernacular style.

A.C.: Yes, a more accessible style. I don't think I ever deliberately sat down to write something in a style that everybody could understand. In the first place you can't be sure that everybody will fall in love with your music even if it is written in such a language. There is no guarantee that the audience is going to want it any more than they would a dissonant piece. I think a more accessible style was brought on by the nature of the things I was asked to do: a ballet score implies that you are looking at something while you are listening to the music, so that you can't give your undivided attention to the music. This suggests a simpler style. The same is true of movie music. As I stress in the new edition of *Our New Music*,[1] it was unfortunate that I wrote my little autobiographical sketch in the first edition just when I was writing these more accessible things, for I gave the false impression that this was the direction I was going to head for in the future. I was just all keyed up by the fact that finally here was a need for our music!

E.T.C.: After the war, you gradually moved toward serial or twelve-tone writing. How did that come about?

A.C.: When I look back now, it seems to me that the Piano Variations was the start of my interest in serial writing. It was Eric Salzman, I think, who said it was almost Webernesque in its concentration on a few notes. Although it doesn't use all twelve tones, it does use seven, and it stays with them throughout in what I hope is a consistently logical way. Also I wrote a song in 1927, recently republished under the title "Poet's Song," which is quite twelve-tony and shows that I was thinking in those terms then. Schoenberg's greater fame after the end of the last war and the continual talk and writing about the technique brought the whole matter to the front of my mind again.

I'd like to explain here one thing about Schoenberg in relation to myself: in the early years, in my own mind, he and Berg and Webern were

[1] Re-titled *The New Music*, W. W. Norton, 1968.

under something of a cloud for the reason that they were still writing German music, and German music was the thing we were trying to get out from under. The expressive quality of their music took precedence over their method, which wasn't clearly understood until much later anyway. (Even Roger, with all his sympathies, didn't come to it until much later.) No matter how significant the method may have seemed, it never occurred to anybody to disconnect the method from the esthetic, which seemed to be basically an old Wagnerian one. The later works of Webern hadn't been written. His cool approach was completely unknown. So it isn't strange that I didn't feel sympathetic. I didn't need the method at the time, for I was busy exploring for myself. It was only later, at the end of the Second World War, the younger fellows, Boulez and such, made it clear that you could keep the method while throwing away the esthetic. This came as a brand new idea to us. Why we didn't think of it for ourselves, I'll never understand.

By 1950, I was involved. The attraction of the method for me was that I began to hear chords that I wouldn't have heard otherwise. Heretofore I had been thinking tonally, but this was a new way of moving tones about. It freshened up one's technique and one's approach. To this very day that remains its main attraction for me.

E.T.C.: Do you use it exclusively?

A.C.: Not necessarily. I wrote an orchestral work this summer entitled *Inscape* in which I used it in a rather more tonal way than I did in my *Connotations*. It still seems to me full of possibilities.

E.T.C.: This might be a good point at which to bring up something I've always been curious about, yet oddly enough have never asked you. The first time I met you was at a reception after some concert or other in 1946. I had submitted an orchestral work for the Gershwin prize, and had been turned down. I was greatly flattered when you told me that you had been on the jury and had been very favorably impressed by my piece. You even described the piece very accurately. "But," you went on to say, "I voted against it. Its melodic line was too German." What did you mean by that? And what did you mean, some years later, when you told me it would be a good idea for me to look at the works of—that name again—Fauré?

A.C.: Did I say that? I suppose I was thinking about the chromaticism of Germanic expressivity, as against a more tonally oriented line—a kind of weltschmerzy quality German music has with its high chromatic content.

E.T.C.: And you would say that even in your twelve-tone music your line is not essentially chromatic?

A.C.: I don't think anybody would ever imagine it as having been written by a German composer. I try to do my own thing using an extended language. Still, there is a difference, even in my own work, because I think of twelve-tone music as having a built-in tenseness. I like to think that the way I use it, it has a certain drama about it, a sense of strain or tension which is inherent in the use of the chromatic. These are new kinds of tensions, different from what I would have dreamt up if I had been thinking tonally.

E.T.C.: Do you think of a series ahead of time, or do you think up a theme and develop your series from it?

A.C.: I'm very much in the Schoenberg line: I always think of a theme. It wouldn't occur to me to pick a series deliberately and then build a theme out of it. I can imagine that being done, but it seems to me quite hard and chancy.

E.T.C.: When you construct the music, do you think of combinatoriality, derivations, etc., or do you proceed more or less intuitively?

A.C.: I've never made any extensive study of current methods, and I'm very vague as to how they all work. The new terminology is Greek to me. I haven't been through the Babbitt school: I haven't that kind of brain. I feel lucky enough if I can add properly. From that standpoint, I'm very much of the old school. But I don't think recent developments are essential to making use of the method as it first developed. No, I am interested in the simple outlines of the theory, and in adapting them to my own purposes.

E.T.C.: Suppose you were commissioned now to write a movie or a ballet score. Would you attempt to use your new idiom, or would you feel that you ought to write something simpler and perhaps more tonal?

A.C.: I couldn't decide in advance; I'd have to know the subject matter. I would want to write a kind of music that seemed appropriate. I'm not married to twelve-tone, and I haven't necessarily given up all contact with tonal music in the usual sense. As always, I would say that any functional music must be influenced by the need you are trying to fulfill.

E.T.C.: You said that in the late Thirties you had a rather rough time until along came the ballets and the movies. But since then you have never wanted for musical commissions, so that you have never had to depend on teaching for a livelihood.

A.C.: No, but I did teach briefly at Harvard, twice, during Walter Piston's sabbaticals, for a half-term in 1934 and again in 1944. True, my film scores helped a lot. Then, in 1938, Boosey and Hawkes became my publishers, guaranteeing me a certain sum each year, so that I wasn't dependent on teaching. Also don't forget that I was at Tanglewood for 21 summers, starting in 1940 and lasting over a span of 25 years. That was income derived from teaching, although it may not be very serious to teach students for just two months of the year. But I did have contact with a great many composition students during that time, perhaps some 400 in all, and I found it very stimulating.

One of the reasons I never thought about teaching in a university is that I had no degree. I graduated from high school and decided not to go to college in order to devote all my time to music. I didn't have the requirements I supposed one needed to teach in a college. Nowadays it's probably freer.

E.T.C.: How do you feel about the fact that today many, perhaps most, young composers look on university teaching as the normal thing to do? They seem to think of this first of all, and even look with wonder on the few who decide against the university career and try to make a go of it in the world at large.

A.C.: It's partly a matter of individual temperament. Certain people are at home and happy within the university, whereas others would not feel comfortable there and shouldn't be there in the first place. If that's the only place they can make a living, so much the worse, for it means a lot of strain. Speaking generally, without relation to personal temperament, I don't think it is healthy for the whole composing community to move within university walls. The protected feeling and the small field of reference are a little worrying. At some point I should think one would want to test everything one does outside, in the big world. Too long and too exclusive a settling into the university musical ambiance might be in individual cases rather upsetting, and as a general trend perhaps not healthy for the musical situation in the country at large—and certainly not healthy for the future of our symphony orchestras. I realize that a good many young composers are not interested in the symphony orchestra, nowadays, but I hope they will be again.

E.T.C.: Do you see any signs, in the kind of music that young composers are now writing, of their university training and orientation?

A.C.: Certainly the orientation has had a serious influence. The concentration on analysis of the innards of all works seems rather special to the present period. There was always analysis going on, but not the kind one is familiar with in the pages of PERSPECTIVES. That's a new manifestation.

E.T.C.: I gather from your tone that you would add, "not an entirely happy one."

A.C.: Well, it's lovely if you like to read the stuff! I don't mind that there's a lot of analysis going on, but I wish it were balanced with a little more interest in, shall we say, the musical content without reference to the analysis content. If a piece gives off absolutely nothing to talk about except the way it's put together, there's something a little funny about the piece. One ought to be able to get some sort of charge out of it just by sitting there and listening to it in a dumb fashion. I think that basically we all listen to music in a rather dumb way, especially when we are presented with a new piece about which we know absolutely nothing. Too often you get the feeling, when reading an analysis, that there isn't much point to the music except the way the darn thing's put together. Well, that's very unsympathetic to me. It worries me a little bit that one doesn't meet up now with the kind of composer we used to think of as being "musical." If you said of someone, "He is terribly musical," that was the highest compliment you could pay. Nowadays, to stress the "musicality" of a composer would seem to be somehow pinning a bad name on him or making him seem lesser or limited or not so interesting.

E.T.C.: What is your own approach to the teaching of composition?

A.C.: I don't think of myself as a teacher in the usual sense. I've never taken anybody from the beginning right straight through to the end. What I try to do is what I used to find valuable in Boulanger: I react. I try to point out what I think are the good things and where the piece seems to flounder or not carry on or to get off the rails. That's very good for summer teaching, but it wouldn't work if you wanted to give a student a four-year course.

E.T.C.: How do you feel now about your association with the MacDowell Colony? Do you think that such places still have something to offer young composers?

A.C.: My interest in the MacDowell Colony was aroused by Paul Rosenfeld. I had received a commission from the League of Composers to write a piece for a concert Koussevitzky was to conduct for the League in the Fall of 1925. I was very anxious to go someplace where I could concentrate on writing this piece, and Rosenfeld suggested the Colony. That was the first I had heard about it.

What it provided, more than the mere place to work, beautiful as it was, was face-to-face contact with people in the other arts. This was new for me. People in New York artistic circles had a chance of meeting one another, but I was pretty naïve and didn't know many people. I had never seen an American poet before I saw Edward Arlington Robinson there that first summer—and William Rose Benét, and Elinor Wylie, and Louis Untermeyer and his wife, Jean. I had never talked with American painters. I knew some American composers but not many. I met Henry Gilbert and Roy Harris there. The Colony was an eye-opener for me. It was immensely stimulating to hear other people talk about their problems in poetry or painting.

I went back four or five times during the Twenties and Thirties, each time meeting different people, and each time being provided with a studio in the woods that was absolutely my own—quiet during the entire day and night (although we didn't work at night, for in those days there were no lights in the studios). I found it invaluable, and I don't see why it wouldn't be invaluable in the same way right now. Not everybody has the perfect situation for writing, and also going away from home for two months and settling down in a new environment can be quite stimulating.

E.T.C.: Young composers can get that at Tanglewood, too.

A.C.: Yes, but not the contact with artists of other kinds. It's one thing to meet casually, at a party, someone who writes poetry. It's another thing to live with him for two months, to see him at breakfast and dinner every day, to talk with him each time. That's much more than a casual encounter. What Tanglewood does, by contrast, is to give you professional stimulation in your own art, with other people working in the same field, which one gets in a broader sense at a place like the Colony or at Yaddo.

I would like to see every state in the Union establish a MacDowell Colony. I don't know why they shouldn't. They've set up these Arts Councils now wanting to do things for their own states, they have affluent citizens with properties who want to do something valuable with them but don't know what, so why not have a colony in every state?

E.T.C.: It's a very good idea. What else might the Arts Councils or foundations do to help us?

A.C.: The best thing would be to get more unplayed music performed. But there's another point that I often think about. I've spent quite a lot of time being what you might call a good citizen of the Republic of Music. I don't find that composers think much about that—about music as an international concern. Take our relations with South America. I had never thought about our southern neighbors until I was offered a trip down there as a kind of cultural ambassador for an official committee set up by Nelson Rockefeller during the war years, in 1941. It was a real eye-opener to go there and make friends with the composers: to see them having the same problems we had up here, to an exaggerated degree, and to see how they understood the problem of their relationship to native musical materials. It extended my idea of what goes into the making of music to find out how it worked in countries like Argentina, Chile, or Brazil; not only was the situation different in each of these countries, but also the types of composers were different. Such an experience enlarges one's field of vision.

I wish there were more of that: moving composers around, letting them bang up against other ideas different from the ones that are current—or even agreeing with the ones that are current. It should be valuable for mature composers and students alike. Look at the influence of French culture on American artists: the fact that so many American artists went to France had an enormous effect. In the same way, it wouldn't hurt anybody to spend a couple of months in Rio—a delightful experience, or an awful experience, but it would be an experience. You wouldn't be left cold by it. I'm a little concerned by a kind of high-class provincialism that seems to be typical of the present-day musical scene. Everybody gets encouragement from a small circle. I realize that encouragement is important, and there are plenty of examples of composers who began with a small circle of admirers; but one can overdo it. The tendency to lean back and depend upon that small-circle encouragement is, I fear, a lessening rather than an enlarging of one's capacities.

I would like to see an extensive foundation program foster this kind of moving about. After all, the Rockefeller and the Ford Foundations do send people abroad all the time. I myself went again to South America, six years later, in 1947, for the State Department. I spent two months in Rio and wrote most of my Clarinet Concerto there.

E.T.C.: Perhaps we can see that copies of this interview fall into the right hands. But, speaking of this interview, it's too bad that we're doing it today and not tomorrow. That would have been very appropriate.

A.C.: Why? Oh, yes, I see. Tomorrow is November 14. No, I'm trying to forget that!

E.T.C. Well, Happy Birthday to you anyway.

—November 13, 1967

COPLAND ON THE SERIAL ROAD:

An Analysis of *Connotations*

PETER EVANS

WHILE IT CANNOT be denied that the postwar revival of interest in serial organization served as no more than a springboard to the European avant-garde, it may well be argued that the most impressive products of that revival are to be found in the work of an older generation, fully formed in its musical ways before the universality of Schoenberg's legacy was yet suspected.[1] There is no place here for talk of "conversions," since the dominating impression created by the serial works concerned is of the composers' reaffirmation of their most characteristic ideals. Dallapiccola's has been the most systematic and leisurely embracing of serial potentialities, Stravinsky's the most notorious; both men have revealed still deeper implications of the method for their own style with each successive score.

When Copland's Piano Quartet (1950) and Piano Fantasy (1955–57), essays in a tentative serialism which I have discussed elsewhere,[2] were followed in 1960 by the Nonet, a work on which serialism has left no more than faint traces, it was possible, if to some listeners disappointing, to conclude that the composer had settled down to that nodding acquaintance with dodecatonic ways of thinking that has sufficed for such a composer as Martin. Yet, Copland's other activities in recent years should have hinted how fundamental has become his involvement in the serial attitude to musical material: his orchestration of the 1930 Piano Variations points up the remarkable parallels between these gaunt early-Copland procedures and the method of construction from the segments of a tone row. At much the same time, Copland revised the 1929 *Symphonic Ode*, a work which strove to achieve palpable unity across a single arch embracing sharply contrasted moods. The same ideal lay behind the Piano Fantasy, a quarter of a century later; but the row could now play a vital role in the unifying process. And now, with *Connotations*, we can see these varied strands of Copland's thought drawn together in a work which, while assimilating the experience of the three earlier scores, at the same time takes his exploration of serial consequences further than ever before.

In the program notes written for the concert performances of *Connotations*, the composer pointed to the "primary meaning" of the new work as summed up in the three four-voiced chords heard at the outset (Ex. 1); from this charting of the "area of exploration," "the subsequent treatment seeks out other implications—connotations that come in a flash or connotations that the composer himself may only gradually uncover." This presentation of the basic set in harmonic conflations means, clearly enough, that there may be drawn from it innumerable melodic lines (by permutations within the three segments) which will still refer to a single source

---

[1] I have attempted to summarize the approach, if not the achievement, of this generation in "Compromises with Serialism," *Proceedings of the Royal Musical Association*, 1961–62, pp. 1–16.

[2] See "The Thematic Technique of Copland's Recent Works," *Tempo* 51 (1959), pp. 2–13.

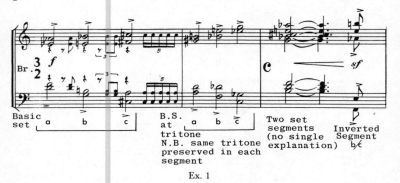

Ex. 1

with some aural immediacy. But this set has further properties that make for a flexible mode of treatment. All three segments have a fund of intervals in common: semitone, two minor thirds forming a tritone, and a perfect fifth; however, the *a* segment's whole tone is replaced (by a major third) in *b* and *c*. The identity, but for transposition, of the last two segments means that in isolation neither defines a single row, for each appears in two of the basic set's twelve transpositions. To transfer from one reading of a segment to another is to sacrifice twelve-tone propriety, but throughout much of the work Copland is not primarily concerned to preserve this; indeed, in some contexts it is simpler to regard the segment, rather than the row, as his building material. Though there may be a predetermined ordering in his changes of attitude to the basic set, it is certainly not rigidly schematic; some indication is given in the following analysis of the important structural function performed by the dialectic between vertical and horizontal serial interpretations, but any oversystematized dissection should be discouraged by Copland's own awareness of those connotations that only gradually reveal themselves. It is wholly typical of the composer of the Piano Fantasy that he can regard a twelve-tone series as simultaneously a generator of precisely determined note relationships and a spur to almost improvisatory fantasy.

The chordal successions of mm. 1 and 2 (Ex. 1), aggressively dissonant in themselves, are soon superimposed one upon the other; the quasicadential formula of m. 3 adds more segments to its repetitions until all twelve notes áre assembled, escaping each time, as if with revulsion, into the comparative consonance of E

Ex. 2a

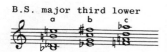

Ex. 2b

major with F in the bass (i.e. the inversion of a *b/c* segment). This furious opening makes clear enough the substance from which the piece is to be fashioned, but presents it in a peculiarly intractable form (the rhythms applied by a second brass group notwithstanding). The first section of the work is devoted to revealing this substance as a more pliable material. The music begins to swing into motion through a rhythmic figure (Ex. 2a) which immediately reveals a close link with the basic set (Ex. 2b); this short-breathed span of oscillating harmonies provides an early example of the ease with which Copland's most idiomatic voice speaks through his new techniques (e.g. the Piano Quartet's non-serial finale in Ex. 2c).

Ex. 2c

The next stage in vitalizing the material is a search for melodic definition: the chords splinter into linear fragments, order being restored by the return of the basic harmonic segments as background support. In performance, the solo piano's intrusion at this point (see the beginning of Ex. 3) is arresting, and indeed, its effect is literally so, for it reverts to the stiff opening harmonic complexes; far more rewarding for the development of the work is the achievement of a relaxed melodic reading of the row which follows (Ex. 3, from m. 10).

Although Copland is to permute his basic set into many other shapes, this first melodic definition (Ex. 3, mm. 10-13) takes priority over all others as a point of reference (the numbering of its note order is used in later examples here). Its importance is underlined by its immediate use, both straight and inverted, as the thread in a passacaglia-like texture. A new balance between melodic and harmonic aspects is then struck in a long section of wind and string antiphony, beginning as

Ex. 3

at Ex. 4, and the first part of the work is rounded off with a return to a more mobile version of the opening brass conflations. Thus, its progress has been roughly arched (from harmonic domination, through the opposition of melody and harmony to melodic domination, and back again); in this way it reflects the shape of the whole work, a structure of five sections arranged in arched correspondence.

After so wide-ranging an exposition of the potentialities of his basic idea, Copland can now settle down to explore a few in greater depth. And it is not surprising that the moods and textural types to which he turns in these middle sections are those which have proved most congenial to him in the past. The restless *Allegro*, juxtaposing short, twitching phrases of angular line in asymmetric rhythms

(B.S. a semitone higher)
(numbered as in melodic set, cf. Ex. 3)

Ex. 4

and lean textures, has been a Copland trait since the Variations (Nos. 14-17) and the *Short Symphony;* the *Fantasy* shows that it has remained a compulsive mode of speech for the emerging serialist. In fact, pitch relationships are subordinate in this style to pithy rhythmic propositions, and in *Connotations,* the orchestral percussion group emphasizes this by establishing the characteristic tone of this scherzo before the cellos introduce the basic set, in a slightly permuted form (Ex. 5a).

B.S. numbered in relation to first melodic statement (cf. Ex.3)

Ex. 5a

As well as simple (often monodic) statements of the set in its four orders, an apparently new twelve-tone shape is introduced that is to return at climactic points of the two scherzos; it is shown, with its derivation, at Ex. 5b. The texture rarely expands beyond two parts, but these are kept in such vigorous rhythmic opposition that the momentum never flags; complete sets are usually offset by the brusquer gestures of single segments. So a momentary conflation (Ex. 5c, m. 1) is enough to provide a vehement punctuation mark. What follows is a continuation of the scherzo-like figuration, at a slower speed, as woodwind commentary on a solemn chordal antiphony of brass and strings (beginning as in Ex. 5c, m. 3); thus, within this section two melodic and harmonic interpretations of the row are balanced.

Ex. 5b

Ex. 5c

A short transition borrows some melodic derivations from the first section and, after a distant echo of the basic harmonies (on muted strings), the middle section begins. Its still, rapt mood is a recurrent quality of Copland's slow movements, created here, as surely as in the most limpid pages of his "popular" style (*Appalachian Spring* inevitably comes to mind), by the composer's hypersensitivity to chordal spacing and to subtleties of instrumental coloring. A wholly convincing explanation in serial terms for each note of these refined textures (Ex. 6a) has so far eluded the present analyst; perhaps we have here struck upon some of those connotations which the composer himself has only gradually uncovered. Certainly the sequel presents no such problems: it consistently plays off half-rows against each other (Ex. 6b.)

Ex. 6a

Ex. 6b

The use of a cadence figure common to the two variations making up this central section prompts a comparison with the "interlude" variations of Brahms's passacaglia in the Fourth Symphony.

And, just as in the Brahms, we are suddenly carried back into the main course of the piece. The fourth section, corresponding to the second, resumes the scherzo pulse, and reversion is taken literally enough for the harmonic version (now oscillating with evident reference to Ex. 2) with background rhythms (restricted now to the percussion) to precede the pure scherzo texture. After some spiky canon and close stretto on segments of the basic set, a return to literal restatement of the earlier purely linear scherzo is made with the reappearance of Ex. 5b; the same theme marks the climax of the crescendo that concludes this section.

The remainder of the work forms, therefore, that part of the arch standing opposite the exposition, and its logical function is to review the first ideas and to provide a summary to the whole work. But its manner of recapitulation only gradually becomes exact as the backward-turning mechanism brings the listener ever closer to the splenetic outburst from which the whole cycle began. At first, the melodic restatement is far more forceful than was its original appearance (see Ex. 3); it is also less painstakingly explanatory, being distributed across a spacious two-part texture (Ex. 7).

Ex. 7

There follow some head-on collisions between different serial forms attempting to run in parallel; here, more than anywhere in the work, there is something suggestive of the serialist's first trial of possibilities about the resultant sound (but the composer may perhaps plead that he is justified in using crude means where he intends a crude effect). It is after this reduction to the simplest linear terms that earlier textures make their literal return—first the splintering fragments through which melody escaped from harmony (and is now to return), then the piano's violent adaptation of the basic chordal proposition (see beginning of Ex. 3). The undulating harmonies of Ex. 2b duly reappear, but Ex. 2a's return is fused with the chordal restatement of Ex. 1's opening bars (Ex. 8a).

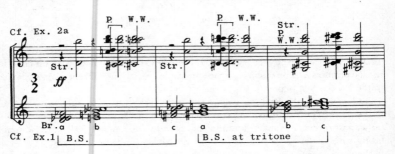

Ex. 8a

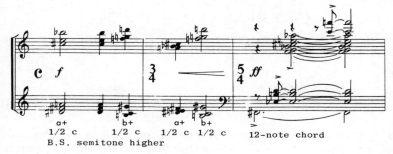

Ex. 8b

This means that the stark yet inert sound of Ex. 1 is still averted, for the rhythmic counteraction of Ex. 2a allows the music to surge past the implied return. Indeed, there is even a bold attempt to launch a coherent melodic superstructure above the extension of the basic harmonies (i.e. a return of that section discussed, though not quoted, between Exx. 2 and 3, a section so far omitted in this restatement). But the climactic pages into which this leads bring back the crucial chords alone, now appropriating rather than opposed by the Ex. 2a rhythm (Ex. 8b) and gradually losing this mobility. And after each appearance, a wall of impenetrable *tutti* sound is erected from the chromatic total (i.e. on the pattern of Ex. 1, m. 3—see Ex. 8b, m. 3), aided by a vast battery of percussion; there is, of course, no clearing of the air with a single consonant segment as at the opening. It would be an academic undertaking to dissect such a twelve-tone chord into segments of the basic set, but the context leaves us in no doubt that we are hearing the material of the entire work, restored to its rawest, most chaotic form.

The mastery with which Copland has executed this splendidly logical structure is not without parallel in his earlier work. That he now brings his own special kind of logic to bear on material already braced by a taut net of serial relationships reaffirms this mastery. If doctrinaire serialists still exist, they will be at liberty to condemn many of Copland's usages as distortions or dilutions of Schoenbergian precept. Such arguments are futile before the one important consideration, that the composer has found through his own reading of the serial idea a signal revivification of his talents. Bearing in mind the unexpected deviation represented by the Nonet's appearance between the embryonic serialism of the Fantasy and the fully committed working-out of a row in *Connotations,* it would be reckless to predict Copland's future course, but the new score suggests that he will not soon tire of the exploration on which he has embarked.

CONVERSATION WITH
WALTER PISTON

PETER WESTERGAARD

PW: Let's begin with some biographical details and let them lead us to more general questions. I know your first training was as a painter and that you had finished your professional training as an artist before you decided to become a composer. How did that happen?

WP: Well, it wasn't exactly as cut and dried as that. My problem came in finding a school beyond high school. My family was far from wealthy, and while I had some talent in music, I was also interested in art. The New England Conservatory cost money, but the Massachusetts School of Art was free. Hence I went to art school, and earned money on the side playing the violin and the piano. I kept getting more and more interested in music, and by the end of the senior year I was entirely devoted to it; but by then I was so near to graduation I decided to finish up school and I got my diploma as a painter.

PW: Were you composing then or just playing the violin?

WP: I wouldn't call it composing. I wrote little tunes. Then when the war came, the First World War, that is, and it became obvious that everybody had to go into the service, I wanted to go in as a musician. I couldn't play any band instrument, but I knew instruments and I knew that the saxophone was very easy. So I went down to Oliver Ditson's and bought a saxophone, and stopped by at the public library to get an instruction book. I learned enough to play by ear. In a very short time I was called and I tried out for the band. I didn't pretend to read the part but just played notes that went with the harmony, and I was accepted. That turned out to be a rather valuable experience for me, because we had all kinds of spare time; with instruments always available in the band room I picked up a moderate ability to play something on each of them. I was proficient enough to play the English horn solo in the *William Tell* Overture on the little soprano saxophone in Symphony Hall.

PW: And after the war? How did you happen to go to Harvard?

WP: By the end of the war I had begun to be more serious about music. I was making my living playing. Having heard about Dr. Davison's counterpoint class at Harvard, I investigated and found there was a category called "special student." So I started the counterpoint class as a special student, and by the end of it Doc was all fired up about getting me to come to Harvard. I think he more or less arranged the whole thing. I didn't have much of any college preparation, and so had to take extra courses, like Greek, and Zoology, etc., for entrance credits. Then I started taking the music courses, and became Doc's assistant.

PW: While you were still an undergraduate?

WP: Yes, and then assistant to other professors in the department.

PW: What kind of musical training were you getting there? Would you call it professional training?

WP: You don't expect professional training in a liberal arts college and you are not supposed to. For that, one goes to a conservatory, although I have noticed in recent years that the conservatories and art schools want to become colleges, offering a minimum liberal arts curriculum. I suppose I was already a professional musician, but being at Harvard helped to rescue me from the kind of music that was narrowing my musical outlook.

PW: What kind was that? Where were you playing?

WP: The familiar, routine popular music, endlessly repeating the platitudes in fashion at the time, occasionally relieved a bit by excerpts from musical shows or even selections from operas. I played in dance halls, hotels, restaurants—and at social events. I remember one colorful and earthy place called Blatz's Palm Garden, first replaced by a parking lot and now by the New Boston City Hall.

The Harvard music department was a new world, where one was in daily contact with great music. Besides, I found especially rewarding the courses I took in subjects outside my field.

PW: You went there for musical education, but you were persuaded to look into other things?

WP: You might say "persuaded" in the way a dean has of persuading you that you can't graduate without those things. But I found them intensely fascinating. You see, I was older than most of the boys, eight years older than my classmates. I graduated with a *summa*, went abroad on a Paine Fellowship, began studying with Nadia Boulanger, and at once found that I lacked a real professional training such as would be needed to be the kind of composer I wanted to become.

PW: What was lacking? What didn't you get at Harvard that you got in France?

WP: You understand that training in the technical branches of the art of composition is never completed. It is a lifetime's continuing pursuit. So I would rather say "I was getting it," not "I got it." For instance, one stayed in the counterpoint class until ready to go on to fugue. Some took years. What we were getting was practice in the handling of notes under given conditions.

PW: Rules?

WP: Yes, rules, if you appreciate what rules mean: that they're purely academic. Rules are not directions how to write music: using rules is something like going to a gymnasium and lifting bars so that you will become strong.

PW: But I would have thought Davison's counterpoint classes were at least a step in the right direction.

WP: Yes, they were. But he sort of frowned on the real training. I often thought that Doc didn't realize what a top-notch natural musician he himself was. He could improvise or write on the blackboard original examples of polyphony of the highest excellence and vitality. But those were the days when it was believed that one studied harmony and counterpoint for the sole purpose of becoming a composer.

PW: What kind of training did Boulanger give you?

WP: I joined her counterpoint class (she wouldn't let me come to the harmony class; said it would be a waste of time for me). We started right at the beginning of the strictest kind of counterpoint, two voices, note against note.

PW: Species counterpoint?

WP: Yes, right up to eight parts. Of course none of that was what I'd ever write in a composition, but I believe it's because of having done it that I have been able to write my music.

PW: And the training in composition? Were you writing compositions on your own that you took to her for criticism, or did she set you specific tasks?

WP: The essential part of composition, the creative part, cannot be taught. A composer is answerable only to himself. It is nevertheless part of the composer's craft to compose according to specific conditions, and he is constantly having to do this as conditions arise in connection with any work he writes. Such exercises can be used to stimulate a student composer, to get him going.

In my case, I did just what I wanted to and then we'd talk it over. Her faculty to perceive what a person was at, or wanted to be at, was nothing less than uncanny. I can remember showing up one time with a page of stems and rests and beams and clefs but no note-heads. She didn't show the slightest hesitation in entering into a discussion of the pros and cons. Now that's a stage in one's groping that one can discuss with oneself, but it's pretty hard for another mind to come into it.

PW: Did you do any performing with Boulanger?

WP: Only in the sense of taking part in bringing to life certain works. She held a gathering of all her students at her apartment on Wednesday afternoons. We'd run through all kinds of things. She would suddenly name five people to do the Franck Quintet the next week. I recall digging into the piano part of that. Also I can remember going down to Fontainebleau to conduct a chorus of her students in *Les Noces,* with her at the piano.

PW: All four?

WP: Well, it sounded that way. Then, I played the viola in the orchestra at the École Normale. It was conducted by the cellist Diran Alexanian, who was Casals' chief assistant in Paris and a very fine musician.

PW: What kind of music were you hearing in Paris? There must have been a lot of music being played there that you couldn't have heard in Boston.

WP: Oh, yes, we were hearing concerts of modern music. Of course, in those days we wouldn't have gone to a Beethoven symphony if you had paid us.

PW: Can you remember anything about the level of performance?

WP: It's difficult to look back now and judge. I understand from my French friends that it was better then than it is now.

PW: Which musicians played the new music?

WP: The best.

PW: Which composers did you hear?

WP: Bartók, Stravinsky, Hindemith, Prokofiev, Ravel, to name a few.

PW: The Viennese composers?

WP: Very little. I studied their music from the scores. I recall a performance of *Pierrot Lunaire,* and one of the Schoenberg Quintet. At the end of it the clarinettist told me he had five measures left over when the others stopped but he thought he had better stop too.

PW: Were there particular pieces you heard then which you've later come to realize had some kind of formative influence on your own pieces?

WP: I think the process of influence is more continuous than can be explained by reference to specific pieces. I've always been interested in everything, and I know I am influenced by it, but I don't know how.

PW: What about that kind of writing we used to call "international counterpoint," the kind of rhythm and lines that are found in your Three Pieces for Flute, Clarinet, and Bassoon from that period? Were you aware of any particular source for that? Many people who studied with Boulanger between the wars have used something like it, but I never heard anyone claim she taught it to him.

WP: She never taught composers particular styles, but rather she influenced them to find their own. I'm trying to think back to that time. Certainly Hindemith had something to do with it . . . , but no, it may sound corny, but I think Bach had a great deal more to do with it. More than that I would say it was in the air.

PW: Why Bach? Was there any reason why you could use the rhythms of Bach and not those of Beethoven or Mozart?

WP: I wouldn't say I used the rhythm of Bach, but that his music stimulated a sense of strong, instrumental counterpoint.

PW: These rhythms seemed the best suited to the idea of contrapuntal independence?

WP: I believe that was at least one of the reasons. A fellow doesn't know much about himself, when you come right down to it.

PW: Did the particular way of using these rhythms come more from Hindemith than from Stravinsky?

WP: I was pretty close to Stravinsky, musically speaking.

PW: Which pieces? The Octet?

WP: Yes. Very much. Then the critics invented the term "neo-classic," a term of scorn in those days.

PW: It was never a rallying cry?

WP: Oh, no, composers never said they were writing neo-classic music. They knew that if it was neo-anything it was neo-baroque.

PW: What brought you back to Harvard?

WP: A job. After two years in Paris I began to think of making a living, and I had already considered teaching in a university. The atmosphere of learning and the association with young people seemed right for me as a composer. So I was happy to accept the opening offered me at Harvard.

PW: Had Harvard changed?

WP: No.

PW: Did you proceed to change it?

WP: Well, I don't know who changed what, but there did begin to be more of a feeling that not only composers but musicians in general ought to have more technical knowledge of music.

PW: What did you think composers needed?

WP: What they needed most was to write music. As for needing harmony, in the ideal sense they don't, you know. A man who has something to say in music spends his life trying to find the best way to say it. I can imagine that such a fellow might bypass the whole subject of harmony—I mean harmony as a summation of a common practice that has come before. The drawback to that plan is that he might lose too much time looking for a chord he could find in Piston's *Harmony*.

PW: Wouldn't you also say that someone who tries to invent his own system without understanding one, like the tonal system, that's been used for a while is apt to invent a rather simple-minded system?

WP: I see this happening all the time, not that I care much about systems. This is a source of worry to me about the young—who don't care whether we're worried about them or not, naturally. I've seen so many of them. They all seem to go through a certain natural evolution. First they are all burned up, the way we were back in the twenties: they want to destroy the past. Then they grow up and say, "Perhaps the past doesn't have to be destroyed after all. I guess I won't destroy it." Then they begin to realize they don't know what the past is, never having studied it. And finally, they get a little older and they look inside themselves to see what they have to say, and they find they have great need for a deep knowledge of their musical heritage. It goes without saying that I except the geniuses.

PW: To get back to your return to the United States, what kind of professional musical life did you find?

WP: That was a great period for new music in this country. It was before the Americana bug bit. Copland, Harris, Sessions, Thomson, et al.—we more or less started out together. We founded the Arrow Press, which we invented for the printing of our own music. We had some help from philanthropists like Alma Wertheim, but I paid for the printing of everything of mine that we published.

PW: Were you involved in the Copland-Sessions concerts?

WP: That trio of mine for flute, clarinet, and bassoon was performed at the first Copland-Sessions concert in a little theater off Broadway.

PW: Were there opportunities for performance in Boston?

WP: Yes, some. Georges Laurent, the first flutist of the Boston Symphony, headed a group of symphony players who gave a series of chamber music concerts. They would get together and rehearse new works, and they didn't get paid for rehearsals, either. Those were very good opportunities.

PW: Were those concerts all new music?

WP: No. But they would average at least one new work on each program. Of course the great event for American music at that time was the coming of Serge Koussevitzky. When I returned from France I felt pretty gloomy about the situation of the composer in America. I knew conductors were not interested in what we composers were doing, so I was writing only chamber music. Edward Burlingame Hill spoke to Koussevitzky about me and Koussevitzky asked to see me. He asked, "Why you no write for orchestra?" I said, "Because nobody would play it." And he said, "Write, and I will play." So I wrote and he played. I would get through with one piece and he would say, "Now what are you writing? Now the next score. Where is the next?" And it was the same story with other American composers.

PW: Did he play the first orchestral works you wrote?

WP: I had written a number of student scores, which I didn't consider good enough even to show him. He did play the first works I was willing to present to the public. Some of these he inveigled me into conducting.

PW: Did you conduct the *Symphonic Piece?*

WP: No. Koussevitzky did.

PW: Would that be the first orchestral piece you still acknowledge?

WP: Yes, but I have never cared to have it published. Hearing it performed by the Boston Symphony was an exciting and enlightening event. The score was so tall you could barely see above the clarinets. After that I wrote and conducted the Suite and the Concerto for Orchestra and then the First Symphony.

PW: You conducted all of them with the B.S.O.?

WP: Yes. And that was a priceless experience for a young composer.

PW: Did your music pose problems to the musicians of that time? Was it new to them?

WP: Not so new, except perhaps some changing meters and dissonant harmony. I must say I've always composed music from the point of view of the performers. I love instruments, and I value the cooperation of the performers. I believe in the contribution of the player to the music as written. I am very old-fashioned that way.

PW: Did you think of yourself as writing specifically for the B.S.O.?

WP: I was writing for a good symphony orchestra music that I knew would be playable. And it was.

PW: Rimski-Korsakov sets up three categories: that which will sound the first time through; that which will sound after an hour of rehearsal; and that which will never sound no matter how much rehearsal time. Were you aiming at the first or the second category?

WP: I was aiming at the first. But you see I was still learning; I wasn't going out on any limbs.

PW: Have you since found it necessary to aim at the second or found yourself confronted with the third?

WP: I have never reached the level of a certain student in my seminar. We were to have three members of the Boston Symphony come over, and I had asked everybody in the seminar to write for that combination. We had an advance look at the pieces, and I had to tell this boy, "You realize this is unplayable." He said, "Oh, do you really think so?" I suggested that he think it over before copying the parts. Well, he didn't. When he put the parts out the musicians took one look and weren't even going to try. I said, "Just try." They tried and could not proceed more than two measures. They finally said, "We are sorry, we just can't do it." I never in my life saw a young man more pleased. He had achieved an unplayable piece.

PW: But that contribution of the player you were talking about — that doesn't mean you have to write easy parts or parts just like ones they've played, does it?

WP: Let me tell you of my experience with the cellist Mstislav Rostropovitch. I met him for the first time when he appeared with the Boston Symphony in 1966. Through an interpreter, he asked me to write a cello concerto for his Carnegie Hall series in February 1967. But for one very short letter thanking me for accepting, not one word of communication took place between us until the rehearsal the day before the concert. He played the rehearsal, and of course the concert, with no music before him, and it sounded just as I had dreamed it would. Also he knew all the orchestra parts, and at the rehearsal he was constantly prompting the members of the London Symphony. As for the contribution, over and above a performance that was a true and faithful statement of my communication, in the process of relaying this to the listeners he gave his own reaction to the communication without in any way altering its musical meaning. A great artist rather intensifies that meaning.

PW: Had you written the concerto specifically for Rostropovitch's playing? What will happen when another cellist plays it?

WP: When he asked me to write it he said, "Please don't write for the player — write for the instrument." I think that's a most unusual request from a virtuoso. He wants to increase the literature for all cellists. Now, I know it is a difficult piece. But it wasn't written to exhibit things that Rostropovitch can do that others can't. You want to write music that you know is playable and that you know will sound as you imagine it, but no creative artist worthy of the name can prevent himself from reaching into the unknown. I have never written a work that doesn't have *something* that I have had to wait to see how it would come out. That was particularly true of this piece because I had no chance to meet with Rostropovitch while I was working on it.

PW: How did you approach the problem of keeping the soloist from being covered by the orchestra?

WP: I approached it first by saying to myself that this isn't always going to be played by Rostropovitch. He's got a tone that simply carries everything before it, but I didn't want to depend on that tone alone. Beyond that, the problem is the same as writing for any combination of instruments. You've got to hear what you put on that page. I have always said it's a waste of time for a composer to touch the piano. It gives you a wrong impression. If you can't hear that note as played by a horn, you had better take some lessons in ear training. I feel now that I can sit in a chair with any score (well maybe not *any* score — there are some that would take an awful lot of concentration) and hear it better than if I were to hear it played.

PW: Suppose you write a score and go to rehearsal only to find you do hear it clearer in your chair — that the actual sounds create confusion that the imagined sounds don't?

WP: That's where experience comes in. It isn't just a question of ear training or hearing mentally, it's a question of knowing what happens when an orchestra takes hold of your piece, or what happens when the conductor is not the best conductor in the world, or, even if he is, he may not care about your piece as long as it doesn't fall apart. If something does not sound the way you thought it was going to, you have to realize the fault may not be yours . . . but also that it *may* be yours. A composer has to write a lot of music. He has to be in it literally up to his ears.

PW: At what point in the process of composition do you begin to consider sonority problems? Can you tell me anything about the order in which the various aspects of a single piece take shape in your mind?

WP: I wish I could. Naturally I try to get the whole thing in mind first.

PW: Before writing any actual notes?

WP: Yes.

PW: What do you mean by "the whole thing"?

WP: A more-or-less nebulous idea of the kind of thing I want; the general shape and proportions; the musical intent of the piece; the kind of sound. Then I go hunting for it.

PW: Do you find you have to backtrack? Does your idea of the kind of sound change in the course of hunting for it?

WP: Certainly. It always makes me smile when the Library of Congress asks me to keep my sketches for their collection. When I get through I don't have any sketches — they're all rubbed out. I write an awful lot of notes that don't stay. Perhaps I decide I want an opening melody. I proceed to write numberless melodies — maybe each a variant of the one before or maybe something totally new — and in that process, I hope, I strike one that suits me. And it's a funny thing; when I get the one I am looking for I know it immediately.

PW: You say "an opening melody"; by that stage do you already know what it's the opening of? Do you first establish the idea of the shape of the movement, or even of the whole piece?

WP: When Rostropovitch asked for a cello concerto I thought, "I've done so many concertos, all in three movements." The plan "fast-slow-fast" is not bad. But I have on occasion heard entire programs of my works, and heard that way I have found it a bit dreary. The idea of movements is a little hackneyed, and I thought, "Wouldn't this be an interesting project: to make one continuous work — variations, but not theme and variations, rather six or seven ways to regard a musical idea, different aspects or facets, each growing out of another."

PW: Six or seven variations of an underlying theme that is never stated, or each variation a variation of the preceding one?

WP: Well, both. I think they are all variations of one another. But I can't sell the idea.

PW: It doesn't sound that different from Schoenberg's notion of perpetual variation.

WP: I suppose you could say that. Probably one could apply it to more music than one might suspect.

PW: Earlier, when we were talking about your return to Harvard in the mid-twenties, I asked you what you thought a young composer needed to know at that time. Before we stop, could you say something about what you think young composers need to know nowadays — or, if you like, what you think they ought at least to be looking into, but aren't?

WP: I remember being young once, and I know a little about how these things go. It saddens me somewhat that the young fellows going into composition seem not to possess sufficient knowledge of what they are turning their backs on. They write, ". . . after the collapse of tonality . . . ," whereas as a matter of fact tonality has not collapsed, and I think it would be useful for them to know it hasn't. Not that it would affect their own way of writing, but it might improve their thinking. A young man comes in with a score and I ask, "What about the harmony?" He says, "I don't use harmony." I say, "As soon as you put two notes together you've got harmony." He says, "Oh, no, I haven't." "Well," I say, "somebody will hear this chord over here and think, hmm, G,B,D. . . . How about that?" He objects, "You aren't supposed to hear it that way." Now, I think that's just whistling in the dark to say you're not supposed to. The fact is you do. It's the same with rhythm. A fellow says to me, "This is a very difficult rhythm: 13½ thirty-seconds for the value of 6½ triplet eighths. It will have to be done by mechanical means." And I'll say, "Aren't you confusing rhythm with the measurement of time?" "They are the same thing," he'll say. I'll ask him, "Haven't you had the experience of hearing two pianists play the same piece and thinking one fellow plays more rhythmically than the other?" He'll say, "Yes, but that's old-fashioned time-beating, and one fellow keeps better time than the other." But the one who plays more rhythmically probably does not "keep time" better, in the mechanical sense. That's just the point. There has never been an adequate treatment of rhythm, and I don't mean to propose that I could do one, but I do believe that rhythm to be rhythm has to be felt. I do not believe that the measuring off of time-values necessarily creates rhythm. As soon as you accept the concept that the only way a rhythm can be performed is by mechanical means you have lost faith in rhythm as I understand it.

PW: Well, I'm all for the idea that rhythm is not just a series of durations, but I'm not so sure about that word "felt." It's the kind of word that makes most of my generation see red and not understand what you're saying. Could I translate it this way? We "feel" the rhythm when the interaction of a number of factors (not just duration but loudness and pitch) makes us expect what's coming next: even if we don't get what we expect, the fact that we expect something affects the way we hear whatever it is we do get.

WP: That's so. But the factors that interact in the playing of the more rhythmic performer we were speaking of are not all written in the music. They are actually subtle distortions of the printed time values (and other values), and they arise from the performer's sensing the musical meaning of what he sees. It is an instinctive and usually unconscious phenomenon. Now I grant you this is old-hat stuff. One says, "The old art of music is gone and we are replacing it with something new." Well, traditions like that are not so easily dismissed. You mentioned dynamics. A while back they were speaking of total organization, or total serialization, for instance, of dynamics. They would write *piano* under an alto flute note, and *piano* under a trombone note, and they seem to have assumed them to be of the same degree of loudness. But *piano* isn't an absolute quantity, it's relative.

PW: But if you wrote p under all the notes of a wind chord you'd expect them to be balanced, wouldn't you?

WP: Probably the chord wouldn't be balanced at the first reading, but good players would adjust as soon as they understood it should be. With mediocre players the chances are against it. The problem of balance is always present because of the disparity in dynamic intensity between instruments and between different parts of the range of individual instruments. It is a responsibility of the orchestra conductor to see that sonorities are in proper equilibrium.

168 PETER WESTERGAARD

PW: Supposing you had players who did understand. Could you conceive of using a loud first chord followed by a second softer chord; then later a third chord that's just the same as the second chord followed by a fourth chord that's just as much softer than the third as the second was softer than the first?

WP: Certainly. But I'd have to make sure that the players understood. Our notation is not accurate enough to show it. A composer friend of mine wrote *fffff*. I asked, "Is that five times as loud as *f*?" He replied, "I don't know. I just want them to play loud." Now, most of the piece gets along with only one *f*, but there are two spots marked *ff*. If you use five *f*'s it raises problems as to what two or three or four *f*'s are supposed to mean to a player. No doubt the question will some day be settled by a notation in decibels.

What interests me even more is the matter of pitch. Here you have all the string players brought up on exercises like Kreutzer's studies and Viotti's concertos—everything in the most elementary tonal style. And even before that, when they learn from their teachers how to play scales, they're told: "In the major, play the third degree high, close to the fourth, and the seventh close to the tonic." The student learns to play in tune by imitating his teacher and listening to other good players. You've never heard of a teacher teaching his students to distinguish between a tempered and an untempered scale. The method has nothing to do with physics; it's just habit forming, but it means that they get to know what scale degree they are playing. It becomes so instinctive that many do not know they do it, and when they play any little phrase they will hear it in some key—it may not be the right one, but the point is they will play it with a tonal sense. I once experimented by asking all the quartets I knew who played the Schoenberg quartets, "How do you go about getting it in tune?" They all seemed puzzled at first, but finally practically all said, "We keep playing until it sounds in tune to us." I said, "Fine," but I wondered if that was what Schoenberg wanted. Although the more I feel I know Schoenberg's music the more I believe he thought that way himself. That brings us back to the question of whether or not tonality has collapsed. And it isn't only the players; it's also the listeners. They will hear tonality in everything.

I would like to illustrate this with an anecdote. Some years ago I noticed a place in an orchestral work, the identity of which I cannot now recall, where the double basses were holding a low A♭, as seventh of the dominant of E♭ sounding above. Meanwhile the chord above changed to a combination sounding as dominant seventh of the key of A♮. This gave the A♭ a new meaning as G♯, leading tone of A.

Now the difference in pitch of these two tones is known to be the comma of Pythagoras, a quite noticeable distance on the string length of the double bass. It was clearly visible to me that all eight players made that small change in the position of the left hand in unison when the new harmony sounded. I spoke to one of them about this and he denied having made any change, but he finally allowed he may have corrected his pitch, feeling it to be a bit out of tune.

An even more interesting side of all this is that many listeners hear a change of pitch when the same example is played on the piano. I have tested this many times. The piano is an instrument that is always out of tune, according to the standards of pitch held by string players, and also by wind players, who continually adjust their pitches to the sound of other instruments. We unconsciously impute pitches to notes of the piano when we understand the musical meaning, and this is based on tonal interpretation. I call it subjective pitch, without which most music would be unintelligible to the average listener.

We must realize that there exists such a concept as musical meaning, and I don't mean, "the grass is green." I mean the kind of meaning you get in a Mozart quartet. Not a representation of anything, but an entity that has been brought into being as languages have been, by common usage, so that all you have to hear is just a little bit, a snatch, to recognize its meaning, its relationship to that usage. Things like that do not go away easily. They're going to be there.

The forces in support of reaction, tradition, conservatism, and preservation of the status quo have been gathered into what has been called, somewhat derisively, "The Establishment." This is something against which all creative artists have always had to struggle, and it is something the listening public, which after all constitutes the receiving end of the artist's communication, believes to be fundamentally right and everlasting. There has never been a time in music history when The Establishment has been so firmly entrenched. It represents the main ingredient in all but a very small part of the vast body of musical literature that is in our libraries and on records, that we hear daily, that we study and play daily, that performers know by heart, and that the public loves. It is inimical to change, or as some would put it, to progress. It will undergo change, as it always has, through the process of evolution, as composers continue to write music according to their personal ideals and convictions, and expressive of their own individuality. It will not be changed by the naïve process of issuing manifestos declaring its demise.

WALTER PISTON

For His Seventieth Birthday

CLIFFORD TAYLOR

THE DIMENSIONS of a creative practice emerge at least as much out of its variables as out of known factors. There is much that we still do not know about the processes of twentieth-century music, perhaps precisely because we are intent on knowing too much. The traditional difference between art and science rests principally on this point, and yet not to know seems to be unthinkable in our time. In the hope of focussing some attention on what might be known, as well as on what is essentially arcane in Walter Piston's music, one might view it as an art not entirely sustained by any total rationality, although it seems to occupy an area about which much can supposedly be known.

Piston, of course, has always been a composer of remarkable circumspection, a formalist who attempts to establish the limitations of a creative vision before giving in to its impulses. His music has always been well made, its thematic materials stated in balance, appropriately reestablished, and presented in the guises in which they appeared most attractive. The times in which he has composed have been both conducive to such a practice and antagonistic to it. Amid the chaos of multiply different ambitions, and the often incomprehensible means by which they are projected, the salvation of sensibility seems to lie in the stability of intelligent formulation. If Piston's work has any meaning, then, beyond the known facts of its construction, it is the symbolization of such an enviable state of sensibility, to which only a few seem to be heir.

With regard to current musical activity, Piston's music is eminently "harmonic," involving, that is, one system of pitch selection. "Implications of harmonic nuance," however, may be a more appropriate expression, since it is always the line, the variable, that functions within the framework of a harmonic structure, and establishes the conditions by which twentieth-century music is fundamentally defined.

We are, in our time, concerned with movement. The single aspect of the triad that most concerns the composer whose music is structurally involved with triadic root implications is its definitive interval, the 3rd. Used in a final cadence, its lack of movement is not problematic; and in any case, the supposition of its static effect is partly unfounded and partly a purely stylistic truth. Thus Bach counterpoint has movement, but not of the kind or degree now required. Within a noncadential textural situation, the stasis of the triadic 3rd causes the other factors of the triadic occurrence to be governed by procedures which no longer fit demands of movement so violently and extensively felt to be not only appropriate but so necessary in our time as to lead directly to the final attitude of chance, the purely fantastic coincidence of immensely varied circumstances.

Harmonic texture in 4ths became a well-established solution by which a primarily diatonic line was maintained. The use of the 4th as a building interval is an obvious cornerstone of Piston's musical practice, but what is more interesting is his judicious handling of it in situations where the presence of the 3rd is simultaneously implicit. At times, a tone functioning in the context of a triadic 3rd does appear directly, but more frequently, in passages with greater forward impulse, it occurs by implication only, as the 4th above an implied root in an unresolved 4-3 suspension (Ex. 1).

Ex. 1 Partita for Violin, Viola, and Organ (1951)

Here, the C of m. 2 would imply the IV of E♭ (major-minor) as the 3rd of the triadic unit, although it might also be conceivable as the added 6th to the E♭ triad itself. The following D with the B♭ suddenly and with deliberate awkwardness, implies the dominant triad. The third measure fulfills the presumption of the subdominant, using the B♭ as nondominant 9th, with a V/I implication. One can hardly dismiss French practice here, that of Milhaud, Honegger, and possibly others coming to mind. The more interesting function of the 3rd comes at the end, however, with the introduction of the G♭ in the next-to-last measure filling the empty E♭-minor 7th implication in the previous measure. The G♭ serves as lower inflection of a presumed G and guarantees the sense of the major triadic third with the concluding E♭. Of course, the line in the original is not explicitly harmonized in this manner. Many other implications are structured into the remaining textural lines of the organ parts, but to a great extent the implications of this principal line are fulfilled or enhanced. The third measure from the end displays a careful avoidance of the 3rd (G♭-G) using the harmonization in 4ths so that the A♭ serves only to imply the forthcoming G♭, and, finally, G, again avoided in the final measure of accompaniment. G does appear in the first measure of the next phrase, however, as the 3rd of an implied E minor, so the sense of movement is preserved throughout by the implication rather than the direct use of the triadic 3rd.

Piston's work is essentially tonal in this sense of implied triadic structure and its association of root and fifth. The traditional corollary of root function, particularly in the large structural sense, is clearly at work; local occurrences of major and minor thirds, especially in melodic context, serve to imply triadic structure, with the lower tones in each configuration taking on the appearance of root structure and function. Texture, too, is essentially conceived in terms of a harmonic order of this general kind, in varying degrees of vertical or diversionary linear projection. This harmonic determinant, moreover, is never displaced by any kind of schematically motivic order, although various forms of serialization are to be found in isolated instances. In the third movement of the Partita for Violin, Viola, and Organ, for example, there are four forms of a 12-tone set exposed in the first 12 measures. Measures 1-6 present O_1 and IR_1, the violin line OR_1, and the upper manual organ part I_1 with G𝄪 embellishment, in the second 6 measures. Underlying the upper manual part of the organ score is a second manual part in triadic forms which essentially harmonizes the upper part. In m. 11, the viola enters with a free scalar design whose last three notes break the stepwise intervallic pattern to complete the I_1 form of the upper manual part (Ex. 2).

Ex. 2

But this is in no sense the definitive practice by which Piston's music is either known or by which he works; its essential consequence in this movement of the Partita is to arbitrarily order chromatic inflection around an apparent F♯ tonality. Still, although Piston's inherent concern for tonality is, for the most part, more directly projected otherwise than in such a serial texture, the problem of movement within a texture is, in fact, the foremost aspect of his thought. The opening of the Violin Concerto, for example, is quite clear in its sense of D, and the introductory material, in the manner of an anacrusis, involves various other degrees of this tonal order in support of its conclusive establishment in m. 10 (Ex. 3). Here, root effect can be determined by the various semblances to traditional practice; when the harmonic situation is overly complex in a polytonal grouping, the lower sonorities prevail. A, at the outset, is tonally predominant. The root implications which follow (G,F,D,A) all serve as introduction to the final D. This context is further supported by the rhythm of these occurrences, in which A has a time length of 4 measures (as a presumed pedal), G, 1 measure, F, 1 measure, D, 2 measures, and A, 1 measure, as the final root of an im-

Ex. 3

plied cadence to D which, as tonic, is sustained for some 12 measures in support of the principal theme of the first movement.

Obviously, however, what occurs above this basic root movement in the lowest range is more important to the whole textural effect than the root implications themselves. The upper designs are certainly selected with a sense of their triadic implications (D, E minor, G, E minor, C major, A major, suspended A over G major, etc.). Aside from considerations of violinistic appropriateness, these "chords" are devised rather freely in terms of traditional practice. Some have no 3rds, and their roots are frequently 3rd-related in a way that produces a weak sense of progression throughout the succession. The point here is clearly not the creation of strong patterns of resolution and relationship through voice movement, but rather the employment of modal voice lines to soften the basic harmonic contrast.

The opening chord itself creates a "polytonal" situation by representing both D and A as roots. But more significantly, the presence of D, the fourth scale-degree of A, in the complex produces a familiar non-triadic configuration whose subsequent treatment defines the modal, rather than traditionally harmonic, nature of the linear figuration and triadic movement. The whole passage could be considered in terms of a flow of lines, beginning with the first chord, and perhaps moving as follows in Ex. 4.

A textural concept is also at work, involving multiple harmonic implications as well as an open spacing of related polytonal units, such as the 5ths over B and D in m. 4, pulse 2, and the 5th over G plus inverted 5th of B on pulse 3 (Ex. 5).

Ex. 4

Ex. 5

This spacing has its basis in overtone resonance, a premise which Roy Harris carried to more extensive conclusions, and with different results, than are evident in Piston's work. In Harris, this overtone resonance is extended to include complete triads, producing a texture as full as Piston's is light.

In the opening theme (Ex. 6), even though the 3rd is present in a clear D major, the presence of E in the sonority creates a multiple harmonic effect and insures movement within the triadic context. The

Ex. 6

Ex. 6 (cont.)

theme itself is a combination of modal scale-degree and harmonic implication with chromatic inflection of certain scale members. Thus the F♯ (3rd
of the D triad) is also treated as an inflection of G, but is always separated
from it by at least one intervening tone, as the C♯ is similarly separated
from the D toward which it inflects. The introduction of the G in m. 6
implies a subdominant relation, but is still working against the multiple
implications of V (A) and I (D) in the bass line. The violin's F♯ in m. 6
is at once the 3rd of the A-D complex, the 7th of G, and the leading-
tone to the scalar fourth degree (G) in the previous measure. This sense
of multiple function and incomplete resolution is finally the essential
point of Piston's harmonic texture and tonal action.

In more volatile melodic textures, the 3rd is given a dynamic ambiguity by the contradictory movement of other parts against it.

Ex. 7. Quintet for Wind Instruments, Second Movement; 1956

This passage begins by implying a V-I root movement with a G♯-minor
tonic. At the bracket marked (x), a movement of voice lines suggests a
triadic structure based on the doubled D of the lower sonorities, with C
as minor 7th, both causing the G above to sound as a traditional 4-3
appogiatura to F♯, a movement which does occur, and a suspended B.
B, however, moves to F♯ in contradiction to traditional practice and this
F♯ moves to G at the same moment that the upper G moves to its
F♯ resolution. Neither F♯ functions clearly as a triadic third. In the next
measure, the D-A 5th groups itself around the F♯, but E, doubled in the
lower lines, impels the F♯ to a resolution upward (to G), contrary to the

D-major triad context around the deserted F♯. The F following creates a suggestion of D minor, and opens the way for a scheme of "naturals" around an F root. From here on the voice movement to m. 5 is both D-minor and F-major oriented. The final chordal structure in this example acquires motion by the direct chromatic inflection of its parts, a simultaneous statement of the kind of action that occurs in varied time patterns in the preceding measures.

The contrapuntal nature of Piston's texture is frequently manifest in a two-part pattern, with two- or three-tone chordal figures added in the harmonic dimension. The opening of the Concerto for Orchestra of 1934 displays this procedure; the Second Symphony begins with this kind of texture, with somber Brahmsian overtones, in the strings; and many passages in the Fourth Symphony are based on it as well.

Ex. 8

To avoid such a familiar term as pandiatonicism in this connection is not easy, but one might say instead that in Ex. 8 the G major modality in both upper and lower parts creates a stable G tonality through scalar means although harmonic implications are also observable in the pitch succession.

Within these contrapuntal textures of two or three parts, lines are guided into and away from triadic incidence, the problematic area of music conceived within the reference of a purely diatonic idiom. Sensitive expressive areas of Piston's thought, however, are often the result of contrapuntal textures which do contain a noticeable incidence of triadic occurrence. The effect within these two-part textures is of motion forward, of consistently changing harmonic conditions, each of which tends to have at least a double tonal implication, triadically or in scalar terms. These implications form the greater part of the process by which linear impulse is maintained. Essentially, movement of this kind is guaranteed by dissonantal occurrence, but this is only possible when the prevailing tonality, either through scalar or root implication of some sort, is sufficiently defined, as it usually is in Piston's work. On the other hand, the scalar tonics are often shifted by these situations, and then the effect is only of one scale degree against another. The force of the linear impulse is to a great extent diminished, establishing instead the pandiatonic condition of interacting modal lines. The harmonic effect of dissonance, more operative in Piston's work, gives it its sharpness and body, where actual pandiatonic writing is often flaccid and without textural substance.

This two-part texture is naturally defined as bass and soprano of the traditional four-part texture. Inner part-writing is often reinforced in triadic form, as in the Second Symphony, (Ex. 9) while in the Quintet for Wind Instruments, true five-part texture predominates because of the complete differentiation of the timbres used.

(x) functional chromaticism

Ex. 9

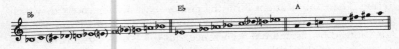

Ex. 9 (cont.)

Here the chromatic inflection of scale degrees is consistently maintained in this example, between C♯ inflection of D and E inflection of F, while the enharmonic notational change of G♭-B♭-D♭ into F♯-A♯-C♯ in m. 3 is a functional chromatic motion toward the A♭ triad in m. 4, an unaltered derivation of the E♭ scalar modality at that point in the phrase.

In Piston's later works his textures remain generally of the same order, slightly more intensified perhaps as in this passage from the first movement of the recent Seventh Symphony.

Ex. 10

This is rather a three-part than a strictly two-part texture, in which a characteristic cell-motive is at work in generating the three lines. Example 11 is from the development section of the movement and effects a tonal move from F to C.

Ex. 11

The linear progress is much more significant than the harmonic, yet the rhythm of the harmonic progression is essentially defined by the rhythm of the bass-line articulations. The cadence creates noticeable harmonic contrast by half-step voice leading, a practice less essential in Piston's work than it was in Hindemith's.

Ex. 12

The bass line following this cadence (Ex. 12) defines the strongest impulse to the A tonality of the recapitulation, although the upper chordal structures are duplications of a second line which goes into the A cadence, the third line stopping three measures earlier (Ex. 13).

Ex. 13

In this final cadence into the A of the recapitulation, the essential three-part design with varied triadic and implied triadic or polytonal doublings for textural fullness establishes emphatic 3- and 4-note patterns which give the cadence its impact beyond the chordal patterns alone. The upper line figure, E, D♯, A♯, changes to E, D♮, A♯, and finally to E♮, D, A, strong tonal degrees of A as destination, while the lower line reiterates a pattern of minor 2nd-major 2nd, the second and third time inverted and preceded by the B-A♯ (B♭) upper leading tone of A. The A is not permitted to appear until the cadence. This is a motivic cadential procedure that achieves its strength essentially through two-part writing and is a more developed technique than that used at a similar point in the Second Symphony, where the plain facts of the harmonic progression—root triads on B♭ from above and on A♭ from below converging on the A—establish A as tonic for the recapitulation.

The tonal scheme of any of Piston's works depends on its method of defining tonal emphasis. Root must be implied in his textures either by the traditional implication of the 5th or by unison, but rarely by polytonal structures unless the bottom tone can arbitrarily be accepted as the strongest member of the group. In the first movement of the Fifth String Quartet, both procedures are used. Unison B♭ establishes the tonal level of the movement, at beginning and end. The last movement, interestingly enough, ends on A, in the sense of a descending cadential resolution from the first movement's B♭.

The neoclassic alternation of themes, characteristic of all Piston's work, shows an indefiniteness in the second theme area of the first movement, from mm. 35-40, in contrast to the clear B♭ unison beginning. The development begins decidedly on G♭, the recapitulation is on D, and the coda, affirms the B♭ again, a statement of original design. The B♭ to G♭ relationship is characteristically that of a 3rd, as are those of both the G♭ and B♭ to the recapitulation D. The second movement ends on D, the third on A, so the large plan finally embraces the 4th, but the significance of all such tonal plans lies in the scalar relationship of selected pitch levels. While the First String Quartet, for example, has a relatively simple tonal plan of movements, C-E-C, the Fifth Quartet's plan is more sensitive to the linear movement of the initial B♭ to the final A. The Seventh Symphony shows a stronger dominant-to-tonic effect in its A-F-D plan, although within the first movement, the A tonality is emphasized, once again, by the more linearly related B♭. What the mind can retain of these tonal levels in terms of the extensive complexity and frequent ambiguity of root implication within the movements is of course questionable, yet other features of formal organization, especially that of phrase clarity by pitch design, are also at work. Since melodic design itself has a tonality relatable to scalar order, i.e., modality, by virtue of tonal repetition and final cadence, the effect of melodic phrasing and melodic or scalar "tonality" is of much greater importance and to a great extent—if not entirely—displaces most considerations of root process. In all these dimensions, Piston's work evidences a consistent avoidance of the triadic third for the sake of linear movement. Any example of his melodic invention displays an intricacy of modal order and chromatic inflection within that kind of order at least equal to, and perhaps more fundamentally significant than, his harmonic predetermination. Under these conditions, the wider range of harmonic implication in his work can only be brought under another form of definition, a theoretical modality, i.e., a generic sense of modality reaching beyond established modal patterns into all scalar possibilities.

Thus this work, in its individual and unostentatious way, also contributes significantly to the defiance of systems of harmonic control in favor of a liberated melodic impulse that has consistently formed the core of contemporary musical thought. Piston's employment of clearly traditional contexts and materials in pursuing this policy has been a remarkable demonstration of how, without abandoning its familiar guises, an art can relate to wholly new cultural-aesthetic impulses such as the Western world has experienced in this century, which in effect alter its traditional definition.

STEFAN WOLPE

For His Sixtieth Birthday

EDWARD LEVY

THE MUSIC OF Stefan Wolpe exemplifies the most significant pre-occupations of contemporary composition. Wolpe has achieved mastery of his own compositional propensities, after long years of intensive self-criticism, directing them, examining his processes, and sharpening his awareness; and this mastery produces music spontaneous sounding and structurally unified, optimally derived yet non-predictable and non-consistent, whose scope encompasses intensely personal yet vastly provocative solutions to contemporary concerns.

Wolpe's *donnée* is an image—a visual-poetic image—and his music is a sound representation of it. Wolpe's music has a characteristic vigor, and in his choice of events, of actions, one cannot help feeling his preferences, his thought, his awareness, his character. In the incisive choice of the core activity and its manifold results, one sees his intense involvement both with his own material and with vital compositional problems.

For instance, Wolpe combines in his work the appeals of the two most publicized directions in music today. The appeal, first, of complete structuring of a piece, is achieved through a personal, contemporary handling of those traditions of organization which are still vital. Although complete reliance on traditional modes of behavior leads only to sterility, an adaptation of traditional criteria or general processes to a unique characteristic usage of contemporary language can be meaningful. The most fundamental criterion here would be economy—non-redundancy and fulfillment of obligation or implication following from that economy; and the most basic general process would be a reliance on traditional ways of establishing an identity which retains its vigor throughout its various projections.

Wolpe acknowledges tradition then, in his characteristic technique of forming tangible shapes and creating variant forms; in his operating within a selected pitch field, carefully introducing into this field new tones that function not to supplant other pitches but to increase, gradually, the availability of pitches; and in his eminent satisfaction of the criterion of economy—the ultimate, most imaginative use of his material.

Wolpe combines this imagination with great control, to achieve the other appeal, non-predictability. His vocabulary of variations must necessarily be vast in order to permit him to work economically within the selected pitch field, but his particular usage of characteristic variations is one of Wolpe's most important original techniques—non-gradual development. This technique, allied with the slow pitch growth, underlies his method of changing densities and overall form. The phenomenon of non-gradual development is also manifested in Wolpe's long line, which is viewed in flashes. First, he creates concrete motivic shapes from a few selected pitches. A complete, resultant, gradually developing line, slowly unfolding in all its steps, would be redundant. Rather, Wolpe works from the basis that all variants inhere in the initial statement of the motivic shape; and, selected segments of the developmental line burst forth as needed, revealing the line's process. On the assumption that there is a basis for a scale of closeness and remoteness in variations, Wolpe does not go from "near" to "far," but chooses particular variants as the context demands. This context is constantly volatile—a least-obvious core element is derived, but so quickly that this new development is also non-predictable. The suggestion of the whole line is sufficient; what point on the line is chosen depends on context, not on progression. Thereby, Wolpe's variations avoid the "perpetual" or "progressive variation" dilemma by being immediate rather than progressive. Since the state, or certainly the implication, of change is an integral part of the material—the material exists in all its varied capabilities as a basic source, and the particular states will be projected in multiple images—the transforms are always available and can be called upon as the situation requires. They are "right" but not "perpetual."

Space in Wolpe's music is permeated with a dynamic activity. The choice of activities is made not only in terms of a non-gradual development, but in terms of immediate transformations of activities, of projections of pitch or motivic material in polar extremes. For example, Wolpe deliberately chooses "material of no consequence." This is actually a variant of pitch, intervallic or motivic material in a shape that, because of its obviousness or even its cliché quality, is generally of minimum freshness. The non-consequential variant is set against other variant shapes which are extremely different in their modes of activity. (See m. 5 of *Form for Piano.*) Because of this juxtaposition, the cliché takes on status and function within the piece. It becomes not banal, but an extreme transformation of the other activities. The non-consequential material still has that essential quality which made it so appealing to so many so often that at length it did become a cliché. This quality retained, the banality is therefore not opposed to freshness; rather, the juxtaposition of the two or more modes of activity creates meaning, i.e. intensity, function, maximum diversity in the context. The concept of extreme difference, of polar complements (in the sense that a positive and negative field complement each other), sets up heights of continual tension in the music, for it is the combination of elements into a total ensemble of events that gives the maximum effective meaning and impact.

This intense communication assumes that all things are possible; therefore, the extremes of a situation are presented, i.e. the pitch situation projects in many specific forms: contained, energetic buzzings, durations of extreme difference, long lines interrupted by motivic lines, intervals or chords in a contrasting articulation. And each presentation produces a changing density of texture—one line projects immediately into multiple simultaneous directions; intervals, motives, pitch groups transform non-gradually into other shapes, in other registral distributions, in other durations, in other timbres, in other phrases with new focal aspects.

The interaction of these varying densities and the constant transformation of the material permit the material to retain its vitality throughout its recurrences. In fact, a correlation seems to exist between the small pitch field used and the transformed projections of it. Though no systematic or direct cause-and-effect is utilized, there is the general attitude that if shapes remain, the context (makeup, composition of these shapes) changes; and when shapes are volatile, the pitch field remains. As the piece progresses, the pitch field increases; but there are always focal pitches, focal intervals, and projections of these pitches in particular shapes so that the pitches are organically incorporated into activities. Basically, pitches are not accompanied by their set complements, but by their cooperative and coexistent motive participants. In this way, Wolpe avoids the non-specific sonority produced by an interminable circulation of tones, by concentrating on smaller pitch constellations. He uses the situation of gradual new pitches, adding pitches organically by projecting each pitch group in a motivic shape, and then having one of two things occur: either the pitch group projects itself in transforms, or new pitches are added as a motivic continuity (Ex. 1).

The slow growth of the pitch field, in sum, means that each new pitch is introduced within an existent situation—as if the pitches which are already members of the set put the newly introduced tone into sufficient situations so that its incorporation into the set results from successful involvements in motivic activities—whereas the existent pitches are found in constantly new involvements, either motivically or texturally, or in new timbres, registers or articulations.

This taking into account of focal pitches, focal intervals and focal motives produces, of course, a much slower rate of pitch circulation and thereby avoids an overall "grayness" of sound by having specific pitches participating in specific types of activity.

Since Wolpe does not present ordered pitches, but rather has pitch groups smaller than a twelve-tone set functioning in multiple involve-

Ex. 1, from *Piece for Two Instrumental Units* (1962)

ments in orderings based on context, these pitches can remain, untransposed, over longer sections. Then, a continuity is established based on this multiplicity of events; certainly, it is not only gradual change that may represent continuity. If an idea is to be picked up later, it must be retained, still "full of promise," so as to produce a counterpoint of activities. Just as an interaction of registers produces a contrapuntal continuity of line over longer areas by having registers picked up again, so the entire interacting ensemble of events produces a long continuity by having particular events or activities picked up and continued later. That continuity within the same type of activity can be established is, of course, as obvious as that continuity can be established by using similar pitches. That the continuity does not have to be immediate has also been observed.

Wolpe uses a restricted pitch field, but he avoids the exasperating redundancy that might result from the meticulous picking up of pitches by constantly involving them in new contexts—articulation, register, density, focus. The material is projected in distinct shapes and not subjected to a series of tricks the master taught it. Rather, a motivic continuity is established in terms of focal aspects. Most often, the least obvious quality of a unit will be extracted to create exactly that result of polar transforms, of complementary extremes, which is wanted. The connection is an unexpected but inherent one. The gradual linking will be called on, but for a function similar to the source's, for when the music leaves out these next-step variants, that next step is still freshly available for use at a later time. Since it has the maximum similarity to the first shape, this variant would serve as a reminder of it, as a new exposition, a new start.

Or this gradual, more obvious extraction will be used as a most unexpected event, since within a context of change, a sudden non-change is the most extreme differentiation in terms of procedure. Moreover, the continuity is both derived and unexpected because the new occurrence will usually contain not just one, but a simultaneous few vital, focal elements.

Wolpe's solution to the problem of textural consistency within the long sections he creates from this complex density is to combine a similar treatment of all voices—each unfolding in its own orbit, each participating in the varied activities—with a contrast of dissimilar activities, all unfolding together within a whirlwind of sound. Such a solution depends on the shapes being always tangible; in this way, the climactic activity, the separation of functions, the unfolding of material are all accounted for—but in a constantly shifting assignment of role. The resultant texture is consistent in its complexity, while avoiding obviousness. It can function unitarily, as does the small pitch field, over longer periods because of its greater multiplicity of action, greater change in densities, and greater interactions.

This maximum differentiation of activities with the maximum similarity of source is capable of maintaining its intensity over long periods. It does not require contrasting sections: it subsumes contrast. Thereby, Wolpe avoids the superimposition on his material of remembered forms. Certainly, it is by now apparent that the borrowed forms took the outer, melodic manifestations of organization rather than its structural foundations and imposed them on systems with intrinsically different behaviors. Wolpe's forms are created from his situation, and the complexity of texture, density and transform permit this situation to last and also prevent its redundancy by demanding time for a perception and absorption of its events. The eruptive quality of the ensemble, the constant newness of projection, the juxtaposition and mixture create long sections and give the form its depth and scope.

Wolpe's most compelling characteristics, the differently acting extreme transforms in a changing complex texture, are, of course, best seen in his latest scores. The characteristic preoccupations and concerns are already visible, however, in his earlier works, two of which I will cite.

Wolpe's first well-known work, *Passacaglia* for piano solo (1936), reveals his concern for intervallic correspondences in complex textures. Moreover, his choice of this form would seem to correlate clearly with his predilection for clear, original shapes and rhythmically vigorous variants derived from them. His concern for intervals is shown in his building the cantus on successively larger intervals from 1 to 11, and forming the eleven countersubjects on expansions of the intervals of this cantus. These countersubjects are early examples of derivative twelve-tone sets, each interval engendering a set built upon it.

In the initial statement, an accompaniment figure disturbs the rhythmic regularity of the cantus, given mostly in even quarters, and thereafter, for the greater part of the piece, each statement of the cantus or its retrograde is presented along with this accompaniment and the successive eleven derived sets.

A special Wolpe trait, along with this complexity, is his exploitation of range, notable in the second variation. The cantus is restated, after the first variation, within its small registral limits, C to A, while the accompaniment opposes this containment by inverting intervals, so that 2's expand into 10's and 1's into 11's and

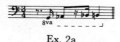

Ex. 2a

becomes

Ex. 2b

This larger range is immediately used in all voices, not only as a contrast in spatial proportions, but with an extra relationship: the beginning of the first derivative set (Ex. 2c)

Ex. 2c

consists of the outer pitch limits of the accompaniment, transposed, extended one more octave. The setting of small against large proportions is used much more rigorously in Wolpe's later works and will perhaps be the subject of future investigations.

The spatial growth of a situation through the use of small pitch groups in multiple projections and the motivic incorporation of new pitches into this situation, which becomes dominant in later pieces, is particularly well illustrated in the *Violin Sonata* (1949). The initial presentation (Ex. 3a) is

Ex. 3a

the rest in both the violin and the piano resulting in the isolation of the G. The three-note motive branches out in many directions, accumulating new pitches around the D and G poles (Ex. 3b)

Ex. 3b

while the violin line expands in space, adding D, then F, G♭, A♭, A and E♭, using the D as a focal pitch from which to grow into new registers (Ex. 3c).

Ex. 3c

When the high D is reached, the expansion of the line focuses on E, E♭, B, B♭, the last pitches to enter, and on the new large range before the line is retracted into its original register and the segment concludes. A new exposition with the original motive using the original pitches then begins, a G-major triad summing up the G-D poles which have dominated so far. This summing precedes the new exposition, exploring other areas of development and much broader pitch inclusions.

It is more revealing, however, to speak of the technique of space and new exposition with reference to one of the later pieces; in the *Form for Piano* (1959). For example, the hexachord is used in a way analogous

f o r m for piano

to the use of a scale—it is identifiable through its unique pitch content, whose order is not maintained in the manner of a set, but is permuted for motivic considerations and for the purpose of revealing the intervallic makeup of the particular hexachord. Since the total intervallic content of a hexachord is equal to that of any of its inversions or transpositions, and since Wolpe is interested in projecting motivic intervals, he uses transpositions less frequently, which results not only in larger harmonic areas, but also in the full exploration of the hexachord's possibilities.

In this work only one major transposition is used, T_5 at m. 30 (Ex. 4a).

Ex. 4a   Ex. 4b

This transposition has the maximum number of new tones possible with this hexachord, four. One minor transposition, used in mm. 8, 9, and 10, has four tones in common (Ex. 4b).

The first hexachord, presented as a non-expressive line in the simplest rhythmic terms, focuses on 3's—Ab-F, G-E, and Bb-A-G. The range limits are a 6, the unique interval of this hexachord, marked by Bb-E. In the next measure the simple line continues, but its flow is suddenly opposed by a new shape which expands the range limits in terms of the previous limits—the Bb-E still are the outer tones, but now three and a half octaves apart. This activity of two contradictory forces results in a containment of each, a non-exhaustion to preserve utility. The dominant interval, 3, remains in the previous limits, with the sustained F moving to the central tone, G. Moreover, a relationship of trichords is achieved among Ab-F-Bb, A-G-E, the two trichords of the first presentation, and Bb-F-G, similar to these, when in normal form, by inversion (Ex. 5a).

Ex. 5a

The linear ordering of the third unit is the fulfillment of linear intervallic possibilities with this trichord, since three combinations of constituent intervals are possible, a 2 and a 3, a 3 and a 5 (presented by the first two), and a 2 and a 5, now presented by the third (Ex. 5b).

Ex. 5b

The difference in articulation which separates the Bb-Ab-E from F-G is, of course, obvious. But pitches can be multiply involved, and any succession of sounds is accepted, no other requisite but contiguity being needed for a perception of continuity. (The significance of the continuity, on the other hand, is the purpose of this analysis.) The fact that the pitches are projected in different registers or in different articulations does no more to dissociate these pitches than the fact of their different durations or timbres. The differences may certainly point to separate functions in separate areas or on different levels, as the location of the high Bb and low E has its own cause and the Ab-E simultaneity has its own consequences; but multiple functions are frequent and in no way preclude hearing the pitches doubly. In fact, the E itself has a double relationship: with the Bb, it marks the range limits, with the Ab, the temporal limits, and is a summary or extreme transform of the previous line. Thus, the Bb belongs doubly to the Bb-Ab-E and to the temporal sequence, Bb-F-G. In fact, the interrelationship of the groups, forming both a functional disparity and a motivic unity, makes the situation more cogent, especially in view of Wolpe's practice of isolating the least obvious in the foreground, the more apparent in the background, as part of his concept of extreme transforms.

The Ab-E is still open for use and continues its interruptive function, combining with another 4, F-A. This tetrachord is a summary situation of the opening of this measure: the two previous central tones, Ab-F, each take part in a 4, from the 4, Ab-E; the new A makes a 13(1) with the Ab, as did the E and F; and the outer limits, E-A, are an exact transposition of the Bb-F limit (Ex. 6).

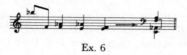

Ex. 6

The next unit is pivotal, being both derived $\left[\dfrac{(F\text{-}A\ \lfloor F\text{-}Bb\text{-}G).}{4\ /\ \text{trichord}}\right]$ and forming two new groups: A-Ab-Bb and A-F-E, which serve to introduce the first four pitches of the complementary hexachord, entering in similar groups: F#-D-C# and C#-D-C. The correlation between new pitches being introduced through established shapes and established pitches always assuming new shapes obtains here.

The remaining two pitches, B and Eb, are similarly introduced in association with two existent pitches, D-B, and C-Eb, through the interval 3. This interval clearly refers to m. 1, but had been put into the background there so as not to exhaust it by an immediate exploitation. Moreover, the new exposure of this 3 brings in the close of this long articulation, emphasized by the static chords; this 3, then, frames the segment. The closing shape functions as such by turning back on itself and halting the forward motion, opposed only by the trichord Ab-Bb-F which precedes the action in the next segment.

The continual extraction of core elements (Ex. 7)

Ex. 7

has created continuity so far, but these elements have been projected in a tremendous variety of types of activity. Within these six measures can be found a long line, short bursts, chords, a trill. The trill, on C-D, is an example of the non-consequential material mentioned earlier. The differentiation between it and other modes of activity removes its banality, while its static quality functions to restrain the growth of activity in order to lead to the closing segment already mentioned.

The 3, now in a new shape, again starts a segment, this one picking up the previous A-A♭-B♭ motive as its next-step extension. This motive also surrounds the E with an F and an E♭, but the E♭ is not a member of this hexachord. Used for motivic reasons, it immediately has a result—the resumed chordal activity is a superimposition of parts of both hexachords, continuing the occurrence which was previously cadential. Now, this total sound is subjected to a transformation, its core being extracted by choosing its limits F-F♯ and its center, B, while its other center, C, operates with an inversion of its previous trichord: C-B-D and C-D♭-B♭.

The piece has two main harmonic areas, T_0 and T_5, with these mm. 8-10 and three parallel measures just before the end, where T_0 reappears within the T_5 area, containing the only other transpositions. The main transposition at m. 30 is made through a common mode of activity, a technique seen in m. 4, where new pitches were introduced through a common motive, and at mm. 6 and 7, where the chordal activity is interrupted and resumed. T_5 contains four new pitches per respective hexachord, which is the maximum available with this particular set and therefore the maximum differentiation; while this transposition, at m. 8, the inversion at T_1, contains four common pitches per hexachord, the maximum available with this set (see Ex. 4).

This transposition around common pitches and common motives marks the end of a segment; and this clear end precedes a new exposition, starting like the beginning, but revealing in greater detail the motives and intervals so far presented but not developed. Each focus is more specific, and the piece gradually becomes denser, leading to the chords in mm. 24-29; the transposition continues the chords to m. 33 from which point on the piece gradually uncoils itself to the simple line at T_0 in mm. 58-60 and a coda at T_5.

The first twelve measures of *Piece for Two Instrumental Units* (1962) illustrates Wolpe's sensitivity to the intervallic situation. The slow pitch growth, through an organic growth of motive, shows the masterful care with which every situation reaches maximum fulfillment and every new pitch is optimally, and gradually, introduced within a situation of quick, non-gradual, imaginative change (Ex. 1).

The first interval, a 4, using the pitches G-B, immediately becomes incorporated into the trichord G-B-A♭. This repetition of the G-B with the A♭, rather than sounding the A♭ alone, sets up the slow growth of the pitch field through the technique of existent pitch situations going into new complexes and the incorporation of new pitches into existent situations. The intervals now are 1 (G-A♭), 3 (A♭-B), and 4 (G-B). The maximum fulfillment of intervallic identity suggests the addition of C to this group because C will produce the following pairs: of 4's, G-B and A♭-C, of 1's, G-A♭ and B-C, and in the particular trichordal presentation used, the inversion built around the 3, G-B-A♭ and B-A♭-C. No other single tone could have at the same time so slightly enlarged the pitch group while exploiting maximum intervallic association.

Now, in addition to the motivic intervals of 1, 3, 4, one new interval, a 5, is created by the addition of C. The pitch material is now projected as a flute line, which functions to expose this new interval within the old pitch field, C-G, to use this same interval to introduce one more new tone, D♭-A♭, and, more importantly, to transform the pitch material into a non-gradual variant. If this were no more than a naive association of the horizontal and the vertical, it would be of little interest. But what is perceived here comes as a result of hearing the same pitch classes in different involvements, and also prepares the continued hearing of such events. The pitches are, and will be, in variously shifting, integrated combinations —in multiple states of being as extreme transforms of a single source situation. The source pitches project as contrasting yet unified forces. The flute line, incidentally, not only sets up linear 5's, but also registral 1's (Ex. 8).

Ex. 8

These are picked up in m. 10 by the oboe.

The newest tone, D♭, immediately presents to our conjecture the new intervals, 6 (D♭-G) and 2 (B-D♭), and the trichord possibilities:

D♭-C-B	D♭-G-C	}
D♭-A♭-B	A♭-D♭-G	} inversions
D♭-G-B	D♭-A♭-C	

The last is the most fruitful, however, since it finds associative possibilities in A♭-C-G and C-G-B. It is, therefore, the most predominant trichord type within this group of five pitches, and is immediately focused on in the flute (G-C-B), cello (D♭-A♭-C) and piano (A♭-C-G and C-G-B). The

flute and cello have, meanwhile, quickly re-represented the older intervals
of 1, 3, 4 and 5 (Ex. 9) but not the newer intervals, 2 and 6.

Ex. 9

In a less imaginative score, the consistent exploration of these intervals
might perhaps take place immediately. But since Wolpe is working with
non-gradual processes, these implied groupings are held off, along with
the relatively unexploited 3, while a quick cut is made to a more pressing
situation, the new Db. The projection of the Db, in one "old" motive
(Db-Ab-C) and two new ones (Db-C-B[+G]), and the violin's sustained
tone, reveal two of Wolpe's methods. One is the thwarted motion, here
accomplished through the shape transform. So far, the rhythmic tendency
has been towards quickening (Ex. 10).

Ex. 10

The results of this familiar technique may be anticipated—quicker,
louder, denser, and finally a climax, followed by a new motion. This
pattern is avoided by the sustaining Db which creates a sharp break in
this quickening; the tension, then, grows by the contiguity of dissimilar
events. Thereby, the existent quick rhythm may unfold slowly, and this
represents economy since the ever-quickening technique uses up material, but the interruption permits it to return with retained freshness. The
sustained tone, then, is not a stoppage of energy ; on the contrary, since it
is a maximum differentiation to the process, the tone is a further gathering
of energy, to be exploded at the end of the sustaining. And this rich variety
of shapes, imaginatively used, may last over long sections and create long
continuities.

The second of Wolpe's methods is his use of "octaves." The quick transformations of shape permit the expanding exposure of pitches to be
gradual. Consequently, members of the same pitch class appear simultaneously. However, they are not duplications. The avoidance of octaves
assumes that the two, or more, tones will reinforce one another, and in a
score utilizing a quick succession of all pitch classes, a duplication requires
some clear motivation or it will seem out of place. But in this case, where
fewer pitch classes are used and members are simply shifting their
associations, it is the association which dominates. Therefore, the pitches
are perceived in terms of their specific involvements in variant forms and

not as duplications or reinforcements. In this way, also, neither contiguous nor simultaneous octaves function as dissonances in Wolpe's music.

It is now, in m. 8, that the previously unexploited intervals, 2, 3, and 6, are developed, bringing in the new tones D and A. Again, the easily reconstructed intervening steps (Ex. 11)

Ex. 11

showing the process as predictable, are considered superfluous and are omitted. The result is produced immediately. In m. 9, the D is held off, while the A becomes part of a situation exactly analogous to the opening, involving 3's, a relatively unexploited interval, rather than 4's (Ex. 12).

Ex. 12

And the oboe in measure 10 picks up the flute activity and intervals of m. 2, bringing the D and A into an analogous 5, along with Db-Ab and G-C. Moreover, the 1's are still kept registrally (Ex. 8), while the trichords are retrogrades, D-A-Db and B-G-C. This line is inverted in the cello, a result of the piano activity in m. 3. This inversion canon is used to offset the condition of constant change prevailing so far, also marked by the piano in m. 11 and the cessation of new tone introduction, the B having to wait until m. 17 for entry.

The piano emphasizes the unused interval 2, in combination with the recently exploited 3 and a resultant 5, functioning as a summary. For a long while, only these eight tones are used, the four others, Eb, E, F and F♯, being introduced in similar motivic association later on.

Thus, Wolpe has found solutions, it seems to me, within the most fertile areas of contemporary thought, some of which I have intended to indicate. His technique and his imagination create a continuity that is non-predictable and yet feels and proves to be eminently logical. His imagination is rich enough to conceive optimally convincing configurations of sound, to grasp the essence and create new opportunities in his music, so that he retains, rather than renounces, the responsibility for his choices.

In an era where one may almost take technical competence for granted, Wolpe's is the voice of imagination, his technical mastery making possible the greatest use of this imagination—the freshness in dealing with the presentation, the projection of material in ever-changing contexts so that the piece is in a continually most intense state, the going beyond predictability. This presumes the setting up of expectations and the more-than-fulfillment of these expectations—the constant state of surprised rightness.

But Wolpe's music goes even further; the very "expectation" itself is that one will always be more-than-fulfilled, that consequences of the overabundant situations will most certainly follow, and that changes and continuities will always surprise. This requires both the technical mastery and the special insight of a trained and original mind to perceive the core relationship of a particular situation, to focus on it, to reveal it and relate it still to the whole. Wolpe does this uniquely and completely, so that our expectations are still more-than-fulfilled.

A CONVERSATION WITH STEUERMANN

GUNTHER SCHULLER

━━━━━━━━━━━ ▪▪▪▪▪▪▪ ━━━━━━━━━━━

EDUARD STEUERMANN, pianist, composer, and teacher, enjoyed the friendship of Schoenberg for nearly forty years, and has been the foremost interpreter of the latter's piano music. Born in Poland when it was still part of the Austro-Hungarian empire, Steuermann moved to Berlin in his teens to study with Busoni who, in 1911, first singled out Steuermann's talent as a composer in the *Signale fuer die Musikalische Welt.*

Despite a full schedule as a performer, teacher, coach, and editor of piano literature, Steuermann has produced an impressive number of compositions. The list includes three Song Cycles, two String Quartets, a Trio, two orchestral works and numerous compositions for piano, many of which have been performed frequently in New York and elsewhere.

As an intimate of the Schoenberg circle and a representative of a European tradition which links the works of Brahms, Wagner, Liszt, and Mahler with the radical innovations of the Schoenberg school, Steuermann exercised a prominent influence upon many younger American musicians and composers, among which the interviewer is honored to include himself.[1]

—G. S.

FIRST ENCOUNTERS

GS: Under what circumstances did you first meet Schoenberg?

ES: It must have been late in 1911 or at the beginning of 1912, after a concert by Busoni, in the restaurant of the Hotel Link in Potsdamer Platz, where we all usually went. Suddenly Busoni got up, took me by the arm and said, "I would like to introduce you to Mr. Schoenberg." Schoenberg was sitting there with his wife and Direktor Hertzka of Universal Edition, and Busoni said, "May I introduce Mr. Steuermann, a very talented pupil who would like to study with you." Schoenberg immediately took out his notebook and said, "When do you want to come?" I was a little surprised—although Busoni had mentioned Schoenberg to me before—but we made an appointment, and two days later I went to Zehlendorf where Schoenberg lived.

GS: Had you heard of Schoenberg at that time?

ES: I hardly knew his music. I had read some reviews in the *Neue Freie Presse* about the performance of his Second Quartet and some other works. The reviews were all negative, but in spite of that, it somehow struck me that this music must be original and interesting.

The lessons started. Schoenberg turned out to be the first person who did not just compliment my music. But he did not teach me in the

---

[1]This note was written in 1964, prior to Steuermann's death in 1966.

orthodox manner at all. He seemed at this time uninterested in teaching counterpoint and thought that I didn't need any further harmony instruction. I simply started to compose; he corrected what I brought and gave me advice—sometimes in an extremely ingenious and precise way, sometimes very much in the "grand manner." You see, he never taught me as he had taught Webern and Berg, and later Eisler and others. Once, for instance, I brought him the beginning of a string quartet, and the introduction was a little too long. He went to his bookshelf, took out Schopenhauer's *Parerga und Paralipomena,* showed me the first sentence which describes the contents of the work, and said, "*That* is an introduction!"

Later in 1912, he wanted me to make piano reductions of his operas, beginning with *Erwartung*. We spent a lot of time and energy on this score, reworking it several times to make it playable without losing the characteristics of the instrumentation. After that I tried *Die Glückliche Hand*. But after many attempts I decided that it could not be reduced for one piano, so it was arranged for two pianos with the main voices in the first piano part.

GS: Had you met Berg and Webern then?

ES: I met them in Berlin. Webern was living in Zehlendorf, not far from Schoenberg—Webern was never far from Schoenberg!—and Berg came once or twice with his young wife. About this time (1912) the first performance of *Gurrelieder* took place.

GS: How many rehearsals did that require?

ES: Actually I don't know, since we heard only the last two or three. It did not sound very satisfactorily in the empty Musikvereinssaal, and there were many mistakes in the parts. Schrecker conducted, and although he was certainly a good musician, his approach was a little *theatralisch,* which was against the spirit of the Schoenberg school. The performance was a great success and made Schoenberg officially famous. I remember sitting in his box when, at the last C major fortissimo with the six trumpets and ten horns, Schoenberg turned to me and asked, "Hoeren Sie das Pizzicato in den Celli?" He was so proud of this pizzicato, but of course one couldn't hear it at all.

PIERROT AND SPRECHSTIMME

Then came *Pierrot Lunaire* with Mrs. Zehme. Twice or three times a week, with the first mail, I received a new piece of *Pierrot* and would go to coach Mrs. Zehme at her home, Olivaerplatz, 40. She was a retired actress who still had artistic ambitions and some strange ideas, including the identification of herself with the character of Pierrot. It was her idea to set a book of poems by Otto Erich Hartleben, allegedly translated from the French of Albert Giraud. First she asked a composer named Friesländer to write some piano accompaniments which she used in her recitation of the *Pierrot* poems. But somehow she was not quite satisfied with this music, and since someone had told her that there was a composer named Schoenberg who was supposed to be a great genius, she asked him to write the music to the Pierrot poems, which he agreed to do.

GS: What was his reaction to the text?

ES: He thought some of it was a little scurrilous. Once I remember being present when he told Mrs. Zehme, "Da schauen Sie, das ist doch nicht wirklich Ernst zu nehmen! Das machen wir doch nicht mit!" But after all, such things seemed somehow to inspire him, and *Pierrot* is of course the best proof of this.

At first Mrs. Zehme wanted Schoenberg to use only a piano; his contract with her also stipulated that there would be a tour in fourteen or fifteen cities, so that the size of the ensemble was a very important consideration. But since Schoenberg was Schoenberg, the first thing he did was to phone Mrs. Zehme to let her know that he had already written the first piece for piano and clarinet (this was "Gebet an Pierrot"). Soon after he phoned her again to ask if he could use a flute as well. Then came the third piece, which is now the first—"Den Wein, den man mit Augen trinkt"—and before long he had clarinet, flute, violin, and cello. And then, since he wanted still more instrumental variety, he had the idea that every piece should have a different ensemble by alternating the flute with piccolo, the clarinet with bass clarinet, and the violin with viola (which was at that time most unusual—our violinist Maliniak was certainly not used to it).

GS: Did Schoenberg himself conduct all the performances on tour?

ES: Schoenberg did not want to travel too much, so he conducted only the principal performances, three in Berlin, one in Hamburg (where we met Klemperer), Prague (his brother-in-law, Zemlinsky, was there) and Vienna. The others were conducted by Scherchen, whom Schoenberg had met just previously.

Scherchen, like Maliniak, was a member of the Blüthner Orchestra. He was one of the young men in whom Mrs. Zehme was interested. He came to rehearsals, where Schoenberg took to him very much, and occasionally asked him to conduct in order to hear how it sounded from a distance. The cellist of the group, Kindler, later, of course, became the well-known conductor; the clarinetist was Essberger, and the flutist was De Vriess, whom I met again years later with the Goldman Band.

GS: What were Schoenberg's rehearsals like?

ES: At first it was largely a matter of experimentation. Everything had to be tried out, and Schoenberg's patience and zeal in exploring all possibilities were incredible. Later, by the time of the Columbia recording in 1940, the situation was different, of course, because the ensemble problems were no longer so great.

GS: Did Schoenberg make any changes based on the experimentation of the premiere rehearsals?

ES: Hardly any; a few dynamic changes, a ritardando in one place. The conception of the piece was very clear.

GS: For a long time many musicians have been deeply curious about the origin of Schoenberg's idea for *Sprechstimme;* how did he come upon it?

ES: It originated in Schoenberg's mind. It was—if you will—an inspiration.

GS: But Humperdinck had already used *Sprechstimme,* perhaps as early as 1895; and Max von Schilling used both normal speech and *Sprechstimme* in his *Mona Lisa.* Didn't Schoenberg know these works?

ES: I don't think he did. Since Schoenberg lived, so to speak, in a completely different world, it is very unlikely that he heard any Humperdinck except perhaps *Hänsel und Gretel.* And I, as Schoenberg's faithful disciple, would also not have listened to such music. The idea of the "melodrama," as it was called, was certainly generally known—Max von Schilling's *Hexenlied* was a kind of "best seller." But the way Schoenberg used it was certainly quite new. The difference is that the word is not "adapted" to the music, nor is the music used to "dramatize" the word, but the speaking is an integral part of the music, "musizieren mit Worten." The explanation Schoenberg gave in his preface to *Pierrot* unfortunately solves only part of the problem.

GS: Yes, it seems to result in a great many slides and glissandos, which I can't believe is what Schoenberg meant.

ES: I worked with many people on it too. It seems to me one has to find the expression of each sentence that will cover an *entire* line. And the emphasis must not be on singing. It seems to me many people sing the *Sprechstimme* too much.

GS: Do you know Lotte Lenya's half-singing, half-speaking delivery in works like *Dreigroschenoper* and *Mahagonny?* She is also an actress rather than a singer; and it seems to me that what she does is interesting and applicable as *Sprechstimme.*

ES: Perhaps, but don't forget that the extraordinary expressions in *Pierrot* are much more complex than Brecht and Weill. Just like Rex

Harrison in *My Fair Lady:* this is also a kind of *Sprechstimme,* but much more natural than *Pierrot* probably ever could or ought to be.

PERFORMANCES IN THE SCHOENBERG CIRCLE: THE GESELLSCHAFT FÜR PRIVATAUFFÜHRUNGEN

GS: Did Schoenberg conduct well enough to make himself clearly understood through his gestures? Did he ever conduct any music but his own?

ES: His ability—perhaps it would be more correct to say his power—as a conductor was sometimes incredible, at other times less convincing. I heard a performance of his *Pelleas* in Barcelona with the Casals orchestra. Casals gave him as many rehearsals as he wanted, but Schoenberg used only six or seven and gave the most perfect performance. Also I never heard more impressive performances of *Verklärte Nacht* and the F♯-minor Quartet than those in a setting for chamber orchestra played by a group of amateurs in Vienna under his direction. One rehearsal detail: the beginning of *Verklärte Nacht* first sounded unclear. Schoenberg started to rehearse only the low Ds of the celli and double basses. When their rhythm was established everything fell into place as if by magic. On the other hand, I remember rehearsing for the first performance of the Opus 29 Clarinet Suite in Paris. The work was then extremely difficult for the performers; no one was very well prepared, and Schoenberg was not too clear. We ended up playing it at a rather slow tempo. Schoenberg used to say in such circumstances: "That is not music for first performances!"

As far as other music is concerned, I particularly remember a concert that Mrs. Mahler arranged in Vienna in 1914 when the war had already broken out. She believed that Schoenberg was a great conductor. He conducted the *Egmont* Overture and the Ninth with the second orchestra in Vienna, the Tonkünstler-Verein, whose musicians were certainly not sympathetic to the great "innovator." For us it was beautiful, although the performance was very adversely criticized. You may ask, what was so beautiful? You know how difficult it is to describe any musical impression; in Schoenberg's "Musizieren" it was primarily the character of his tempi, especially his ability to make the music move and stand still at the same time, which I will never forget. It was never a "tempo" as such—the contrary of "motoric."

GS: When did you first play the Opus 11?

ES: In 1911 or 1912, but I played Opus 19 in public even before then. I had barely started to study with Schoenberg when he told me about a concert of his compositions in the Choralionsaal and asked me to play the newly composed Opus 19. I was also to accompany Mrs. Winternitz-Dorda, a very beautiful soprano from Hamburg, in the *George-Lieder*. I had to go to Hamburg, hardly knowing the music, to rehearse with her. But since she had absolute pitch, it was not too difficult. We also played the first, second, and fourth of the Five Orchestra Pieces in a version for two pianos, eight hands, arranged by Webern and Schoenberg. My partner was Louis Closson, a Belgian pupil of Busoni; the other piano team was really interesting: Webern and Louis Gruenberg. There was strong opposition to these "heresies," but also enthusiasm. Later, I remember I played the Opus 11 in Regensburg in a horribly cold and bare Turnhalle, and remember the faces of all those *Bierphilister*. To play the Opus 11, No. 2 as slowly as Schoenberg wanted for such an audience was quite something in those days! This was in 1913; then the war broke out, and we all went into the Army.

But immediately after the war Schoenberg started the Society for Private Performances. The first concert seems in retrospect an historic event since the Society was probably the first to be devoted to twentieth-century music. At the opening I played the fourth and seventh Scriabin Sonatas, then the four-hand arrangement of the Mahler Seventh symphony with the pianist, Bachrich, rehearsed by Schoenberg. We had a hierarchy of supervision for performances in our "Verein": there were three so-called "Vortragsmeister" whose task it was to coach with the performers—Webern, Berg, and myself, and later Erwin Stein. The highest authority over all of us was, of course, Schoenberg.

GS: Had you played much music other than Schoenberg's before this?

ES: Actually, I played Schoenberg only at special concerts. But I gave many other recitals, especially when I was a student in Berlin, where I played at the Bechsteinsaal.

GS: What other music did you play for the Society? Did you play any works by Debussy, Bartók, Stravinsky, for example?

ES: Of course, I played Busoni's Elegies and the Sonatina; Ravel's *Gaspard de la nuit;* the Berg Sonata, etc. I don't remember doing any Bartók, but I performed Stravinsky's *Piano Rag Music,* as well as the *Easy Pieces* for four hands. Once I even played *Petrouchka* with Serkin in a four-hand arrangement, but that was later, after Schoenberg had left Vienna. And I was probably one of the first to play Book I of the Debussy Etudes, first for the Society and later on tour. There was also a great deal of contemporary music that I played without memorizing it, in readings, or special performances, or for publishers. For instance, I was the first to play the Sonata by Ludwig Zenk, who was a pupil and,

I think, also a cousin of Webern. Zenk was very grateful to me because I had played his Sonata for Universal Edition, and they accepted it for publication. I found out later that he was at the same time a convinced Nazi. That was just a brand of the Viennese "double counterpoint." Before Webern's Variations were published, Webern sent them to me with a very cordial dedication in a manuscript beautifully copied by Zenk.

GS: Despite the dedication, however, I understand you have never played the Variations in public.

ES: I have taught them to students. Apart from some personal reasons, I have not yet found the time to study them to the perfection they require. Nowadays I feel that I would like to play the work, especially when I hear some of the awful performances by younger pianists.

GS: Webern's pupil, Peter Stadlen, seems to agree with you. He wrote rather negatively about present-day Webern performances by "serial-conscious" pianists.

ES: It is certainly true that they are much too rigid. Webern himself was the freest interpreter of his own music that could be imagined.

GS: Did you ever play in any of Webern's ensemble works, and did he work with you in realizing the piano parts?

ES: I played the first performances of the Concerto for Nine Instruments and the Saxophone Quartet. In fact, I was almost present when Webern composed the Concerto. One day he came to me and said, "You know, I have found a row that is unique!—three tones, their inversion, retrograde and retrograde inversion!" He thought this had something to do with the ancient palindrome—"Amor, Roma," etc. (he was rather naïve in this respect). After the first movement was finished, he played a little of it for me at his house in Maria-Enzersdorf. He played so freely that I hardly could follow the music, but it was extraordinary. When he conducted, however, he was not so free; I suppose one cannot be, or at least, he could not. But as far as the piano was concerned, he said very little, even when I first accompanied his songs.

I also played a lot of other music with Webern conducting: the *Emperor* Concerto in Barcelona and Vienna, the Mozart E-flat in Vienna and Berlin, and a Bach Concerto—for me, he conducted Bach best of all. He combined a projection of the motivic structure, which made the music vibrant with inner life, with a sense of the great line, always supported by simple and clear dynamics. I must say that he influenced my approach to Bach strongly.

GS: Under what kind of social and economic circumstances did all of these performances take place? For instance, you must have had to engage outside players for the Society; how were you able to afford this?

ES: Hiring players was the most difficult part of managing the Society. Schoenberg always insisted on some payment for the musicians, but we had practically no money because of the inflation. There were no individual tickets sold; the concerts were only for subscribers. Since the Viennese are famous for their gatecrashing, everyone had to have a membership card with a photo and signature. Our friend, Dr. Polnauer, would stand at the door checking everyone. The programs were never announced in advance either, because Schoenberg didn't want people to be able to "pick the candies from the cakes." Applause was forbidden; the audience was not supposed to create "success" or "no success," but only to accept what was offered.

Once, when the finances of the Society were at their lowest, Schoenberg had the idea of raising money with a "Johann Strauss Evening." Our "orchestra" consisted of the Kolisch Quartet, piano (me), and —since we had no money to hire wind players—a harmonium played by Hans Gal's sister, Erna. In Austria we had those huge Kunstharmoniums —not like the little harmoniums here—and Schoenberg's instrumentations of *Rosen aus dem Suden* and *Eine Nacht in Venedig,* especially in the way he used the harmonium, are absolute masterpieces.

GS: Are these waltzes extant?

ES: I wish I knew—the manuscripts were sold at an auction, but nobody seems to know where they disappeared during the Nazi period. Webern did *Zigeunerbaron Waltz* and Berg did *Wein, Weib, und Gesang.* Webern's instrumentation was nice, but it was very light and clear. I remember the piano always played the brass fanfares.

GS: Do you recall any of the other instrumentalists who played for the Society?

ES: We could rarely afford to use wind players, but there was, for instance, a Faisst Quartet in Vienna that performed the D-minor Quartet by Zemlinsky. Webern coached them endlessly in this. Singers, of course, were always hard to find; but at this time Felicie Michacek, who became rather famous in Europe, was singing Webern's songs and Debussy's *Proses lyriques* for us.

Actually we tried to get anyone who was good enough to play our music. It was not too difficult: the lesser-known musicians always, especially in the difficult postwar period, were glad to have the opportunity to be heard in public. Some were only semi-professional; for instance, one of our violinists, Dr. Oskar Adler, a childhood friend of Schoenberg, was a physician and also a famous astrologer. He played Reger especially well, a little *altmodish*, probably in the Joachim tradition. The Debussy Sonata was less authentic but, perhaps just because of this peculiar "clumsiness," touching.

GS: Did you ever know Stiegler, the first horn of the Opera and the Philharmonic? Schoenberg once told me that he was the greatest horn player he had ever heard.

ES: I didn't know Stiegler personally, but Schoenberg's son studied horn with him. In general, the older players were not available to us. We could not have asked Stiegler to play for the Society.

GS: Did you ever hear Schoenberg play the cello?

ES: Of course; and also the viola. During the period of the Society, he was very fond of playing chamber music. This was during the years when he was developing the twelve-tone technique and was not publishing new works so that he had more time for other activities.

GS: If he played the viola, he must have studied all the string instruments at some time. Did he play any other instruments?

ES: A little piano, but I think that was all.

GS: I ask this because Schoenberg was one of the great orchestrators. His insight into instruments—especially strings—was remarkable. And George Szell once told me that everyone who studied in Vienna had to learn and play every instrument for some part of his student years.

ES: But Schoenberg did not study composition in Vienna; he was entirely an autodidact, and he was never really a music student at all. Once, in Hollywood, we had a discussion about a questionable spot in Beethoven's Ninth Symphony—the place in the last movement where the clarinet plays C-sharp against the chorus' C. When I asked Schoenberg about it, he looked at his score—he had already marked that particular place—and said that it was a mistake. I wanted, of course, to defend Beethoven, but he said that everyone could make a mistake. "For instance, you know that I never wrote a single note for a string instrument without trying it out." I knew how true this was—one has only to consider his use of harmonics in the Phantasy, for example. Then he brought out a score of the *Gurrelieder* and, in the last part, pointed to a low C-flat in the violas. I asked him what had happened at rehearsals; he said, "Nobody seemed to notice."

GS: But all the performances by the Society were of chamber works. Were Schoenberg's stage works ever performed? For example, was *Erwartung* known even to the members of the inner circle?

ES: *Erwartung* was composed before I met Schoenberg. Handwritten copies were made; Webern, Berg certainly knew it, probably other friends in Vienna too. In Berlin, where I was, hardly anybody knew the work. But in the spring of 1914 we went with Schoenberg to Dresden, which had the most progressive opera house in Germany. The conductor was Ernst von Schuch, who did all the first performances of Strauss. He was a very charming old *Hof-Mann*. The *Intendant* was Graf von Seebach. They were very interested in hearing something by Schoenberg to see whether they might perform it. I played all of *Erwartung* for them on the piano, with Schuch following the score. They were even more interested in *Die Glückliche Hand,* and Schuch asked Schoenberg to tell them about the plot. Schoenberg started to talk, but Seebach, the old monarchist, interrupted and told it himself extremely well. I was quite amazed. The directors of the Dresden Opera were obviously planning to perform a Schoenberg work, but then the war started and nothing ever came of it. They were very fine artists and showed a great deal of courage and independence at a time when people, especially in Berlin, ignored Schoenberg, with the notable exceptions of Busoni, Schnabel and, to some extent, previously, Richard Strauss.

ENCOUNTERS WITH COMPOSERS AND CONDUCTORS

GS: When you were in Vienna in the Twenties, did you meet any of the important composers of the time—Stravinsky, Milhaud, Hindemith, etc?

ES: Milhaud once came to Vienna. He had performed *Pierrot* in Paris, and Mrs. Mahler gave a reception for him and Poulenc at which I played my *Kammersymphonie* arrangement and Schoenberg conducted *Pierrot*. Then Milhaud responded by also conducting parts of *Pierrot* to show how he had done it. My most unforgettable memory, however, was that Milhaud and Poulenc invited me to the Hotel Bristol for a wonderful lunch. It was 1920, during the inflation, and there was practically no food in Vienna; this was my first real meal in years!

I also met Ravel during that period, and even played four hands with him. We met at Mrs. Mahler's and played through *Ma Mere l'Oye* and the *Rhapsodie Espagnole* for the conductor, Oskar Fried, who was planning a Ravel concert and always wanted to hear new pieces played first on the piano. By the way, Webern once did the Mallarmé songs; he adored them, especially the last, which is very close to Schoenberg.

GS: Did you ever meet Hindemith?

ES: Yes, we once appeared together on a program of the BBC in London. I remember, I played the E-minor Toccata by Bach, and he performed as a member of the Amar Quartet. We had an interesting conversation afterwards, among other things about the much-discussed Haba quarter-tone system. Hindemith, who was as little convinced about this kind of development as I was, said in a direct and radical way, "Why not take the bull by the horns and indicate the exact number of vibrations for every tone. With electric instruments it will be possible."

GS: What about Stravinsky?

ES: I had not met Stravinsky then. There is some confusion about this. Last year a secretary of Stravinsky called me to ask if I remembered that Stravinsky was present at the performance of *Pierrot* in Berlin. I told her that I didn't remember ever having met Stravinsky there.

GS: But the recent books give the impression that Stravinsky was always a great admirer of Schoenberg.

ES: Schoenberg was rather interested in Stravinsky; he found his instrumentation very clever. We performed *Pribaoutki,* and Schoenberg said, "He always writes mezzo-forte, and how well it sounds." (Schoenberg always advised his students never to write mezzo-forte, but either forte or piano.) Then there appeared an interview by Stravinsky in which he said that Schoenberg's music was a dead-end. Of course, Schoenberg, in his usual tempermental way, was infuriated, and turned against Stravinsky.

GS: Did this episode generate the *Drei Satiren?*

ES: Schoenberg wrote the *Satiren* later, and one of them is about "Modernsky." As we know, this choral piece, one of the most "virtuoso" achievements in counterpoint, is written in four clefs and reads the same when the page is turned upside down.

But Stravinsky is most unprejudiced and really practices the artistic independence he preaches. For instance, after Gerhard Eisler was deported, there was a reaction here in the United States, and certain people wanted Hanns Eisler, his brother, to leave the country as well, which he did. When a concert of Eisler's works was arranged to protest this action and a petition circulated, the very first person to sign it was Stravinsky.

GS: Was Krenek involved with the Schoenberg circle during the Twenties?

ES: No, because he lived mostly in Berlin; but Schoenberg considered him very talented and used to say, "That is a man whose mother tongue is music." He was a wild atonalist then—in his Chaconne for piano, for example—before *Jonny spielt auf.*

GS: Did you know Varèse in Berlin in 1912?

ES: Yes, and I even heard a piece of his then called, I think, *Bourgogne.*

GS: That was one of the works destroyed in a fire before Varèse came to America, so you heard a composition that no longer exists.

ES: I can hardly remember what it was like, except that there was one particular passage for terrifically divisi strings—I don't know how many individual parts—that made a tremendous forest of string sound. The performance was by the Blüthner Orchestra.

GS: Did the Berlin orchestras do much contemporary music?

ES: Quite a bit, I remember Strauss conducting the Mahler Third at the Königliche Kapelle, and a performance of *Rosenkavalier* with Muck that was completely without Viennese Schmalz or sentimentality, and very clear. Later I heard it played by Klemens Krauss and others, but the Muck performance still stays in my memory.

GS: Can we talk about the pianistic problems in Schoenberg's music? Coming from the Busoni and Liszt tradition, as you did, were there problems that you had to solve personally? Did Schoenberg help you in any specific way?

ES: Hardly at all. When he heard me play the Opus 11 for the first time, he made some slight changes in the first edition. He added some marcato signs, indications "without Pedal," etc. I remember he wanted the second piece very slow, which was astonishing to me in view of the indication, "Massige Achtel." When I had to play these pieces the first time in Regensburg, he gave me this memorable advice: "Don't be afraid that the audience might become nervous because of the slow tempo. If you believe in your tempo wholeheartedly, the piece will not seem long; if you are unsure of it, it will become boring." But in the second edition the metronome mark indicates a faster tempo. Otherwise, as far as style is concerned, the Brahms tradition (from which I also came) is the main influence on Schoenberg in the first piano works. Later, in Opus 23, Opus 25, and Opus 33a and b, the twelve-tone system brought a very different approach to the piano style, especially in terms of the identity of harmony and melody. How far my interpretations were the full realization of Schoenberg's ideas I don't know. A composer like Schoenberg has a very far-reaching imaginary vision of his music. The interpreter can only try to reach the sphere of this imagination, to bring the dead signs on the paper to life. But that goes for any music, except perhaps electronic music, and that is something which I hold against electronic music: that it denies the possibility of perpetual rejuvenation through enacting a meaning in a variety of ways.

GS: What about the pedaling in Schoenberg? I know that you have very specific ideas on this subject.

ES: Schoenberg always insisted that his music be played almost without pedal which, frankly, I obeyed only half-heartedly. You cannot play the modern piano without pedal. You have to use it, of course, so that the tones are not blurred, and to make sure that the "sober" sonority without pedal vibration, which is so characteristic, comes through.

GS: Would you care to say something about today's music?

ES: To talk about contemporary avant-garde music is difficult since it changes almost every year. First, there was a kind of super-serialism, the "totally predetermined" music; then, as Dr. Steinecke told me, as a *reaction to all of that,* the aleatoric music; and probably something else by now. In Darmstadt I heard the music of Nono, whom I consider very talented; Stockhausen is certainly a very remarkable man; Boulez is an excellent craftsman. But I never understood why, after the establishment of the twelve-tone system, one had to go on serializing all the parameters of music. To me, serializing in some way the fixed tones of the twelve-tone reservoir is like using an Ariadne's thread to lead out of the labyrinth of so-called "free atonality" which, without a guiding principle, might become confused, repetitious, uncharacteristic. Whether this serializing is indispensable for building larger forms one cannot say. An inspired composer might at any time prove that it is not. Anyway, to serialize a *given quantity* of fixed tones is something entirely different from trying to do the same with an *infinity* of time-lengths (rhythm), dynamics, timbres. It always seemed to me a mechanical application of the principle.

For me, twelve-tone composition has two aspects: one is harmonic, the other contrapuntal. The harmonic aspect consists of the urge of the chromatic complex to achieve completion, to close the circle of the 12 tones. (This urge, by the way, does not always have to be satisfied—just as the dominant 7th doesn't always have to resolve to the triad of the first degree.) The contrapuntal aspect I compared years ago with Freud's conception of the eternal repetition of the first pre-natal experiences. This contrapuntal aspect is, by the way, as old as music itself. We have only to think of the augmentation and diminution techniques of earlier times. The idea of rhythmic series is used, to some extent, in Berg's Double Concerto, in the "Rondo Ritmico." It is also obviously anticipated by the iso-rhythmic structures which, incidentally, always seemed to me examples of schematic thinking. Schoenberg generally used serialism with more liberty than Webern, but then, Webern did not write such long and involved works.

As for aleatoric music, I don't understand why one does it. Nietzsche says that for the seeker of truth the rule is more important than the exception. For me, no pursuit of reason is as frustrating as the experiments of "chance." But so many people are interested in it: even my friend Adorno writes that he was impressed by Cage's Piano Concerto. It probably has to do with our time and its philosophy—our nuclear Dark Ages. Maybe a new religion will emerge from it, but at present it is more "Credo quia absurdum."

GS: In general, then, what do you think is the significance of Schoenberg's music in the context of today's musical situation?

ES: First of all, there is hardly a living musician who has not been influenced by Schoenberg in some way or other; even writers of radio and television commercials have appropriated his atonal idiom. But serialism, to which even his most bitter adversaries are now converted, seems to stem more clearly from him. It would be more important perhaps to distinguish what is *not* due to Schoenberg's influence. There has been since Schoenberg's death a trend to stress the differences between him and Webern, to emphasize Webern's independence. The battle-cry was post-Webernism. In my old-fashioned opinion, it would be important to examine these trends and evaluate them as artistic questions, i.e. more as questions of personality than of "style." But to pursue this point would try the patience of even as sympathetic an interviewer as you have been.

May 20, 1964

ELLIOTT CARTER AND THE
POSTWAR COMPOSERS

MARTIN BOYKAN

T HERE ARE CERTAIN WORKS which stand in a peculiarly intimate relation to the time in which they are born; they give articulate form to those ideas which, in some ill-defined way, haunt a generation of composers. Judged by absolute standards, Carter's First Quartet is, of course, a work of the first rank, and one that will last; there is hardly any need now to reiterate this. But if it was so electrifying to the postwar generation, it was not merely because of its quality (there are fine works which create hardly a stir when they first appear); it was also because this quartet was the kind of work that was very much needed and desired. It spoke, in fact, for the America of the Fifties, in the same way that the *Sacre* spoke for the Europe of a half-century ago.

Just as we can see the European sensibility changing in preparation for the *Sacre,* just as there are a few isolated works that anticipate it, so American music began to move in the direction of the First Quartet in the early fifties. The most obvious example of this is the first of Billy Jim Layton's Five Studies for Violin and Piano. Here, in a work written in 1952 (but apparently without knowledge of the First Quartet), are all the devices which were to become famous as Carter patents: independence of the instrumental parts, rhythmic modulation, polyrhythms, even the gigue-like motives of Carter's last movement. I do not mean to imply that the total effect of Layton's piece is like Carter; obviously the First Quartet seemed no less astonishing and original because it answered to a need. The point is simply that the encounter with Carter has deeply marked the postwar generation. It is, I think, of more than merely historical interest to probe—as far as one dares—into the nature of this encounter.

American sensibility. Because of its extraordinary originality, one tends to forget that many of its gestures have haunted the American imagination for a long time. Long melodies of equal note values were once strongly associated with Roy Harris; the device of dialoguing sustained music with loud, rapid interjections has been used by William Schuman; Ruth Crawford's Quartet of 1931 hints at some of Carter's organizational procedures. Even the celebrated device of rhythmic modulation was not entirely novel; an early example occurs in Sessions's 1942 Duo.

For people accustomed to thinking of American music in terms of lively rhythm, syncopation, or folk song, it is easy to miss the peculiarly American flavor of

Carter's pathos. Actually, the professional cheerfulness of much Americana was a
false note; the poets have always thought of America as a haunted and tragic place
—and Copland was never as truly American as in the Piano Variations or the
Piano Fantasy. It has been remarked that where English literature tends to precise
and objective description, a dominant strain in American literature is the tortured
confessional; a similar comparison might be made between the arithmetic systems
of the Europeans and Carter's psychological and dramatic methods of organization
—methods which resemble literary programs without texts. In any case, no one
seriously debates the problem of an "American music" any more, not merely
because fashions have changed, but because the problem no longer exists, and if
an iron curtain sometimes seems to separate America and Europe, perhaps that is
the price we have to pay.

I doubt if the very young today can fully appreciate the peculiar ideological
battles of Carter's generation. Nowadays, a composer is called upon to defend his
methods of organization, his aesthetic, even his seriousness as an artist; formerly,
he swore allegiance to particular chords. On the one hand, there was the diatonic
vocabulary of the neoclassicists; on the other, the "chromaticism" of expressionism.
Even those who infiltrated both camps tended to use "chromaticism" for its familiar
emotional connotations; Hindemith's designation of chords with tritones as
Dionysian, and chords built on fourths or fifths as Apollonian pretty well summed
up the feeling of the time. The expressionistic associations of "chromaticism"
derive their meaning, of course, from the common-practice style and have no
relevance outside of this context. But music between the wars was haunted by
ghosts. Today it is self-evident that the classical phraseology of Schoenberg's
twelve-tone works is not a mask; a generation ago this was impossible to understand.
The masters who continued to explore may not have been harmed by this ideological division, but for most composers, it engendered an unhealthy atmosphere. It
makes all the difference in the world whether a composer is born into a tradition
and explores within it because he does not know anything else, or whether he
consciously avoids a whole area of musical material simply because it is too
"radical" or too "conservative" or ideologically on the wrong side of the fence; the
latter course leads inevitably to artificiality. I do not mean to suggest that one
should use all the chords all the time. There is no coherent musical language
which is not in some way restricted; indeed, there are certain effects which can
only be achieved by an extreme restriction. But it is one thing to make a particular choice for a particular piece, and quite another to choose out of an abstract
loyalty to a Style. This is why so much of the neoclassic music of Stravinsky's
imitators—in many cases the work of composers of considerable talent—now seems
mannered and false. Inevitably, the idiom of an explorer is softened and diluted in
the hands of his followers, but I doubt that we should find the same peculiar
quality of artificiality in the derivative music of the past.

The power of ideological associations was so strong that some of Carter's first
listeners undoubtedly thought at once of Berg or Schoenberg. Actually, the First
Quartet—in spite of some Bartókian influences—has little to do with Central
European harmony; it is rather the result of a direct and logical evolution from the
Coplandesque idiom of Carter's earlier music. Already in an early song like the

"Voyage" of Hart Crane, we can see Carter extending Copland's vocabulary; one can draw a straight line from there—through the Piano Sonata and the Cello Sonata—to the Quartet. The serial works of Copland and (to a lesser extent) Stravinsky left their harmonic languages relatively intact. But Carter's development out of Copland was an object lesson to the postwar generation, for with it the old superstitions finally disappeared.

It is a striking fact that much of the music written in the first half of our century (always excepting Schoenberg) shows a severe harmonic restriction, not only in vocabulary, but also in the constant use of ostinati, extended accompaniment figures, etc. From the technical point of view, this was undoubtedly wise at the time; when a common practice has been swept aside, it is necessary to listen intently to the new chords before one can begin to explore possibilities of enrichment and refinement. Perhaps an analogy might be made with that other moment when a common practice was swept aside, the Monteverdian revolution; for here, too, we find a very thin diet of musical materials. But having stripped music to bare essentials, the later Monteverdi begins the opposite process—the linear elaboration of his style. I do not wish to press this analogy too far; Monteverdi pointed toward a new common practice, and we have left Arcadia for good. But something of the same tendency is represented by Carter's elaboration of the materials of Copland and Stravinsky. If there is any common ground on which many American composers today could meet, it is in the avoidance of ostinati, accompaniment figures, broad patches of static harmony—in short, in the desire for a harmony which *inflects*. In a sense, where one starts from is less important. The tonal idiom of Shifrin's *Oedipus Cantata,* for instance, may be astonishing in view of the prevalent style, but it is totally different from the "Neoclassicism" of the Forties. In place of a broad tonal design, we have a harmony that moves quickly and inflects constantly; the vocabulary may be Stravinskian in origin, but it has been nourished by contact with Webern and Sessions, and as a result has a new richness of tonal implication.

Works which carry as heavy an historical weight as the First Quartet are frequently constricting in their influence; one need only think of how many composers became entangled in the coils of *Tristan* or the *Sacre.* I have tried to indicate some of the reasons why Carter has, on the contrary, been so liberating. The fact is that although every young composer has been deeply involved with him, few show traces of his influence in their work. Billy Jim Layton has perhaps remained closest to Carter, but though his Quartet or his Septet may occasionally employ Carterian polyrhythms or Carterian gestures, his language is more akin to that of the earlier Stravinsky (an important source for Carter as well). Yehudi Wyner shows the direct influence of Carter only in the first movement of his *Concert Duo;* his Serenade moves more in the direction of Berg and Schoenberg. And Shifrin's music shows that in this freer postwar atmosphere, even a tonal language may acquire an unexpected freshness. For where the European tendency has been to reject all of the music written between the wars, Carter has, on the other hand, made the whole of the twentieth century available.

"Poe and Baudelaire," W. H. Auden has written, "are the fathers of modern poetry in that they were the first poets . . . who, born into the modern age—that is to say, after the mutation of the closed society of tradition and inheritance into the open society of fashion and choice—realized what a decisive change this was. This change was not instantaneous and even now it is still incomplete . . . poetry may have reached modernity while music is still unreflective." The trouble, I think, is not so much that music has been unreflective, as that it has been afflicted by a failure of nerve. In spite of a few composers of the first rank, and a number of unquestioned masterpieces, music between the wars was haunted by an unhealthy nostalgia for some common practice, some system or style that would substitute for a stable tradition. Old habits die hard, and there are still people who speak of "advanced" music, "traditional" music, and music of the "middle ground," although these terms have become meaningless even in the chronological sense. And curiously enough, similar attitudes linger on even in the thinking of those who would abolish the past altogether. In a recent article, for example, Boulez writes that ". . . music currently possesses a broad range of means, a vocabulary which once again attains universality of conception and comprehension. Admittedly, this equipment still requires a great deal of improvement, and must be given time to be broken in, acquire more flexibility, become standard. *Nevertheless the essential discoveries have been made*"[1] (italics mine). Now, language of this kind conjures up the specter of a new common practice; we are not unacquainted with the beauties of that "permanent revolution" which has its discoveries behind it. Unconscious ties with attitudes from the past are potentially dangerous; when "tradition" is a matter of conscious choice, it remains fruitful. Carter's work is of importance to the postwar generation not only because of its artistic power, but also because it provides a moral lesson, because it reminds the composer that it is his task—painful, perhaps, but inescapable—to *choose* his language freshly for each work, and to choose from the whole range of musical possibilities.

[1] PERSPECTIVES, Spring 1963, p. 33.

EXPRESSIONISM AND AMERICAN MUSIC

ELLIOTT CARTER

THE TENDENCY for each generation in America to wipe away the memory of the previous one, and the general neglect of our own recent past, which we treat as a curiosity useful for young scholars in exercising their research techniques—so characteristic of American treatment of the work of its important artists—is partly responsible for the general neglect of the rather sizable number of composers who in their day were called "ultramodern," and who wrote in this country during the early decades of our century. And it is also part of this unfortunate pattern that interest in these composers is being awakened now because their music fits into a new frame of reference imported from Europe since the war, thus confirming the disturbing fact that the world of serious music here is still thought of as an outpost of that European world which Americans have so often found more attractive than the reality of what they have at home. In fact, it often seems as if we have no genuine interest in looking at our own situation realistically—at least in music—and developing ourselves for what we really are, but are always trying to gain admission into the European musical world (which, at present, is rapidly losing its inner impetus and is fading into a lifeless shadow of what it was).

When interest in Schoenberg and his circle began to be imported into America some years after the war and various of our agencies sent Americans abroad to learn what Europeans were doing and invited Europeans over here to reveal their secrets to us, those who had been close to this music all along began to be treated with a little more respect, while previously their efforts (including those of Schoenberg and his followers living in this country) had been dismissed as meaningless. Thus with the introduction of the post-Webern music and aesthetic here, it was only natural that we should begin to take more interest in our early ultramoderns whose techniques and outlook had much in common with the Viennese school of about the same time.

The long neglect of these American composers has resulted in a lack of information about them, an unfamiliarity with their ideas and music and often a falsification of facts, so that it now is important to reconsider our attitude about them in the light of actual information in order to understand our own musical situation more clearly. The purpose of the series of articles which PERSPECTIVES OF NEW MUSIC is devoting to various composers of that time is not a nationalistic one in the European sense at all. It is undertaken in the attempt to clarify the special attitudes these creators developed in relation to the unusual musical situation of America, which gave an entirely different direction to this group than that of its counterparts in Europe. For they came at a time when ideas that were to change the face of each of the arts were widespread, and the same sort of thinking which formed the background of the Central European Expressionist movement also informed the thinking of artists both in Russia (which does not concern us here) and in the United States.

Because of many similarities of outlook, the great amount of analytical and philosophical thought which has been recently lavished on German Expressionism by European and even American scholars can perhaps be helpful in filling the large empty gap of serious criticism which surrounds the work under consideration, and can be helpful in understanding what went on in this country almost independently. The works produced at that time here, some of clearly great interest, others simply curiosities, have the special traits of the artistic milieu out of which they came, which has not changed much in the intervening years. Very little serious thought and criticism is devoted to our music even today except by composers themselves, and this can be laid partially to the conflict between the American reality and the American dream of Europe which patrons of music try to perpetuate in our musical institutions.

During the period with which we are concerned a great deal of contemporary music was performed in New York, Chicago, Boston, and San Francisco. The Metropolitan Opera House kept *Pétrouchka, Le Rossignol,* de Falla's *Vida Breve,* Gruenberg's *Emperor Jones,* and Carpenter's *Skyscrapers* in its repertory. The International Composers' Guild and the League of Composers organized many important performances including *Wozzeck,* Schoenberg's *Glückliche Hand,* and Ives' Prelude and second movement from his Fourth Symphony. There was an interest in microtonal music,[1] and besides the concert of Hans Barth and Ives discussed by Howard Boatwright,[2] the League of Composers presented a *Sonata casi Fantasia* in quarter, eighth and sixteenth tones by the Mexican composer Julian Carillo for guitar, octavina, arpa-citera and a

[1] F. Busoni, *Entwurf einer neuen Aesthetik der Tonkunst,* Leipzig, 1907. References to English translation by T. Baker: *The New Aesthetic of Music,* New York, 1911. On pp. 31–33, Busoni makes out a case for the division of the whole tone into sixths and refers to an American acoustician, Thaddeus Cahill, whose Dynamophone cöuld produce any division of pitch required of it. Also see D. Rudhyar, "The Relativity of our Musical Conceptions," *Musical Quarterly* (January, 1922) for a discussion of microtones.

[2] See above, pp. 3–12.

French horn made in New York that could play sixteenth tones, in 1926, on the same program as the first U. S. performance of Schoenberg's Wind Quintet. In the next year Carillo appeared with a larger ensemble of microtonal instruments and recorded his *Preludio a Cristobal Colón* for Columbia Records. But the two important rivals in presenting modern music to the large musical public were Leopold Stokowski—an irrepressible experimenter, in those days, who played Schoenberg, Varèse and Ruggles, and was a supporter of the more extreme "ultramodernists,"—and Serge Koussevitzky, also dedicated to the new, but really most interested in the Franco-Russian schools and in launching the (then) younger generation of American composers, giving them the kind of enthusiastic support he had previously given to young Russians in Europe. At that time these institutions felt it their obligation to keep their audience abreast of new developments—especially those coming from abroad, and in the case of Koussevitzky of the American composers he sponsored, just as art museums still do today. Few good scores (given, of course, the particular tastes of the conductors) had to wait for any length of time to be heard. Each new work of Stravinsky, for instance, was heard within a year after it was composed, performed with serious devotion by one of the outstanding orchestras, quite contrary to the situation today. In the end Koussevitzky's energy and persistence won a larger audience for the new American neoclassical, folk-loric, and populist school and adherents of other aesthetics were more and more bypassed and forgotten.[3]

It was in the early, more advanced stages of this period that the American ultramodern school was especially active, but when the Boston Symphony composers began to dominate the scene in the mid-thirties most of this activity came to a standstill. If there had not been such a drastic change, it is possible that Ives, Varèse, Ruggles, Rudhyar, Cowell, Riegger, Ornstein, Becker, Tremblay and those a bit younger like Crawford, Strang, and Weiss among many others who are beginning to be heard again, would have had an entirely different development. In any case, Cowell's *New Music Edition* carried on valiantly from 1927 to the present, keeping the scores of this group in circulation and thus enlivened the sometimes very pessimistic outlook for the "ultras."

It is at first surprising that the American group seems to have been but dimly aware of its counterparts in Vienna and Russia, but on closer familiarity with the period, it becomes clear that the general opinion here of the Viennese school, particularly as regards Schoenberg

[3] Ives was a subscriber to a box at the Saturday afternoon concerts of the Boston Symphony at Carnegie Hall, and the author of this article remembers being invited to join him and Mrs. Ives at concerts where Scriabin's *Poème de l'Extase, Prométhée,* Stravinsky's *Sacre,* and Ravel's *Daphnis* were performed.

and Webern, was of a kind that would lead few to become deeply involved in their music. Paul Rosenfeld, for instance, whose enthusiastic
and sympathetic criticism was influential even among musicians in
the twenties found that Schoenberg's works "baffle with their apparently
willful ugliness, and bewilder with their geometric cruelty and coldness.
. . . It is only in regarding him as primarily an experimenter that the
later Schoenberg loses his incomprehensibility."[24] When one realizes
that Rosenfeld knew the early tonal works and Opp. 11, 16, and 19
when he wrote this, it is easy to see how the appearance of twelve-tone
works must have strengthened this opinion which is still widely held in
America, despite the evident fact revealed by a number of recordings
that quite the opposite is true. This attitude persisted to the very end of
Schoenberg's life in this country and succeeded in restricting his influence to a much smaller circle than he deserved, and kept most of the
composers discussed from coming to grips with his music. Cowell, however, did publish the second of Webern's *Drei Volkstexte,* Op. 17, in 1930
(in a slightly different version from the one now published by Universal
Edition) and Schoenberg's Op. 33b in 1932 in *New Music Edition,* yet in
his book, *New Musical Resources,*[5] he mentions a new system of tonal
organization used by Schoenberg but shows no understanding of it,
perhaps because the book had been written, so the author explains in a
preface, in 1919. Until around 1930, and even after, it is hard to escape
the impression that the Viennese music left very little impression on
most of the ultramoderns. Riegger, it is true, did start to use a very simplified version of the twelve-tone system then and wrote his *Dichotomy*
(published 1932) incorporating this method but in a way utterly different from the Viennese.

The reverse influence is interesting to speculate about. We do know
that Webern directed works of Cowell, Ruggles, and Ives in Vienna in
1932, that Slonimsky conducted works of this school in various places in
Europe and that Schoenberg left among his posthumous papers an oft-
quoted statement about Ives. Certainly an American is tempted to be
reminded of the tone-cluster writing of Ives and Cowell when it appears
so baldly on the piano in Berg's *Lulu* (mm. 16, 79, and in a number of
other places particularly during Rodrigo, the athlete's, recitative,
mm. 722-768—perhaps to characterize and develop the idea of "Das
wahre Tier," which is introduced by the tone-cluster in the Prologue.
There may even be a reminiscence of Henry Cowell's *Tiger* here).

To clarify certain aesthetic, artistic, and technical matters central to

[4] P. Rosenfeld, *Musical Portraits,* New York, 1920, pp. 233ff, but compare his praise a few
years later: *Musical Chronicle,* New York, 1923, pp. 300–314.
[5] H. Cowell, *New Musical Resources,* New York, 1930.

this group, it is useful to compare them with those central to the composers associated with German Expressionism. A number of papers presented at the Convegno Internazionale di Studi sull'Espressionismo of the Maggio Fiorentino of 1964 are particularly relevant.[6] The problem of trying to define and delineate the special features of this movement is troublesome, naturally, and there has been a tendency by German musical scholars and Luigi Rognoni to insist that it be limited only to the works of the Viennese—and to all of their works, although the paper of Dr. Stuckenschmidt was inclined to include some Russian and a few of the American composers to be discussed in this series. In any case, the basic manifesto of the movement, *Der blaue Reiter,*[7] was the first attempt to clarify its aims. In this pamphlet, music holds a central position since by its very nature music is not a representational art but an expressive art[8] (a point of view derived from the type of thinking that put music at the top of the hierarchy of the arts, as in Walter Pater, in Busoni, and in Ives). *Der blaue Reiter* contained four important articles on music: Schoenberg's *Das Verhältnis zum Text;* Sabanieff's *"Prometheus" von Skrjabin;* von Hartmann's *Über die Anarchie in der Musik;* and Kulbin's *Die Freie Musik.* Other statements about expressionism and music are to be found in Kandinsky's *Über das Geistige in der Kunst*[9] in Schoenberg's *Aphorismen*[10] and his *Harmonielehre*[11] and more peripherally in Busoni's *Entwurf einer Neuen Aesthetik der Tonkunst.* Comparison with the general tenor of statements in these works and those made in Ives' *Essays Before a Sonata,*[12] as well as the critical writings of James Huneker and Paul Rosenfeld reveals many similarities.

The main difference, as always, is that the state of American musical life was so inchoate that a revolutionary movement in this art would necessarily be less well thought out, less focused and more of an affair of individuals only agreeing in a general way, hence less corrosive of the fundamental aspects of what seemed to all a moribund musical tradi-

---

[6] L. Rognoni, *Il Significato dell'Espressionismo come Fenomenologia del Linguaggio Musicale.* J. Rufer, *Das Erbe des Expressionismus in der Zwölftonmusik.* H. H. Stuckenschmidt, *Expressionismus in der Musik.* L. Mittner, *L'Espressionismo fra l'Impressionismo e la Neue Sachlickeit: Fratture e Continuità.*

[7] *Der Blaue Reiter,* Munich, 1912. English translation of Schoenberg's "Das Verhältnis zum Text" in *Style and Idea,* New York, Philosophical Library, 1950.

[8] W. Sokel, *The Writer in Extremis* (*Expressionism in German Literature*), Stanford, California, Stanford University Press, 1959 (McGraw-Hill Paperback, 1964) devotes a whole chapter, "Music and Existence," to this subject.

[9] W. Kandinsky, *Über das Geistige in der Kunst,* Munich, 1912. English transl., *Concerning the Spiritual in Art,* New York, 1947.

[10] A. Schoenberg, *Aphorismen,* "Die Musik," Berlin, 1909–1910. Italian transl. in L. Rognoni, *Espressionismo e Dodecaphonia,* Milan, 1954.

[11] A. Schoenberg, *Harmonielehre,* third ed., Vienna, 1922.

[12] C. Ives, *Essays Before a Sonata and other Writings,* ed. by Howard Boatwright, New York: W. W. Norton & Co., Inc., 1962.

tion since the situation was not seen with any clarity—and for that reason tended to dissipate itself in superficialities and absurdities, as so often happens even today.

The basic point of agreement is Hegel's statement (quoted partially by Ives)[13] that "The universal need for expression in art lies, therefore, in man's rational impulse to exalt the inner and outer world into a spiritual consciousness for himself, as an object in which he recognizes his own self." This statement as quoted by Ives omits the words "and outer" and the last phrase "as an object . . ." Both of these omissions are very significant, for they reveal how close Ives' thinking was to that of the expressionists, for whom the inner world was of prime importance, and for whom art was not an object but a means of embodying his own spiritual vision, for himself, and, in view of other statements, for others to share, through what was later called an "intersubjective relationship."[14]

Rufer's excellent paper attempts to give a general definition:[15]

> There too (in painting and music) is an eruption into chaos, a state of total unrelatedness (which, however, manifests itself in formlessness!), intoxication, ecstasy, the undermining of the very foundations of representative art. "There are no 'objects' or 'colors' in art; only expression." (Franz Marc, 1911). . . . Music of intensely romantic—one might as well say expressionistic—character, with an increasingly pronounced tendency toward breaking the bounds of tonality, toward apparent destruction of musical coherence and traditional formal schemata. Everything was called into question and always seemed to lead into chaos. Today, in retrospect, it seems self-evident that so many fine talents were destroyed in this atmosphere. Only a chosen few, through the force of their genius and the strengthening effect of constant trials, found themselves again. And here I can do no better than quote Gottfried Benn: "The expressionists in particular experienced the profound, objective necessities demanded by craftsmanship in art: the ethos of professionalism, the morality of form."

The actual texts of the period stress truthfulness of expression and the inner necessity of the artist to express his transcendent experiences, as Kandinsky writes:[16]

> (This) inner beauty arises from the pressure of subjective necessity

[13] *Ibid.*, p. 81 and editor's note, p. 141.

[14] L. Rognoni, *Il Significato*, p. 9. "Just as expression is only possible in spoken language if an 'intersubjective relationship' is established, so it is in an even more direct and immediate way in musical language."

[15] Rufer, *op. cit.*, pp. 3–4.

[16] Kandinsky, *op. cit.*, pp. 31–32 (my translation from the German).

and the renunciation of the conventional forms of the beautiful. To those unaccustomed to it, it appears as ugliness. Humanity, in general, is drawn to external things, today more than ever, and does not willingly recognize subjective necessity. The refusal to employ the habitual forms of the beautiful leads one to hold as sacred all the procedures which permit the artist to manifest his personality. The Viennese composer, Arnold Schoenberg, follows this direction alone, scarcely recognized by a few rare and enthusiastic admirers.

Schoenberg himself writes:[17]

> Beauty begins to appear at that moment when the noncreative become aware of its absence. It does not exist earlier because the artist has no need of it. For him, truth suffices. It is enough for him to have expressed himself, to say what had to be said according to the laws of his nature. The laws of the nature of men of genius, however, are the laws of future humanity. . . . Nevertheless, beauty gives itself to the artist even though he did not seek it, having striven only toward truthfulness.

Ives, in an elaborate discussion of form versus content and manner versus substance—a discussion which identifies form and manners with the generally accepted traditional forms and styles of music language and content and substance with the artist's feelings and vision seeking expression:[18]

> Beauty in its common conception has nothing to do with it (substance). . . . Substance can be expressed in music, and that is the only valuable thing in it; and, moreover, that in two separate pieces of music in which the notes are almost identical, one can be of substance with little manner and the other can be of manner with little substance. . . . The substance of a tune comes from somewhere near the soul, and the manner comes from—God knows where.

Curiously enough although the expressionists were very aware in their writings that an inner vision was the driving force behind their search for new artistic means, Ives and Cowell, who were the only ones who wrote extensively about this music did not state this idea directly in words. It must also be pointed out that the influence of mysticism—in Kandinsky,[19] the theosophy of Blavatsky (which is also partially evident in certain ideas of the Viennese composers) and in Ives, the trans-

[17] Schoenberg, *Harmonielehre*, p. 393.
[18] Ives, *op. cit.*, p. 77.
[19] Kandinsky, *op. cit.*

cendentalism of Emerson[20]—formed the basis for this sense of the importance of the inner vision and the disdain for the "material" world. Ruggles, to judge by the titles of his works, and Rudhyar also were deeply influenced by mystical thought. The power of the inner experience to force these composers to find a new means of expression led in two apparently opposite directions, called by Benn, "chaos and geometry" (recalling, oddly, Pascal's *l'esprit de sagesse et l'esprit de géometrie*). The former was the direction toward the basic, elemental aspects of human experience (and the elemental materials of art): Whitman's "barbaric yawp"—the baby's first cry at birth—what was sometimes called the *Urschrei* or the *Urlaut* (Busoni also discusses, in another sense, *Urmusik*)[21]—the primeval immediate expression of basic human emotion. Mittner's paper is valuable on this point:[22]

> The two main artistic procedures of expressionism are the primordial utterance (*Urschrei,* or in the terminology of Edschmid, *geballter Schrei,* almost "compressed cry") and the imposition of an abstract structure, often specifically geometric, on reality. These two procedures seem, and often are, diametrically opposed, since the 'cry' arises in the soul of the seer who envisions or witnesses the destruction of his world, while 'abstraction' is, primarily, the work of an ideal architect who strives to reconstruct the world or construct a completely new one. The relationship, however, is reversible, since geometry can deform and even disintegrate, while the 'cry' can turn into an ecstatic shout of jubilation which invokes or creates a new world, an ideal world. . . . The *Urschrei* of German expressionism almost never realizes the "We," and thus reveals the tragic position of uncertainty of the bewildered bourgeoisie. It is rarely the vaunted shout of rebellion and liberation, but primarily a cry of anguish and horror. The parallel with atonal music is significant. The *Urschrei* is most tellingly evoked in the monodrama *Erwartung,* which records with the precision of a psychograph the various moments of spasmodic expectation indicated by the title, followed by a series of cries of horror and desperation.

Mittner also points out the relation of the *Urschrei* to silence:[23]

> In contrast to this concern for the lacerating, primordial 'cry,' a new power is found in *silence* which, paradoxically, is considered its meta-

[20] Ives, *op. cit.,* p. 36.

[21] Busoni, *op. cit.,* p. 8.

[22] Mittner, *op. cit.,* pp. 43ff. On this point Mittner has a footnote referring another interpretation of the dichotomy by Sokel (*op. cit.*) who traces, as he calls it, "Pure Form and Pure Formlessness" back through German literary history in an attempt to show that it is a special product of the German cultural situation.

[23] Mittner, *op. cit.,* p. 36.

morphosis, since a tragic occurrence is presaged or experienced in a silence analogous to an internal 'cry' of the soul.

Among the American ultramoderns, the urge for such intensification of expression is particularly in evidence in Ruggles, in Rudhyar and to a certain extent in Ives. Certainly his song, *Walt Whitman,* which has something of a caricature about it, perhaps, strikes a character of expressionistic intensity in its first measures, that is similar to the opening pages of the "Emerson" movement of the Concord Sonata and to the first movement of Ruggles' *Men and Mountains.*

The opposing expressionist tendency, as Mittner points out, is that of constructivism, familiar to Americans as an attitude through the aesthetic comments of Poe. In the American period under consideration many kinds of "geometrical" schemata were applied to music, as they were also in Europe and Russia. The rhythmic experiments of Ives partly come out of this thinking, as do those of Varèse, while Ruggles, Ives, Varèse, seem to have experimented with pitch organization. Ruth Crawford, in particular, developed all kinds of patterns of this sort. Her *Piano Study in Mixed Accents* (1930) uses variable meters and a retrograde pitch plan that reminds one of similar methods of Boris Blacher, while her String Quartet (1931), especially the last movement, juggles with quite a number of different "geometric" systems, one governing pitch, another dynamics, and still another the number of consecutive notes before a rest in any given passage, besides, the whole movement is divided into two parts, the second a retrograde of the first a semitone higher. Cowell's book, *New Musical Resources,*[24] has a chapter dealing with the association of pitch-interval ratios with speed ratios after the manner "discovered" later by certain Europeans. During the late twenties and thirties, Joseph Schillinger, who had come to America from Russia, bringing with him the fruits of similar thinking there, taught here; and after his death, his *The Schillinger System of Musical Composition* was published (1946) with an introduction by Cowell, which although attempting to be an all-embracing method of explaining the technique of music of all types is, ultimately, simply another example of this aspect of expressionist "geometry" in that it applies "extrinsic" patterns derived from other fields of systematization and theoretical description to music, often without taking into account the "intrinsic" patterns of musical discourse sufficiently. As Mittner points out in this connection, "geometry" can be a way of building an entirely new world or a way of deforming or dissolving the old. It is possible that an illogical, disorganized geometry or a totally irrelevant one can be just as much

[24] Cowell, *op. cit.*

of a deforming or even constructive pattern as one more obviously relevant and logical (although the chances are obviously higher that the latter will be more fruitful) in the hands of an imaginative composer. The history of the canon in all its phases is a clear demonstration of this.

To get down to actual musical practice, the most obvious similarity is that of the "emancipation of dissonance." Just when this began has not yet been explored and hence it is difficult to say as is often said, that Ives worked independently and before Schoenberg at this, since there may have been a prior obscure source, as there is to microtonal music. Certainly René Lenormand's *Étude sur l'Harmonie Moderne*[25] gives examples from Fanelli's *Tableaux Symphoniques* of 1883 containing whole-tone progressions, Erik Satie's chords constructed on fourths in 1891, and a twelve-tone chord used by Jean Huré in 1910. It is true that Ives seems to have tried a tremendous variety of harmonic methods from about 1900 on. With his point of view, he experimented not only with passages of consistent harmonic structure (such as is common in Scriabin) in works such as the songs *Evening, Two Little Flowers, Harpalus, Walking, Soliloquy,* and with very great diversity of harmonic structure, as in *Majority, Lincoln,* as well as polyphonic textures derived from these opposing attitudes toward harmony. Ruggles, Ornstein, Rudhyar maintained a very much more consistent harmonic approach. Ruggles, in particular, shows a great sensitivity to the handling of major sevenths and minor ninths, and their interrelationships with other intervals. The fourth *Evocation* is a particularly fine example of this. Tone-clusters which might be considered a reduction of harmony to its most primitive and undifferentiated state, may have been first used by Ives in his First Piano Sonata of 1902 and then by Cowell in 1917. By 1912, Ives was writing large tone-clusters for divided strings in his orchestra music, especially in the *Fourth of July* in which several streams of tone clusters rush up and down scales in contrary motion simultaneously. Berg uses clusters in the men's chorus in the first tavern scene in *Wozzeck.* Indeed both tavern scenes in this opera have a strikingly similar character to those works of Ives that suggest crowd scenes, as the one mentioned above, and the second movement of the Fourth Symphony. The strings divided into tone-clusters, which seems to have been one of Ives' discoveries, did not come into wide usage until very recently in the works of Xenakis, Ligeti, Penderecki, and Cerha. Ives' attitude toward dissonance is summed up:[26]

> Many sounds we are used to do not bother us, and for that reason we are inclined to call them beautiful. Possibly the fondness for in-

25 R. Lenormand, *Étude sur l'Harmonie Moderne,* Paris, 1912.
26 Ives, *op. cit.,* p. 98.

dividual utterance may throw out a skin-deep arrangement which is readily accepted as beautiful—formulae that weaken rather than toughen up the musical muscles.

Although Cowell wrote a number of piano works exploring poly-rhythms (and using a notation devised by him for the purpose) and Ornstein used irregular bar lengths—and Rudhyar and Ruggles used irrational note divisions in order to give the impression of rubato and rhythmic freedom—it was again Ives who explored the field of rhythm most extensively, using precompositional patterns of note values, all types of polyrhythms, of approximately coordinated instrumental groups, of passages more or less improvised rhythmically, carrying such explora-tion much further than any composer of his time. In a desire to make the performance situation vivid, Ives sometimes wrote remarks in the score directed to the performer to encourage him to give free rein to his fantasy. His remark: "Perhaps music is the art of speaking extrava-gantly,"[27] gives some clue to his general approach and links him once again to the expressionists.

One of Ives' most puzzling aspects is his extreme heterogeneity, a characteristic of some of Cowell's and Ornstein's music, not shared by the other Americans who resemble much more closely the more accept-able attitude Schoenberg stated in his early essay, indicating the kind of thinking which would eventually lead him to adopt the twelve-tone method:[28]

Inspired by the first words of the text, I had composed many of my songs straight through to the end. It turned out that I had never done greater justice to the poet than when, guided by my first direct contact with the sound of the beginning, I divined everything that obviously had to follow the first sound with inevitability.

Thence it became clear to me that the work of art is like every other complete organism. It is so homogeneous in its composition that in every detail it reveals its truest, inmost essence.

Such a sense of inner cohesion is closely allied with the general tendency among expressionists toward "reduction" in technique, to finding the basic material of any given work. This method became acutely impor-tant to musicians as the form-building function of tonality was elimi-nated, obviously, and also as various familiar methods of beginning, stating, developing, and ending began to seem outworn because they weakened the intensity and vibrant immediacy of individual musical moments. As in literature, much concern and invention was lavished on

[27] Ives, op. cit., p. 52.
[28] Schoenberg, Style and Idea, p. 4.

new methods of fragmentary presentation, such as starting *in medias res* or ending with an incompleted phrase. Closely allied with this was the tendency toward very short, concentrated totalities after the analogy of a Chinese character or a hieroglyph. The works of Schoenberg and Webern of this type are well known. It is interesting that among the Americans only Ives attempted this in works such as the songs, *Anne Street, Maple Leaves, 1,2,3,* and *Soliloquy.*

But not only this type of fragmentation was common among expressionists but also the fragmentation of the materials of the work. In this respect the music of Varèse is particularly significant in that its material is made up of small fragments for the most part and these fragments are generally reduced to very basic, elemental shapes— melodic material made of repeated notes, repeated chordal sounds depending for their telling effect on their instrumentation, vertical spacing, and timing. Varèse's music corresponds very closely to Mittner's delineation of several stages in the development of the expressionistic vision as seen in poetry and painting:[29]

> The visionary power of expressionism did not result in a sudden turning away from the observation of reality, but reached this goal through a series of steps. The first was a reduction of sense data. Barlach, in his sculptures, took a most important step in this direction in 1901 . . . he began to reduce methodically the lines of his figures to those which seemed to him the most important, and so achieved a new, vigorous, and very plastic presentation of the essence of his subjects. The second step consisted of the extraction and separate use of each aspect of the total sense perception as a thing in itself, detaching it from the object to which it belongs, with the consequent deformation of reality as an entity. Such a procedure evolved also in poetry through means specifically derived from painting, where it had caused a revolution in the field of color. . . . Color was no longer added to figure, but figure to color. From such an unnaturalistic coupling of color and figure, it is but a short step to the unnaturalistic coupling of any of the other elements of reality.

The dissociation of the various elements of reality and their reassembling in new ways, isolating, as Kandinsky did, color from shape, etc. is paralleled by the dissociation, first, of the various so-called "elements" of music—melody, harmony, rhythm. The next step was the more subtle one of dissociating certain qualities from others, such as tonecolor from the above three, and finally the dissociation of all the presently called "parameters" from each other. All of these tendencies along with the "reductive" method are evident in Varèse.

[29] Mittner, *op. cit.,* pp. 32ff.

In passing it is interesting to point out that the development of the resources of instrumental techniques, which was not so common in Europe until recently, had during this period an important exponent in America. Carlos Salzédo's *Modern Study of the Harp* (New York, 1921) presents a whole new repertory of effects for that instrument that are still not incorporated into our composers' vocabulary as are the latest tapping and scraping of the violin from France and Poland.

Perhaps the other striking feature of resemblance between these two groups is the avoidance of repetition and the sense of continuous variation. Ives' statements about this are very indicative:

> Unity is too generally conceived of, or too easily accepted, as analogous to form, and form as analogous to custom, and custom to habit.[30]

> Coherence, to a certain extent, must bear some relation to the listener's subconscious perspective. But is this its only function? Has it not another of bringing outer or new things into wider coherence?[31]

> There may be an analogy—and on first sight there seems to be— between the state and power of artistic perceptions and the law of perpetual change, that ever-flowing stream, partly biological, partly cosmic, ever going on in ourselves, in nature, in all life . . . Perhaps this is why conformity in art (a conformity which we seem naturally to look for) appears so unrealizable, if not impossible.[32]

[30] Ives, *op. cit.*, p. 98.
[31] *Ibid.*, p. 98.
[32] *Ibid.*, p. 71.

ARTHUR BERGER: THE COMPOSER AS MANNERIST

JOHN MAC IVOR PERKINS

THE WORD "mannerism" is not particularly frequent in music criticism. When it appears, it often denotes some specific idiosyncrasy of style and tends to suggest "artificiality" in the most pejorative sense of that word. A closely related but less popular, more complex, more powerful, non-pejorative meaning has become current through the writings of art historians. The simplest definition would probably be "the sharing of one or more characteristics of style or aesthetic positions with those sixteenth-century painters, sculptors, and architects frequently identified as Mannerists." If this useful term, which is best spelled with a capital M, is to find application in music criticism, an enumeration of the style characteristics and aesthetic positions of the Mannerists, in terms which are meaningful in a musical context, would be most desirable. At best, this is a difficult undertaking. Nevertheless, at least one author has pointed to Mannerism as a useful critical approach to the work of Gesualdo.[1]

The same author suggests that twentieth-century understanding of and sensitivity to the works of the sixteenth-century Mannerists may indicate that we are experiencing something of a second Mannerist age.[2] In the field of music, a fair case could be made for this, at least for the period roughly between 1920 and 1955. By its very nature, however, Mannerism is a personal thing, and attaches more appropriately to individuals than to ages. One contemporary composer whose work is seen to good advantage in a Mannerist light is Arthur Berger.

To avoid a lengthy historical analogy it will be necessary to attempt a generalized description of the Mannerist concept, even at the risk (or, indeed, the certainty) of oversimplification. The following points seem most important: (1) The Mannerist stands in a very special, intimate relation to the past, and notably to the immediate past of his own art. This relationship may often be described as a conscious mixture of rejection and exaggeration. There may be a tendency toward parody, occasionally in the sense of "burlesque" but usually in a highly serious spirit. Mannerists are thus neither conservative

[1] Daniel B. Rowland, *Mannerism—Style and Mood*, Yale University Press, 1964, pp. 23-47.
[2] *Ibid.*, p. 82.

nor revolutionary in attitude; and, although they may of course attract a few imitators, and their works may embody striking, imaginative novelties, they are characteristically neither system builders nor far-reaching historical innovators. (2) Mannerist works of art show a tendency toward discontinuity or "fragmentation" on many levels. In Daniel Rowland's words, "any sense of smoothness or flow is purposely destroyed."[3] (3) The over-all structure of Mannerist works is rarely simple or obvious. Indeed, the Mannerist work taken as a whole, as well as many of its parts, is likely to be characterized by an acutely insecure order. Symmetries and unambiguous subordinations seem to be avoided.

> Each of the works we have studied shows a strong tendency to break into parts because there are no obvious patterns left to hold it together. . . . "Unreadable" is an accurate term to describe Mannerist structure, because it is more obvious to the mind than it is to the eye or the ear. It is a structure which always emerges when a work is studied, but is seldom obvious because of the complication and refinement of the very elements which constitute it. Only those sensitive to this type of structure can perceive it. . . . Mannerism is characterized by a lack of focus, a condition of unstable equilibrium. The result is that the eye or ear remains in ceaseless but apparently aimless motion.[4]

(4) On the other hand, Mannerism does not imply mere submission to chaos. Insecurity is not disengagement, and the Mannerist is not likely to be mistaken for a "disengaged" artist. The conflict between order and chaos may be uncertain in outcome, but there are signs that it has been an intensely experienced conflict.

> There seems to be no order inherent in the materials themselves; instead we get an impression of the artist struggling against the elements of his art, trying to establish a pattern among parts . . . which exist in a condition of tension one with the other. This tension is unresolved and nondirectional. Like the dissonances in Gesualdo's madrigal, it does not lead to a resolution; it does not lead anywhere, but, for the first time, exists for its own sake. This more than anything else defines Mannerism: tension is created not to be resolved but to remain. . . .[5]

If Arthur Berger is to be considered as a New Mannerist, it will be expeditious to examine his work in relation to each of these four points in turn.

[3] *Ibid.*, p. 75.   [4] *Ibid.*, pp. 77-78.   [5] *Ibid.*, p. 77.

I

The music of the immediate past, which has been an important part of the environment during every composer's formation, is subjected in Berger's case to a continuing, habitual process of critical reexamination, selection, and rejection. Few composers are so consciously, even self-consciously, historical in approach, and few are so disinclined to accept discovered solutions as inviolate.

In his diatonic phase, Berger seemed to make use of some of the devices of the neoclassicists without actually joining the party. Indeed, in a review of Berger's Duo for cello and piano, a work composed in 1951, Milton Babbitt wrote that "in its emphasis on registrational differentiation and intricacy of ensemble, the Duo has been justifiably characterized as 'diatonic Webern.' "[6] The gradual shift to twelve-tone method in the 1950's is fully consistent with Berger's personality: the twelve-tone method had by then become something not only of the present but also of the past; it had become available in a new sense. This was not a simple case of a composer "going twelve-tone." A new stylistic parody became possible: Berger himself described the Chamber Music for Thirteen Players (1956) as "neoclassic twelve-tone."

Furthermore, there was no question of accepting uncritically every aspect of the spirit of the twelve-tone "classics" or any one of several possible versions of orthodox twelve-tone technique. George Perle has pointed to the heterodox procedures manifested in the 1958 String Quartet.[7] There are two related but distinct melodic sets, while the chords and figurations are derived independently, according to a scheme of unordered pitch sets. The Chamber Concerto (1959) and the 3 Pieces for 2 Pianos (1961), are, in different ways, still less routine in their approach to systematic pitch choice. The original title of the latter work, "Improvisations," was meant to suggest that the composer "improvised" the pieces in composing them, that the choice of pitch and register was made on a purely contextual basis. Nevertheless, it is clear that the experience of composing the Chamber Concerto, as well as the other twelve-tone works, played an important role in guiding these contextual choices, even if a partly unconscious one.

The directions of Berger's highly developed critical faculty, especially his uncompromising rejection of certain aspects of much of the music of the recent past, has led him to a very personal, "tight,"

[6] *The Saturday Review*, March 13, 1954.
[7] *Musical Quarterly*, October 1960, p. 522.

stylistic position. What remains, after so much is rejected, is necessarily subject to strict limitations: limitations so consistently imposed
as to seem the result of systematic "stylization." At the same time,
the rejection of certain possibilities focuses attention on others; and
these other unrejected possibilities may be transformed into something
fundamentally new, or may be derived by a process of magnification,
extension, or exaggeration of materials and procedures from the past.

Increasingly in recent years, Berger's harmonic vocabulary has been
dominated by the five "dissonant" source trichords (i.e., three-note
sets defined by total interval-class content) presented singly and in
numerous combinations, as chords, arpeggios, and melodic fragments (Ex. 1).

Ex. 1, 3 Pieces for 2 Pianos

The current Work in Progress, a piano piece, is quite uncompromising in this respect, and the first trichord plays a very prominent role
(see Exx. 6a and 6b). Quite significantly, Berger had been employing the "dissonant" trichords as primary building blocks or basic
cells well before his return to the twelve-tone method. (They are
more characteristic of his diatonic music, in fact, than of his brief
twelve-tone period in the thirties.)

In contrapuntal textures, all registers are generally kept active.
In the Chamber Concerto and the Work in Progress, this is forced by
intricate precompositional mechanisms, but it is equally true of earlier
and later works: exclusively low-register, high-register, and even
middle-register passages of more than a very few seconds' duration
are almost impossible to find. As another style characteristic dating
from Berger's diatonic period, it is probable that this derives, by
extension, from the widely spaced chords and open textures of Copland and from Stravinsky's middle-period music, rather than from
Babbitt or Boulez. Berger, however, goes well beyond the neoclassicists in persistently exploiting the whole instrumental range (Ex. 2).

In almost every work written before the Work in Progress, Berger
has stressed binary rhythmic subdivisions. Even triplets are com-

Ex. 2, 3 Pieces for 2 Pianos

paratively uncommon, and where they do occur they are generally fast and tend to coincide with the beat rather than overlap it.

The regular metrical pulse is thus maintained as a "felt" rhythmic element or framework. In the most recent works, periods of fixed meter are frequently alternated with periods during which the meter changes in nearly every bar; these changing meters, however, disrupt the underlying steady beat or tactus only in climactic or other unusual situations. In the String Quartet, the opposition between simple and compound meters, with equal sixteenth-notes, provides a dichotomy of great importance in the generation of the form not only of the first movement (where the initial simple meter never returns) but of the entire quartet (Exx. 3 and 4).

Against the mechanical rigidity of metrical pulse, Berger employs irregular accents and rests, distributed very liberally (see Ex. 10). Irregular tied-over note values are not common except perhaps for well-isolated chords or single tones.

What might be called the normal background texture in Berger is characterized by successions of staccato sixteenth-notes (eighths in fast tempi, thirty-seconds in slow movements) punctuated and fragmented by displaced accents, short rests every few notes, occasional legato snatches and briefly sustained notes. Characteristically, three or more such instrumental lines combine to form a web of such animation and color that performers must make a special effort both to identify and to "bring out" any foreground line which may be present (See Ex. 3). The effect was compared by Peggy Glanville-Hicks to "the pen dots and etched patches which surround and shade

Ex. 3, String Quartet

Ex. 4, String Quartet

a line drawing of Paul Klee."[8] The leading cantabile melodic element of the String Quartet is first announced as a series of dotted eighth-notes, which stands in relief against such a background, and also provides a link between the simple and compound meters mentioned above (Ex. 5).

The rhythmic language of Stravinsky is clearly one source for most of this. Berger is more drastic however: the "straight" rhythms which regularly introduce and prepare the "twitches," unexpected syncopations, and dislocations in Stravinsky are often not present in Berger's music. It is not that there are no accented downbeats, but

[8] *A C A Bulletin*, 1953.

that when these occur, they are usually offset almost immediately by counter-accents. The result is a state of almost uniform "nervous" syncopation, roughly analogous to the condition of constant dissonance which also prevails. The effect of Berger's music is less theatrical, less "balletic," more abstract than that of Stravinsky's; this difference of rhythmic conception is one reason.

Ex. 5, String Quartet

Despite the brevity of the only available movement, the current Work in Progress is undeniably the most elaborate of Berger's compositions. This is most striking with respect to rhythm. Not only are the surface duration relationships more intricate than in any previous work, but the larger rhythmic relationships, within the phrase and between phrases, and the timing and balancing of events in general are less symmetrical and predictable, more complex and refined than before (Exx. 6a and 6b).

Ex. 6a, Work in Progress

Ex. 6b, Work in Progress

It would appear that as the harmonic limitations of Berger's style are becoming more and more stringent, the rhythmic conception is broadening, i.e., becoming more inclusive. On the basis of the one movement, however, the Work in Progress is not an entirely "new departure" in Berger's development; rather, it embodies a logical enrichment of style, in a direction suggested in earlier works, and certainly not without distinct traces of the former manner carried over into the new context.[9]

II

Many of the essential characteristics of Berger's style are reflected in his treatment of cantabile melodies. Almost invariably they cover a wide range (more than two octaves) and almost invariably intervals of a seventh and a ninth are prominently included. More individual is the manner in which these lines are often cut off abruptly, almost arbitrarily. Phrases are not allowed to proceed to a "natural" cadence but are interrupted in midstream (Ex. 7).

The pronounced snatch-like quality or discontinuity which results is played up harmonically and by instrumentation. Indeed, the state or condition of discontinuity—for when discontinuities are emphasized frequently enough over a long span they cease to be heard as events and are better described as a condition—is clearly a leading aspect of Berger's style on many levels. It is also characteristic of much contemporary music; in this case, however, one is aware that it has been

[9] I have not seen the recent, unpublished Septet.

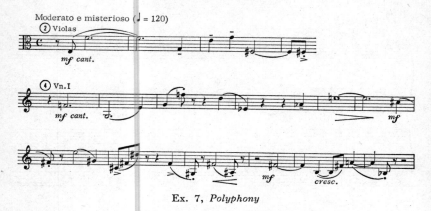

Ex. 7, *Polyphony*

actively cultivated as a stylistic virtue. Comparatively smooth, continuous passages or even whole movements exist, of course, as exceptions. The degree of discontinuity even becomes a structural element in the largest forms. But the most relaxed slow movements and most resigned pianissimo codas still show clear signs of (undoubtedly deliberate) roughening in phrase structure and linear surface.

Of the five trichords of Ex. 1, the last is the least frequent in Berger's recent music. No doubt the presence of the tritone is partially responsible: chords derived from this trichord tend to function as dominants, and in any case the tritone usually demands respectful treatment. Another possible explanation for the slighting of this trichord is that it is not so well adapted as the others to the kind of spacing Berger often prefers for sustained chords: it tends to fill in the vertical gaps rather smoothly and evenly.

As can be seen in many of the examples, Berger's approach to spacing and registration is personal and highly fastidious. In chords, obvious, symmetrical, opaque, and close spacings all are avoided. Wide vertical gaps are frequent, as are vertical alternations of large and small intervals. Emphasis is placed upon transparency and variety rather than fusion; indeed, performers, especially string players, must attend very carefully to intonation and simultaneity of attack to avoid a wispy, spidery effect. Progressions of similarly spaced chords are exceptional; in general, the spacing of each chord gives the impression of having been worked out individually. This is a false impression, of course: the spacings interact. For example, registers left vacant in any given chord tend to be occupied in the next, and vice versa (see Ex. 10). As one consequence of this, chords seem rather to succeed one another than to progress. At least, the powerful bonds of harmonic progression are appreciably relaxed and underplayed, sometimes to the point of obscurity.

Berger's writing for orchestra is ultra-transparent and almost thin. Individual instrumental qualities, as well as simultaneous or successive oppositions of sharply contrasting sonorities (such as secco against legato sounds) are emphasized, rather than fused combinations, mixed colors, or gradual, "organic" sonorous developments. The scoring of chords, like their spacing and structure, changes from chord to chord; most of the instruments are kept "active" most of the time (although the individual parts have many rests, the rests are seldom very long). Percussion is used sparingly and generally for accent rather than in an independent role.[10] The resulting over-all effect is intricate, kaleidoscopic, and light.

III

Berger is so anti-prolific, and his works offer such a variety of formal conceptions, that it is difficult to generalize about their nature. It is safe to state, however, that despite the lucid, consistent, and relatively unbewildering surface of his music—or perhaps because of it—it is by no means easy to hear and follow large-scale structures. The parts, united by a common tightly defined style, bear a superficial but sometimes irrelevant and distracting resemblance to one another; there are no full-fledged themes to use as points of reference; contrasts are not gross; oppositions and other interactions may be very intricate. A further difficulty is provided by the fact that neat, symmetrically balanced, well-isolated sections on the one hand and overwhelming (and thus unifying) climaxes on the other, are equally foreign to Berger's language. The climax of the String Quartet seems powerful enough out of context; in context it becomes so only after the listener has familiarized himself with the whole work, that is, in retrospect. Even then, it is not the sort of climax that pulls everything together (Ex. 8).

In Ex. 9, the opening measures of the Chamber Concerto have been reduced so that the "foreground" and "background" elements (A and B, respectively) are separated.

In this section element A generally appears in the violins and celli,

[10] Berger's is a language of pitch relationships above all. Special mention must be made, however, of the delicate and ingenious use of prepared sounds in the 3 Pieces for 2 Pianos. Here, Cage's invention is "unrejected." It is not exaggerated or extended either, but scattered, dispersed, and relieved. The rich variety of effects (single and double wood screws inserted between the strings, rubber wedges, "blocked" strings, pizzicato, forearm and palm clusters, etc.) becomes part of the music, not the reverse, as the result of a clearly evident rhythmic framework and an uncommon exercise of restraint.

Ex. 8, String Quartet

but it is not always easy to distinguish the elements aurally. Element
A is a strict conventional twelve-tone structure, but the series itself
(which represents the chromatic all-combinatorial source set, has a
very restricted vocabulary of adjacent intervals and a second hexa-

Ex. 9, Chamber Concerto

Ex. 9 Chamber Concerto (cont.)

chord which is a transposition of the first) is characteristic. In element B the order of appearance and succession of pitches is not systematic, but the registers in which each pitch-class appears is fixed for the duration of each short period. These periods are indicated by circled Roman numbers in Ex. 9; their beginnings and endings sometimes coincide with the beginnings and endings of musical phrases, but usually do not. Circled Arabic numbers refer to the octave assignments (the octaves are measured from C to B). By this reckoning, C passes, in the first 7 periods, through octaves 1, 2, 3, 4, 5, 6, and 7; F♯ appears in octaves 7, 6, 5, 4, 3, 2, and 1. The other pitches follow more devious routes according to an involved scheme. The pitches are not, of course, distributed equally among the octaves; the actual distribution in any given period is related to events in element A and to the structure of the tone row.

As an ordering or unifying element, the scheme is fragile in the extreme. Indeed, the precompositional apparatus of this piece would seem to be little more than an intellectual conceit or a compositional scaffolding which is dissolved in the finished work. Berger's larger, more realistic structural devices are often elusive as well.

In the given excerpt from the opening section of *Polyphony* for orchestra (1955) the original basic cell (second source trichord) is later expanded by moving the minor second outside the minor third;

Ex. 10, Polyphony

Ex. 10 *Polyphony* (cont.)

that is, by shifting to the third trichord (Ex. 10). Thus the careful manipulation and selection of these elementary units is an important aspect of the over-all design of the composition.

The pitch-selection technique of the Work in Progress constitutes a considerable extension and refinement of the method employed in element B of the Chamber Concerto. A consciously controlled and balanced network of routes governs register choices of individual pitches and (in a more complex but essentially similar way) certain specific two- and three-note pitch collections. The available short movement is divided into eighteen very brief sections (these are indicated in the manuscript copy and usually coincide with musical articulations). The route of G, for example, is as follows:

section number:	1 2 3 4 5 6 7 8	9	10 11	12		13	14		15	16	17	18
octave number:	5		3	5		4	6		2	3	7		1	5	6	3

Since in this work octave 8 = octave 1 (mod 7), the processes involved here are made easier to grasp by visualizing the registers as diatonic degrees:

Ex. 11

There are at least two examples here of an orderly process (indicated by connected stems) interrupted by an "arbitrary" event (marked +) or rather an event responsive to considerations outside the established local symmetry. In each case, however, the "random" event becomes an element in a new symmetrical (i.e., orderly) pattern which governs subsequent choices. The routes of the other pitches and collections provide numerous other examples of this technique. (The second "orderly process" indicated above [stems down], a wedge-shaped non-repetitive tour of the octaves, may seem far-fetched; it was suggested by simpler examples of this pattern governing other pitches.)

The inherent flexibility of this system, which enables the individual routes to be "bent" or guided in certain directions, makes possible the forecasting and proper timing of certain over-all conditions. Thus, to cite only the most unequivocal examples, the "low" (except for G) condition of Section 2 (see Ex. 6a) and the "empty middle" condition of Section 15 (see Ex. 6b) have evidently been planned, if not "precompositionally" then at a very early stage of the compositional process. Conceptually then—and also, to a remarkable degree, to the ear—these states represent organic formal elements, not simply coloristic effects or "gestures." Naturally, they are not approached gradually, by an obvious diagonal movement: the composer, in a public lecture at Brandeis, has stated that one of his intentions was to "avoid the hill-and-dale treatment of registers."

Because of the brevity of the sections, and the high level of independence of the pitch routes (which is of course promoted by their internal symmetries), no given registral concentration can prevail more than a few seconds, so that all registers remain alive. Thus two of the most immediately effective pianistic devices employed by contemporary composers—namely, the quasi-improvisational, *bravura* "sweep" up (or down) the keyboard, and the prolonged, intensive exploration of extreme (and/or extremely limited) ranges—are precluded by the pitch-selection technique of this composition. They would, in any case, be ruled out as alien to Berger's style.

IV

Certain features of Berger's designs, certain ordering and unifying elements, recur frequently enough to be called characteristic. Because of the unfamiliar manner in which these devices operate—their unusually long time span, for example—and because of the unavailability of much of the music itself, it is quite difficult to illustrate them by short excerpts. They should at least be mentioned, however:

1. Several works start with a crucially important vertical structure, a built-up (non-simultaneous) chord and/or motive-complex which, even if it is never repeated in its original form, acts as a point of reference and a source for the entire movement or composition. If the significance of the often very brief opening gesture is overlooked, the meaning of the whole work may be distorted. 2. Specific polarities (contrasts maximized within the limits of the style) are established at the outset; the body of the composition can frequently be analyzed as a struggle between and among these polarities. For example: one tonal center or "pole" vs. another; chords vs. active contrapuntal textures; pizzicato vs. cantabile melodies; simple vs. compound meter; fixed vs. changing meter; etc. 3. Quasi-arbitrary interruptions are frequent: these are simply large-scale manifestations of the spirit of discontinuity which characterizes Berger's rhythm and phrase structure. As a special instance of such interruptions, recapitulations are always at least partially frustrated. Several of Berger's major works may be analyzed as a prolonged and ultimately futile "struggle" to return. The tension generated by this struggle is left unresolved. The

String Quartet is the clearest example.[11] The sense of closure which would be provided by a true recapitulation is entirely missing; instead, the motivating energy is gradully dissipated or "bled off" during the second half of the work. Fragmentary or well-disguised recapitulations do take place, of course. In the second of the 3 Pieces for 2 Pianos the mysterious, atypical opening chord (Ex. 12a) reappears near the end in a disguised version (Ex. 12b).

Ex. 12a, 3 Pieces for 2 Pianos

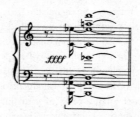

Ex. 12b, 3 Pieces for 2 Pianos

In the book quoted at the beginning of this article, Daniel Rowland summarized the aesthetic and underlying metaphysical assumptions of Mannerism in the following way:

> The world is in essence disunified. Any order that exists is one of precarious balance imposed by man's ingenuity. This order is fragile, liable to destruction at the slightest movement, because the events or parts have an existence of their own antagonistic to the order imposed. . . . The only order in the universe outside of God exists in man's creative, intuitive intellect. For the Mannerist, however, man is incapable of dominating hostile nature, of recreating his own order in it. The pattern he imposes is a pattern of wit and cleverness which is in constant conflict with the material world, and this conflict is plainly manifested in the Mannerist style.[12]

[11] See Benjamin Boretz, in *The Nation*, February 17, 1962, and George Perle, *op.cit.*
[12] Rowland, *op.cit.*, pp. 81-82.

Arthur Berger is one American composer who has found himself and at the same time has persisted in enriching his musical language and enlarging his scope. He does not thrash around wildly in many directions, nor does he continue year after year to manufacture insignificant variations upon a single good piece. In discovering himself, he has found not an overwhelming voice, but a civilized, persuasive one: to allow it to go unheard because it is taken for something it is not would indeed be unfortunate.

ASPECTS OF TONALITY IN THE MUSIC
OF ROSS LEE FINNEY

HENRY ONDERDONK

I

ROSS LEE FINNEY's first composition using the twelve-tone technic was written in 1950. American composers, like their European colleagues, showed a new interest in all forms of serialism after World War II. By and large this interest emerged in the generation after the war, and one might have expected that a composer who matured in the '30's, as Finney did, would resist new kinds of musical syntax. The fact that Finney studied in the early '30's with Alban Berg is undoubtedly important, for his music is much closer to Berg than to Schoenberg or Webern. But of equal importance were two events: his service in the war and his move in 1948 to the University of Michigan as Composer-in-Residence after nineteen years on the faculty of Smith College.

His early music is diatonic and reflects his concern for melody. His studies in the '20's with Nadia Boulanger and in the '30's with Roger Sessions (who has remained a lifelong friend) strongly influenced his musical thought. To develop a style, an artist must be strongly committed in at least one of three directions: to himself, to his time, or to his tradition. Finney's commitment is to all three. When he adopted twelve-tone practice, he maintained his belief in the tonality that had dominated his early scores. As a teacher he compelled students, not necessarily to compose tonally, but at least to account for tonality, to know what they ignored if they chose to do so. He uses the word frequently and in colorful, persuasive metaphor.[1] Thus, he demanded of himself, when he adopted twelve-tone practice in the '50's, that his music also reflect his tonal concern. Since these two have not routinely formed a companionship, it is of interest to see how it is managed.

In making this investigation I shall examine the first movements of two works: the Sixth String Quartet (Finney's first twelve-tone composition),

---

[1] I know of no one quite so able to speak compellingly about music as Finney. He achieves that delicate balance between persuasion, example, and demand which nourishes a student's self-belief through self-criticism. The number of his successful students, who exhibit a wide range of musical characteristics, is extensive and testifies to his impressive skill as a teacher.

composed in 1950, and his Third Symphony, composed a decade later in 1960.[2] The two works are similar in several ways: they are both concerned with a tonal plan (both focusing on the tonality of E), and they both use more than a single twelve-tone row. There is, of course, a fundamental difference in the way in which the rows are derived and the manner in which they are used. The technic of the symphony is a refinement over the earlier work.

II

The four movements of the quartet are sectional and traditional in their organization, and they are framed by an introduction and a conclusion. Three rows are presented in the introduction (Ex. 1).

Ex. 1

These rows are not interrelated as permutations of one another and therefore represent a rather lavish display of source material, but each provides a certain tonal[3] possibility that is dependent on the interval of a minor second (Ex. 2). In Row II, the tonal center E is supported through emphasis on its fifth and the leading tones, F and D♯. In using Row I, whose opening triad furnishes an F root,[4] Finney will reverse the roles that F and E are given

---

[2] String Quartet No. 6 (E) (C. F. Peters: parts [P6458], study score [P6459]; Composers Recordings, Inc. [CRI-116]). Symphony No. 3 (C. F. Peters [P6667]; Louisville First Edition Records [400–672]).

[3] In this article, the word "tonality," should be understood to signify not merely the relations between notes but also the presence of centers of attraction (tonal centers) whose recurrence throughout a work provides articulation and cohesiveness. Tonal operations or procedures would then denote the means by which tonal centers are promoted or rejected.

[4] The word "root" in this article refers to that note of an interval which gives it stability, specifically: the lower note of the perfect fifth, the higher note of the perfect fourth; the lower note of a major and minor third, the higher note of a major and minor sixth. The tritone and the major and minor second would not of themselves possess a root in this sense.

in Row II. D♯ becomes associated with B, and the resulting B root stands juxtaposed, in the third movement, to the F root. The ensuing tonal polarity can be heard to require resolution since these two roots are a tritone apart. Movement IV, through its concentration upon the tonal center E, will supply the resolution. Row III divides into "white keys" and "black keys," and of course each segment is in a half-step relationship to the other. The second movement, which uses this row, is a scherzo in which the first segment of seven notes is given more emphasis in the first and the last sections, while the second segment of five notes dominates the "trio." The listener should hear these uses of the rows, so essential to the fabric of the music, quite clearly.

Ex. 2

The first movement, following the short introduction, illustrates two ways in which a row can be used to achieve tonal functions: to establish and maintain a tonal center (stabilizing), and to disestablish it and move to another (excursive). In this work these functions correspond to traditional practice, the first (stabilizing) used in the main- and sub-thematic sections of the exposition and recapitulation, and the second (excursive) in the bridge passages and the development. The main theme begins as follows (Ex. 3):

Ex. 3

One could hear the first few measures in the following way. In the foreground of emphasis E, by its low placement in the cello part and its association with pitches which make it a root (B and G—m. 15), as well as by its resolution of the leading tone (D♯ or E♭) in the outer voices, emerges as the tonal center. This fact, deriving from melodic arrangement, is reinforced by the ostinato-like recurrence which discloses the above emphasis in the most rhythmically emphatic manner. As a combatant against this array of force, the F has no chance and is reduced to subordination (upper leading tone). The C root (at *a*) exists as the only other challenger, both because of the precise clarity of its exposure and its forcible declaration by the cello in m. 17. But though furnishing contrast, it is made, by rhythm, to be that which throws the E into relief and does not undermine E. C serves an important role in the subsequent bridge passage.

Now we may confront the remaining, somewhat more problematic processes, for which the sample at *x* can be taken as illustrative. How can this material, so complex and self-contradictory, be understood tonally? The explanation in part, I think, must depend upon the linear logic of the outer voices which, in connection with rhythm, insist upon the tonality of E as follows (Ex. 4):

Ex. 4

Finney always carefully controls what he calls the "floor" and "ceiling" in this way, but to make this the sole explanation of the passage in question is to evade the issue. We may begin by rearranging the vertical sonorities at *x* into more compact chords in order to expose more clearly the movement of intervals and reduce the voice leading to an essential simplicity (Ex. 5). (In twelve-tone music, verticality has always been a vexing problem.) The sonority at (1) and (2) by virtue of the use of the tritone, seventh, and ninth (and by implication second, fourteenth, and so forth) predicts change. A following sonority which includes new tones, as in this case, will create change and satisfy the requirement of the prediction. Progression thus results from displacement. That the sonority at (2) is of the same kind as that at (1) merely keeps alive the nature of the moment: a prediction of, or a command to, change. The sonority at (3) displaces that at (2) by

which event the tritone is resolved by step. The sonority at (3) asserts a D♯
root which must be displaced. Undoubtedly the D♮, its simultaneously
applied leading tone, helps to do this; for although a subject tone, it is also
an irritant. Finally the C root of sonority (4) replaces the D♯ of (3), at
once fulfilling the cause and effect of displacement (with help from D♮).
In the latter two sonorities, change is not so easy to predict; they exist side
by side, self-enclosed. Altogether (1) and (2) may clearly be seen as leading onward, while (3) and (4) combine with the preceding C root to form
a curious, equivocal situation. They need the recurrent E to subdue the
D♯ and absorb the more closely related C♯ and C♮.

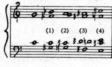

(1)   (2)   (3)   (4)

Ex. 5

The rest of the main thematic section proceeds according to the same
principles and need not concern us, though it illustrates these principles
through different textures. The texture disperses and thins, allowing for
much conversational chatter and imitation in the manner of the sixteenth
century. Finney's sense of counterpoint, to my mind, resembles Renaissance style more than any other, even taking into account the instrumental
quality of the medium. The sub-theme, in fact, is pure madrigal and very
beautiful (cf. the composer's lovely choruses, *Six Spherical Madrigals*
[1947]).

As an example of centrifugal function (i.e., proceeding away from the
center: excursive), the bridge passage makes use of one of the frequently
employed varieties of twelve-tone procedure: hexachordal segmentation.
The first four measures sufficiently show its import (Ex. 6a).

Ex. 6

For some the practice here may seem whimsical, for this quartet does not employ a combinatorial row and therefore no pair of hexachords (except the original) completes an aggregate. The hexachord is treated as a motive in an imitative texture. The desire for a common-tone relationship and the delineation of progression dictate the choice of transposition.

In order to understand how the hexachord functions in this example, one should distinguish its two parts: one is the perfect fifth which gives the tonal location of the hexachord and specifies its place in the progression, and the other is a group of notes which leads the ear to the fifth (Ex. 6b, where white notes indicate the former and black notes the latter). Bear in mind that the initial condition of this passage is the realization of the tonal center, E, at the beginning of m. 41. Our first inkling that E is about to be abandoned develops when the D♮, in the same measure, places E in an unstable position. In fact, the preceding cadence, wherein D♯ collides with its note of resolution, does not lend E much security. This D♯ is reiterated as a root by 0–10 and the insecurity is heightened. 0–9 would seem to restore E, but by this time the implications are clear (note that the possible qualification by A of the C root is removed by A's incorporation into a tritone—m. 42). 0–8 places E firmly in a tritone of its own, and the final blow is administered by the D root in m. 45, implied initially by the diminished triad of 0–8 and subsequently by 0–4 in m. 44 until it is realized. The sense of the whole is that of a sequence (Ex. 6c) with the initial tone of each pattern being related to the note of reference, E, by half-step below and above, and the final D emerging as goal of the sequence and the new basis for procedure along the terrain being explored.

The development reveals more elaborate examples of the process of excursion. In the first part of the development (mm. 83–95) segments, combined with full statements, are deployed in a sequential manner (Ex. 7).

Ex. 7

The choice of transpositions is determined by the possibility for adjacent
minor seconds, provided by 1–2 and 11–12, by which one row is hinged to
another in a descending scalar arrangement; thus, from Ex. 7 at *x*, we may
extract the resultant scheme (Ex. 8):

Ex. 8

Segmentation derives from an intent to echo; 0–12 generates an echo in
the upper stratum and 0–1, though postponed, in the lower in measure
86.[5] In this phrase the tonal instability of the minor second, present at the
origin and termination of each pattern of the sequence, enhances the
inherent ambiguity of the sequential idea (ambiguous because the destination of a sequential progression cannot be known during its course)
while, at the same time, the systematic transposition of the patterns main-
tains a sense of control. This example finds analogy in harmonic practice
where the outcome of each pattern of a sequence is an unstable sonority,
such as a dominant seventh chord (cf. Mozart: *Menuetto*, K. 355, mm.
5–10, 33–38).

The second part of the development contains a different sort of ambiguity. The music has given an impression of circuity that is eventually
mirrored in one compact unit of contradiction whereby matters become
stuck, as if in frustration (Ex. 9).

Ex. 9

[5] I should mention here, because of the exchange in the lower voices between mm. 87
and 88, Finney's disagreement with the prohibition of octave doubling. Because, at least,
of his belief in tonality, he is indifferent to apprehensions about traditional reference and
employs the octave for all of the customary contrapuntal situations: imitation, reinforcement, and emphasis. Several examples occur in the quotations I have made, e.g., Ex. 3,
m. 15.

These chords may be interpreted in a number of ways of which the following seem to me the most appropriate:

Ex. 10

When they cease, they seem to be in the process of alternating (indefinitely). Part III of the development then sustains D♭ (as C♯) as tonal axis in a prolonged, static moment of release (letdown) prior to the gathered renewal of energy in the recapitulation. Whereas the minor second of Part I requires interpretation in several directions at once, here we encounter ambiguity by bewilderment or confusion. This is one of Finney's favorite means of achieving climax and of generating the need for solution.

III

In the many works that Finney composed between 1950 and 1960, one finds a growing interest in variation much more loosely tied to a tonal origin, an increasing presence of "fantasy" with a consequent disruption of the periodic phrase structure which his music ordinarily assumed, segments of a hundred measures or more retrograded as a means of recapitulation, and a formal framework far less traditional and more various than that projected by the Sixth Quartet. His language becomes increasingly dissonant and chromatic; rhythm, above all, experiences a growth into more diverse forms of his individual sense of gesture.

These developments occur mainly in chamber music, Finney's special preserve, and though they illustrate growth, they do not produce a mode of expression essentially changed from his earlier work. Obviously they emerge, not only because of inner necessity, but also in response to contemporary thought: the focus on Webern, the ubiquitous experiments with rhythm, and the like. Finney often regretted the fact that he had been unable to hear his early orchestral works and was determined once again to compose for that medium; so the three scores, crowded into the end of the decade—the Variations for Orchestra (1957), the Second Symphony (1959), and the Third Symphony (1960)—come as no surprise.

That the last work was composed so soon after the Second Symphony is symptomatic, for it seems to gather the achievements of the '50's into a straightforward, spontaneous statement, unfolding with certainty. It has its uniquenesses, notably in form. It is based on the following four rows (Ex. 11).

Ex. 11

In his score the composer has this to say about them: ". . . It [the symphony] is based on four variants of the same twelve-tone row, all of which are introduced in the first few measures. One variant is melodic [Row I]; another is scalewise [Row II] and furnishes much of the momentum of the work. The other two are harmonic—one emphasizing fifths, the other, thirds [Rows III and IV]."[6] In general, Row I furnishes the main thematic substance, and whereas Row II has its moments of thematic prominence, it usually provides contrapuntal filler or material for connecting passages. Its intervallic blandness makes it readily absorbable into structures featuring larger intervals (any of the other three rows, for instance). Rows III and IV, occurring less often, serve to characterize cadential moments or to act as substructure. Row IV is a source set for Row III. Although it is true that each of these rows is all-combinatorial, this has no bearing on their tonal usage.

I have thought it best to discuss events in their order of appearance with reference to extracted segments, self-enclosed and complete, wherein musical possibilities are introduced and then carried forward to fulfillment. These segments bear upon one another so as to create a continuity which is essential to the form of the first movement as a whole and also symptomatic of the point of view or the kind of technical control that guides the composer's ear throughout. Examples 12, 15, 17, and 19 represent four such segments and cover the first 77 measures of the score.

In the beginning, the symphony unfolds a large tapestry, richly colored and variegated, which has none of the compact, incisive single-mindedness of the corresponding moment in the Sixth Quartet (Ex. 12). This material operates on three levels of which the highest, as Row I, states the principal theme. The purpose of the opening is to establish the tonal center, E. In this light, Rows III and IV combine to offer support,

[6] This quotation is taken from the published score of the symphony (cited above in n. 2) on the page facing page 1.

Ex. 12. Initial numbers refer to rows in Ex. 11

as well as challenge, while Row II lends notes (the sustained ones) to both functions and a certain connective tissue of motion. At the outset, E is by no means secure. E operates tonally in m. 1, Row I (as a possibility); in m. 6, fourth beat, between Rows I and II (a subtle, subdued forecast); in m. 14, Row I (where E insistently intrudes into surroundings foreign to it); finally in mm. 18 to 22, Row II, then IV, then I (where E gradually gains the mastery of its antagonists and, by the new beginning of m. 22, a realization of its primacy).

Within this outline, tonality operates either by agreement among the levels, where two or three coincide to make the same achievement, or by disagreement, where materials, antipathetic though occurring simultaneously, relate to the tonal environment by cross reference. Instances of agreement occur in mm. 4 and 5, where the C root is stated (seen emerging through mm. 2 and 3); in mm. 9–11 where D is stated by Rows III and IV; in mm. 12–15, where G is stated by Rows III and IV and reinforced by the entrance of Row I in mm. 14 and 15; and in m. 22 where E finally stands alone.

Examples of disagreement function in two ways: materials refer either to a previous existence (a sort of summing-up) or to a future appearance, hence possible outcome. Thus, Row III in m. 4 summarizes the previous progression from E to the C root, clinching the latter by its own G♮ (common tones make the reference easy to grasp). However in mm. 6–8, Row I introduces a new entity challenging the sustained C material (Ex. 13):

Ex. 13

This is picked up and reinforced by the notes sustained from Row II, mm. 7–9: B♭, G♭, and E♭. Here the F♯ and A♯, antipathetic to the C material over which they are introduced, eventually assume a commanding position in the tonal environment.

In addition to these operations, there is a system of leading-tone or, on the other hand, parenthetical relationships which relate some of the elements of the environment. From this point of view, the materials of the E♭ root eventually move to E by half-step (manifest throughout mm. 16–22) but they also move downward to the materials of the D root (m. 9). Precisely because of the dominance of the D environment from mm. 9–11, D absorbs the E♭ materials and makes parenthetical the central triadic group in m. 10 (that D♭ here replaces E♭ merely pushes the reference further backward to its original emergence as C♯ in Row I, mm. 6–7). A similar parenthetical position and reference of the E♭ materials (as D♯) within the G environment may be seen in mm. 13–14 where they also have a specific, if subdued, tie to their eventual move to E. This whole complex of relationships may be symbolized as follows (Ex. 14):

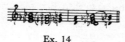

Ex. 14

The above analyses are by no means exhaustive but should serve to expose the principal tonal elements of the beginning, to explain their interaction and the relative position of authority to its subjects. One should note how the subsidiary roots are either displaced or are systematically eroded throughout mm. 15–22 by becoming one note of a tritone. Indeed, E itself seems about to suffer this fate of its companions (mm. 18) but, by its persistence, finds its authority secured. Of the subsidiary roots, D and C play substantial roles in the form of the movement.

From m. 22, the movement is toward D, though the final and decisive arrival is delayed for some 55 measures. The D is heard periodically en route in a process analogous to sighting a destination through enshrouding mists which lift their cover from time to time. The first and customary step is to jeopardize E as a tonal center, accomplished between mm. 22 and 33 (Ex. 15).

Ex. 15

The intervallic core of this phrase is indicated below the example by letters and may be reduced to the following scheme (Ex. 16):

Ex. 16

The principle here is twofold: (1) to base sonorities on the interval of the second, and (2) to spread them outward from a centrally located E according to melodic contours, so that E is placed in a variety of ambiguous positions. The idea suggests a symmetrical expansion, but though there are some symmetrical structures—notably at (d), (f), and (g)—no exact

(initial numbers refer to rows in Ex. 11)

Ex. 17

symmetrical scheme results. These methods tend to continue movement toward stability, and the structure at (g) insures D as the basis of that stability.

The next step is to sight a destination and head for it (Ex. 17). To bring this about, three interacting principles are at work in this segment. The first may be called that of melodic emphasis, whereby a note in a line becomes prominent and then is allowed to linger so as to be absorbed and assessed. Thus in m. 35, the D of the main melody is clearly heard, is supported by the D sustained from m. 36 in the bass, and eventually assumes the position of a root.

The second principle, a corollary to the first, is, by the piling-up of sustained tones, to achieve a sonority which has directional indication (function). Thus by m. 38, a completed sonority, actually a full dominant ninth indicates a G destination. In turn, G occurs in m. 38 (Row I, middle beat) but its security as a point of resolution is prejudiced by its immediate association with C♯. From m. 38 to 43, the resultant sonority focuses on this tritone so that D is suggested once again. But in m. 43, C replaces C♯ and, together with the remaining B and F, assumes command of the progression. In the end, D reappears but in association with first B♭ and then B♮ (bassoons) so that its authority remains uncertain. We are left in doubt, though D as the final destination is strongly suggested.

The third principle is a variation of the second and may be seen within mm. 43–45. Whereas the second principle operates through an additive process in which an accumulation of tones realizes an intervallic entity which may then act in a certain way, the third operates through a reductive process in which the ingredients of an entity are deleted, by simple choice, so that the material causes of action are removed or the indicated course of action is altered. In the present instance, the full entity exists in m. 42 (Ex. 18):

Ex. 18

Here the two tritones provide the most evident causes for action (C♯–G, B–F). First the C♯ is removed, then the G, then the E, thus allowing the remaining tritone to assert its potentiality which the added C above (second principle) fully realizes.

The final stage in the progression to D begins in m. 51 where it would be normal to introduce a new theme, a new section of the form, a new milieu, that is, as downbeat and to confirm the goal of the preceding transition. What happens is quite different. While the horns state D in m. 51, that D is immediately rendered unstable by the entering bass, and this poised moment of upbeat is *prolonged* and then *transformed* into a new milieu, but not one that might have been anticipated (Ex. 19).

(initial numbers refer to rows in Ex. II; ref. = reference)

Ex. 19

Ex. 19 (cont.)

The effect is diversionary. It is as though the protagonist, pursuing his way toward D, is diverted into a channel which opens for him an unexpected world wherein he strolls rather than strides, pauses, as it were, to contemplate and absorb its sensuous delights. The slowed tempo, the delicacy of orchestration, the filigree of solistic gestures which hang about the environment he is contemplating all arrest the straightforward momentum by which he has hitherto progressed. There is a certain dramatic irony in this situation. For while D is eventually and finally attained in m. 77, it is made, at that very moment, the point of departure toward other goals; D, as tonal center, is never permitted to have a section of the form all to itself. The tonal events of Ex. 19 illustrate the nature of this diversion and its relationship to D.

Texturally, the diversion presents four layers of counterpoint of which the highest and lowest represent Row I and the two in between, Row IV. All have different roles though they sometimes support one another. Row I above continues 0–2 from the previous section and is primarily decorative. While it is sometimes antithetical to events below, it always eventually comes to terms with them (for example: mm. 51–53: its F$\sharp$ and D$\sharp$ lend support to the brass; mm. 59–61: its line finds its way to D, likewise in agreement with the brass). The second and third layers (reading down) combine to present Row IV in its most obvious character, that is, with its hexachords intact and distinct. But Row IV above is decorative of Row IV below, and it too always comes to agreement with the lower line (for example: Row IV above literally anticipates the succeeding brass hexachords from m. 58 to 59, 62 to 63, 68 to 69). The fourth and lowest layer is the bass line (again Row I).

Viewed as a whole the passage, by analogy, may be seen as a kind of concertato texture wherein the recurring brass statements, together with Row I above, represent the ritornello, Row IV above offers solistic com-

mentary in alternation, and the bass line stands as a foundation in the
nature of a cantus firmus. Precisely because the upper two layers furnish
embellishment or parenthetical commentary and are brought to terms
with the lower, the latter embody the substance of the progression. Thus
one may consider them apart from the rest (Ex. 20; in this example, each
hexachord is represented by two adjacent augmented triads connected by
a beam; white notes stand for the brass, black notes for the solo strings;
the cantus firmus lies below and letters outline the phrases by which one
may relate this example to Ex. 19).

One should notice that the cantus firmus always lends one note to the
brass hexachords for their completion. Now, since each hexachord contains

Ex. 20

three perfect fifths and no qualifying, undermining agent (such as a tritone), it strongly suggests the possibility of root progression. If this is pursued, the question will be, which of the fifths determines *the* functioning root? Excepting only two instances—at (c) and perhaps in the last hexachord—the cantus firmus contributes one of the roots. Following this observation and taking into account the commanding position of the cantus firmus as bass, we may isolate the following root progression (Ex. 21). This analysis is quite verifiable by ear. The sense of the progression accords nicely with the atmosphere of the diversion as D is not reached until the diversion has run its course.

Ex. 21

The purpose of Row IV may also be understood from another of its elements, the augmented triad, and here both proponents of the row contribute. While each hexachord asserts a root deriving from a perfect fifth, that root still exists in an augmented triad. An augmented triad may imply an uncertainty and this quality of mystery is often exploited in a tonal context. Each hexachord of Row IV contains two such triads, shown in their adjacency in Ex. 20 (beams between staves indicate common-tone relationships). These triads may be understood to represent tonal purpose as follows: first, each triad (or pair of triads) embodies uncertainty and therefore predicts either resolution or displacement; second, each retains this character until the end when resolution occurs through melodic displacement. Ex. 20 clearly shows that this succession of triads moves strictly by half-step from its origin in 0–6, m. 51, back and forth between two triads of the same pitch-class content (at least Ex. 22 is one way to exhibit the facts):

Ex. 22

Sometimes the movement forward is seen to begin over again, as, in phrase (a), 1–6 takes its point of departure from within 0–6 preceding. Nevertheless, the melodic progression thus defined consistently moves between these two triads which may be reduced to one). In consequence, the tonal resultant is oscillatory, static as with an ostinato. Because forward momentum seems to be reduced to a very low degree of urgency thereby, this, too, accords with the character of the diversion as a moment of pause within the movement as a whole.

In this example we see that two different tonal purposes, evidenced by the same series of intervals, promote the general character of the formal fragment between m. 51 and m. 77. This type of ambiguity, where a single element embodies two or more distinct implications which, by their correlative weight and equal importance, resolve to one reinforced implication, is perhaps not so common in music as in poetry where the symbolic function of the word, through concrete reference to visible experience in connection with imagined consequences, occasions such embodiment quite naturally. The pivot chord (the pivotal progression or phrase, in short, the pivotal situation) represents a variety of this type of ambiguity. The pivot chord embodies two or more implications, only one of which will be chosen, so that its relevance is not only to the present but to the future.[7] The diversion also may be understood in this sense.

I do not propose to go beyond this point except to note briefly the tonal form of the whole movement which is brought about according to the methods described above. Example 23 shows the centers of tonal

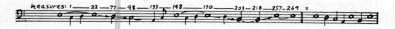

Ex. 23

attraction in their relative importance. Measures 148–70 seem to imply recapitulation, an aspect of sonata form, but this is not the case. Each moment of tonal realization inaugurates a restless furtherance of exploration so that m. 148 is like beginning over again. It is by no means recapitulatory. The fullest, grandest such moment of search begins with B in m. 203 and this, the climactic segment of the score, ultimately reaches E at m. 238 more by resignation than achievement or perhaps, in some sense, by both. One can speculate on the extent to which the pervasive chromaticism of row structure realizes these two qualities. But the first movement as a whole rests on the simplest tonal basis, each moment of which provides a sound foundation for further action and which coheres in an obvious logic, so that the constructive power of this logic grants both freedom for expansion and the necessities for purposeful direction. The music is fervent in its romanticism and at the same time exposed with the clear precision of Finney's best manner.

IV

From the above observations one may draw the following conclusions. Finney's accommodation of tonality to twelve-tone procedure seems to

[7] Those familiar with William Empson's *Seven Types of Ambiguity* will recognize several analytical approaches in this article. The writer wishes not only to honor his debt to that fascinating book but also to recommend it for its many and diverse relevances to musical procedures.

rest on the fundamental distinction, as a premise, that tonality is a concept, hence ideological, whereas twelve-tone practice provides a method of operation and therefore is technological. Twelve-tone practice might be considered as one of the latest methods through which tonality has been realized. This in turn makes an implicit assertion about the pitch content of a row: one of the twelve notes will dominate the others, and it follows that the composer would have to order this content so that it forges, dissolves, and reforges the loyalties which he has conceived. Here we confront a conceptual confusion. Is not a functional order already embodied in the row? Must the composer not resign himself to it, wherever it lead? Not exactly. He would control the given order so as to permit it, as opposed to force it, to realize the tonal purposes he wishes. Doubtless in practice the tonal result of a serialized order may become indistinguishable, in the composer's mind, from his tonal purposes, but this should not equate tonality with twelve-tone procedure, that is, ends with means.

It follows, too, that once a single note of a row has been selected as tonal center, it becomes a constant in authority and therefore the remaining eleven must be relegated to the status of passing phenomena. As centers of attraction change during the course of a large form, then so will the directional purpose of these phenomena change from passing between a tonal center and its reestablishment to passing between different centers, thus conditioning the composer's choice of row transpositions. But, assuming that the passing is successful, then the success of the emergent edifice, as a structure, will depend upon the relationship of the tonal centers. The row, the choice of row transpositions, may promote this success but will not ultimately determine it. Of course, the once-recommended belief that twelve distinct pitches should exist with equality in a chromatic environment has no meaning when, according to the above concepts, row practice realizes tonality.

Finney so frequently resorts to more than one row in a single composition that one must consider his purpose. Obviously, an operative tonality may be realized by one row or several rows together, so that this practice must have another intention. Apparently it is an attempt to avoid one of the greatest hazards of twelve-tone music, namely its monotony. In reality, the functioning order within a row arises not from an order of pitches but from an order of intervals, and, while a transposition may rearrange the order of pitches thus guaranteeing some variety of companionship, the functioning intervallic order will remain the same. By resorting to more than one row, Finney is able to draw upon a greater variety of intervallic orderings and at the same time to enrich his contrapuntal fabric with an equal variety of melodic contours.

In an address at Scripps College, California, in 1959, Finney said:

> The artist lives today in a vastly different world than he did a hundred years ago, and almost certainly a different world than he will live in a hundred years hence. He lives in a world in transition, a world in which change is the most certain quality of culture. Each artist must adapt himself in his own way to this changing culture, holding only those traditions valid that actually aid expression.[8]

It is characteristic of him to advise, by implication at least, the artist to be expressive, and just as characteristic that he advocate a blending of the new and the traditional. His own music perfectly reflects his belief in these recommendations.

[8] Ross Lee Finney, "Analysis and the Creative Process," *Scripps College Bulletin*, Vol. XXXIII, No. 2 (1959), 3.